Praise for Joel Turtel's
Public Schools, Public Menace

"This book is a must-read for every parent. It is sad but true that the public school system in America threatens the values of families and the welfare of students. It is for that reason that Dr. James Dobson and I urge parents to take their children out of public school and either home-school or find private, traditionally religious schools."

> — **Dr. Laura Schlessinger,** internationally syndicated Radio talk host, and author of *Stupid Things Parents Do To Mess Up Their Kids*

"*Public Schools, Public Menace* is a great resource for any parents who are interested in better education for their children. It is written with passion and insight."

> — **Alan Bonsteel, M.D.**, author of *A Choice For Our Children: Curing the Crisis In America's Schools*

"This is an excellent, thoroughly documented and detailed exposition of what's wrong with the public schools. The author makes it clear that parents have a responsibility to make sure that their children get a good education, which is no longer to be had in a government school. His chapters on the widespread drugging of children by the 'educators' and the negative effects of such medication should be read by every parent with a child in a public school. What can parents do about it? The author outlines the benefits of homeschooling, which is no doubt the best alternative to the public schools available to parents. How can a parent homeschool if he or she has to work? The author addresses that problem and provides some very creative suggestions. If you are a parent wrestling with the problem of education for your children, this book is for you . . . ."

> — **Samuel L. Blumenfeld**, syndicated columnist, and author of *"Homeschooling: A Parent's Guide To Teaching Children"* and seven other books on education and public schools.

Excerpts from *Public Schools, Public Menace*

• For parents who think they have no alternatives, my book will explain why you don't have to settle for a third-rate public-school education for your children. You do have alternatives, many excellent, low-cost alternatives that can give your children a first-rate education and a rewarding future.

• The [public school] system cannot be fixed because it depends on compulsion and monopoly government control.

• A student teacher for a fifth-grade class in Minneapolis wrote the following letter to the local newspaper: ". . . I was told [that] children are not to be expected to spell the following words correctly: back, big, call, came, can, day, did, dog, down, get, good, if, in, is, it, have, he, home, like, little, man, morning, mother, my, night, off, out, over, people, play, ran, said, saw, she, some, soon, their, them, there, time, two, too, up, us, very, water, we, went, where, when, will, would, etc. Is this nuts?"

• By the 1850s, *before* we had compulsory, government-controlled public schools, child and adult literacy rates averaged over 90 percent, making illiteracy rates less than 10 percent. Today, as shown by the New York State Education Department's annual report and other studies, student illiteracy rates in many public schools range from 30 to 75 percent. This is an education horror story.

• Compulsory public schools, by their nature, are anti-parent, despite school officials' calls for more parental involvement and cooperation.

• Is there anything wrong with lying, cheating, stealing, shoplifting, taking drugs, premarital sex, insulting your parents, pornography, irresponsibility, or getting pregnant in junior high school? Not according to the values taught to children in many public schools today . . . In classrooms throughout the country, Judeo-Christian beliefs are cast aside or ridiculed.

• Mr. Gatto, an award-winning English teacher for twenty-six years, learned that it only takes about a hundred hours to teach a willing child to read, write, and do basic arithmetic. If this is so, what are public schools doing with our children for *twelve years*, while they turn them into functional illiterates?

• Today, many parents pin their hopes for better schools on government-sponsored alternatives such as vouchers, charter schools, Supreme Court decisions, or the No Child Left Behind Act . . . I'm sorry to say that these are mostly false hopes. If parents wait for these alternatives to finally give their children the education they need and deserve, they will be waiting for a very long time. Parents, don't hold your breath on these options.

• A public-school system that coerces parents into giving their children mind-altering drugs that are potentially addictive, dangerous, or even lethal, is a moral abomination.

• In effect, public-school employees say to parents: "You have to pay our salary and benefits, but how dare you demand proof that we know how to teach your children? How dare you judge our merit? How dare you demand that you get your money's worth?"

Public Schools, Public Menace:

*How Public Schools
Lie to Parents and
Betray Our Children*

Public Schools, Public Menace:

How Public Schools Lie to Parents and Betray Our Children

Joel Turtel

Liberty Books
New York

Library of Congress Control Number: 2004094548

Printed in the United States of America

Turtel, Joel
Public Schools, Public Menace: How Public Schools Lie
To Parents and Betray Our Children.
Includes bibliographical references and index
ISBN # 0-9645693-2-9
1. Public Schools — Nature of and problems with.   2.
Education — Aims and objectives — United States.   3.
Home-schooling — Nature of and Benefits   4. Education
and Public schools — History and Changes   5. Privatization
of Education.   6. Comparative education systems

Published by Liberty Books, New York

To Helen,
my brave, clever girl

Contents

viii   **Contents**

Acknowledgments

During the three years it took me to research and write *Public Schools, Public Menace*, there were times that I felt daunted by the size and difficulty of the project. Without the help and support of my friends and editors, I could not have completed this book.

I would like to express grateful appreciation to my editor, Carol Thoma. She demanded the best in my writing, introduced ideas and issues I had not thought of, showed me the value of presenting different points of view, and made me prove my arguments with greater clarity.

I am also grateful to Joseph L. Bast, President of the Heartland Institute, for editing my manuscript. His thoughtful and thorough editing was invaluable in helping me to address important issues about public schools and education that I had not previously dealt with in the manuscript.

I would like to express my deep appreciation to the authors of the many books I used in my research for writing *Public Schools, Public Menace*—John Gatto, Charl es J. Sykes, Sheldon Richman, Peter R. Breggin, M.D., the late John Holt, and many others. Without their brilliant and illuminating books, ideas, and research to guide me, I could not have completed this book.

ix

Finally, I wish to thank Helen for her psychological insights about children and parents, and for her excellent editorial contributions to the manuscript.

Preface

Many parents have children who do poorly in public school, fail in their studies, or can't adjust to crowded, impersonal classrooms or indifferent teachers. Millions of other parents have children who find school boring, frustrating, or meaningless. I will argue in this book that in most cases the problem lies with the public schools, *not* with our children. It turns out that millions of children have good reasons to hate public school, reasons that parents should not ignore.

Parents whose children are doing well in their studies often don't see a problem with their local public school. But for these parents, what if the school has been deceiving you? What if school authorities dumb-down the textbooks and manipulate test and report-card grades to make you believe your children are doing well in school, when in fact they are not?

What if, despite your children's good grades and glowing report cards, your public school cripples your children's ability to read, smothers their desire to learn, warps their values, and wastes twelve years of their lives? Worse, what if these schools betray your children so school employees get to keep their tenure-guaranteed jobs?

One glaring indication that our public schools have become an educational menace to our children is the frightening lit-

1

eracy statistics we read about in study after study. For example, in 2002, New York State's Education Department issued its second annual Report that included public-school students' math and reading scores. The Report found that 65 percent of elementary-school students, 90 percent of middle-school students, and 84 percent of high-school students failed to meet *minimum* New York State math and reading standards.[1] This appalling illiteracy is not confined to New York students—other studies show similar results from public schools across the country.

Most public-school teachers, principals, and administrators are intelligent, hardworking, and dedicated people. Also, most children are intelligent and literally born with a burning desire to learn about the world around them. So why do public schools keep failing millions of children, year after year, no matter how hard school officials try or how much tax money we give them?

If public schools keep failing our children despite the best efforts of well-intentioned educators, perhaps it is time we ask some fundamental questions about the system itself. Why do we need public schools at all? Why can't parents simply buy education for their children in an open, unregulated free-market, the same way they buy food or clothing for their children or a car for themselves? Is there something unique about education that we should make it a compulsory government monopoly like the Post Office? Has education always been controlled by the government? What does "education" really mean, and what is the best way to give our children a low-cost, quality education? These are the kinds of questions that led me to investigate our public-school system and write this book.

When a social, economic, or political system has seemingly intractable problems, there are usually deep, underlying reasons at fault. Usually, the foundation of the system is rotten. To find out why public schools continually fail, and to find better alternatives, I examined the foundations of our public-school system.

In doing my research, I soon realized that the fundamental problem with our public schools is not ill-trained teachers, lack of money, broken-down school buildings, or overcrowded classrooms. These are only secondary effects of the root problem. The main reason our public schools fail, and will continue to fail, is because they are a compulsory, government-run, near-total education monopoly. The root problem is that local and state *governments* control 1st through 12th grade education in our country and suppress a voluntary free-market education system.

I also researched alternative education systems that succeeded in the past, before we had public schools. I discovered that government-run, compulsory public schools are a fairly new phenomenon in this country, and became fully entrenched only after the late 1890's. For over two hundred years before public schools came along, education in America was voluntary, and literacy rates were far higher than they are today. For over two hundred years before we had public schools, parents controlled how, when, and where to educate their children, with little government interference. Parents were free to buy education in a vibrant education free market of unlicensed, low-cost local tutors, private schools, church schools, and colleges. Millions of average parents taught their kids to read at home with the Bible or inexpensive learn-to-read primers such as *McGuffy's Readers*.

If this voluntary education system succeeded for over two hundred years, why not bring it back? I realized that if we gave parents this same precious freedom today, our children could get a quality education most parents could afford and most kids would enjoy.

The problem, however, is that we've now had public schools for over a hundred years, so many parents today find it hard to imagine better alternatives. As bad as public schools are, parents think of them as the norm, as American as apple pie. One purpose of my book is to show parents that they should *not* accept these schools and the failed education they give our children as the norm, and that in many ways public schools are deeply unAmerican.

The second goal of my book is to show parents there are real, exciting, low-cost alternatives to public schools. These alternatives work, and I will argue that parents can and should embrace these alternatives to give their children the education they need and deserve.

However, the *idea* of public schools is still deeply embedded in most parents' minds. As a result, I believe that only when parents understand how destructive public schools can be to their children, will they consider the alternatives available to them right now.

Parents have different opinions about our public schools today. Many low-income minority parents are fed up with the violent, drug-infested schools in their neighborhood, schools that barely teach their children to read. Year after year, these parents plead with school authorities to do something about the schools, but to no avail.

Many middle-class parents also believe that public schools do a poor job educating their children, but they can't afford expensive private schools or are not aware of other education options for their kids. So these parents often suffer with their local schools as best they can.

Other parents believe *their* local schools are doing a good job, especially parents whose children get good test and report card grades. However, as we will discover later in the book, these parents don't realize how school authorities deceive them into thinking their children are doing better than they really are.

For low-income minority parents, my book will confirm your worst fears about our public schools. You will see how and why these schools betray your children. But I will show you how to rescue your children from these schools, a way out that is in your power right now.

For middle-class parents who think they have no alternatives, my book will explain why you don't have to settle for a third-rate education for your children. You do have alternatives, many excellent, low-cost alternatives that can give your children a first-rate education and a rewarding future.

For those parents who believe that their local school does a good job, this book will explain how many public schools deceive parents into thinking their children are getting a good education, when that is hardly the case.

For all parents, no matter what your current opinion of our public schools, I will endeavor to show that public schools have become a menace to your children, a menace far more dangerous than you might realize. Yes, "menace" is a strong word, but it is a word that fits many public schools today.

Chapter 1 will explore the surprising history of literacy and education in America. We'll see how public schools cripple children's ability to read. We'll also explore why literacy is so important, and how illiteracy can ruin your children's lives.

Chapters 2 through 6 will examine other dangers that threaten children in public schools. We will see how many schools indoctrinate children with anti-parent, anti-Judeo-Christian, and anti-American values. I will explain how public schools especially hurt low-income minority children. We'll discover that many public schools coerce parents into giving their children mind-altering drugs like Ritalin, and expose innocent children to shocking sexual material in sex-education classes. These chapters will examine why public schools get away with their continuing failure, year after year, and why the public-school system is beyond repair.

In Chapter 7, we will explore why the public-school system's real function is to protect the jobs of school bureaucrats and employees. I will also dissect the many excuses school authorities use to rationalize their ongoing failure to give our children a decent education.

For those parents who wish to take their children out of public school, Chapters 8, 9, and the Resources section will help you find and use many alternative education resources available to you right now. I will also explore many options that let parents educate their kids at home, even if both parents work. These options include Internet schools, Internet charter schools, low-cost teaching books, computer learning software, bookstores, public libraries, and home-schooling.

Over a million parents today homeschool their children with great success. In Chapters 8 and 9, I will answer many important questions parents have about home-schooling, questions such as "is it worth it?," "can I do it?," "how can I manage the time to homeschool?," and "how do I homeschool if I've never done it before?" We'll also examine twenty-two danger signals from your children that tell you it's time to think about taking them out of public school and looking for better alternatives.

We'll see why and how home-schooling can give your children a great education, and can be *much faster, easier, and more affordable* than you think. We'll also see how home-schooling can be the most rewarding experience of your life and your children's lives.

Parent-directed home-schooling is only one of many options parents have right now. Internet schools and Internet Charter schools are a new, exciting, and mostly untapped education resource for parents. These schools give children individualized instruction that *takes most of the home-schooling load from parents' backs*. Most Internet schools cost much less than brick-and-mortar private schools (including Catholic or Protestant-affiliated schools), yet they can give children a high-quality education leading to an accredited diploma and college admission.

It is my hope that this book will convince parents to seriously consider taking their children out of public school, *permanently*, and take advantage of the many excellent, low-cost education alternatives available to them right now.

Part I

Public Schools, Public Menace

1

A Child's Mind Is a
Terrible Thing To Waste

From the time the Mayflower landed at Plymouth Rock in 1620 until the 1850s, most parents taught their children to read at home or sent their children to small private or religious grammar schools. Education was voluntary and local governments did not force parents to send their children to school. Yet, literacy rates in colonial America were far higher than they are today.

In 1765, John Adams wrote that "a native of America, especially of New England, who cannot read and write is as rare a Phenomenon as a Comet."[1] Jacob Duche, the chaplain of Congress in 1772, said of his countrymen, "Almost every man is a reader."[2] Daniel Webster confirmed that the product of home education was near-universal literacy when he stated, "a youth of fifteen, of either sex, who cannot read and write, is very seldom to be found."[3]

After the Revolutionary War, literacy rates continued to rise in all the colonies. There were many affordable, innovative local schools parents could send their children to. Literacy data from that early period show that from 1650 to 1795, the literacy rate among white men rose from 60 to 90 percent. Literacy among women went from 30 to 45 percent.[4]

In the early 1800s, Pierre Samuel Dupont, an influential French citizen who helped Thomas Jefferson negotiate for the Louisiana Purchase, came to America and surveyed education here. He found that most young Americans could read, write, and "cipher" (do arithmetic), and that Americans of all ages could and did read the Bible. He estimated that fewer than four Americans in a thousand were unable to write neatly and legibly.[5]

From 1800 to 1840, literacy rates in the North increased from 75 percent to between 91 and 97 percent. In the South, the white literacy rate grew from about 50 to 60 percent, to 81 percent. By 1850, literacy rates in Massachusetts and other New England states for both men *and* women were close to 97 percent. This was *before* Massachusetts created the first compulsory public-school system in America in 1852.[6] Of course, these literacy numbers did not apply to black slaves since many colonies had laws that forbid teaching slaves to read.

Another sign of high literacy rates in early America was book sales. By 1776, the colonies had a population of about three million people. Thomas Paine's pamphlet *Common Sense*, published in 1776, sold 120,000 copies. That was equivalent to selling ten million copies today. By 1818, the population in the the United States was about twenty million. Between 1813 and 1823, Noah Webster's *Spelling Book* and Walter Scott's novels sold over five million copies. That would be the equivalent of selling sixty million copies today. Europeans who visited America in the 1820s and 1830s, such as Alexis de Tocqueville (author of the great classic, *Democracy in America*) and Pierre du Pont de Nemours, marveled at how well educated Americans were.[7]

Declining Literacy Rates

Fast forward to the 1930s. Before World War II, public schools demanded hard work, dedication, and accountability from their students. In the 1930s, we still had a high literacy rate. However, by the 1940s, public-school education had started to deteriorate. The rapid deterioration of literacy after the 1940s showed up clearly when tracked through Army admissions tests, as explained by John Taylor Gatto in his book, *The Underground History of American Education*:

At the start of WWII millions of men showed up at registration offices to take low-level academic tests before being inducted. The years of maximum mobilization were 1942 to 1944; the fighting force had been mostly schooled in the 1930s, both those inducted and those turned away. Eighteen million men were tested; seventeen million, two hundred-and-eighty-thousand of them were judged to have the minimum competence in reading required to be a soldier, a 96 percent literacy rate. Although this was a 2 percent fall-off from the 98 percent among voluntary military applicants ten years before, the dip was so small it didn't worry anybody.

World War II was over in 1945. Six years later another war began in Korea. Several million men were tested for military service, but this time 600,000 were rejected. Literacy in the draft pool had dropped to 81 percent even though all that was needed to classify a soldier as literate was fourth grade reading proficiency. In a few short years from the beginning of WWII to Korea, a terrifying problem of adult illiteracy had appeared. The Korean War group received most of *its* schooling in the 1940s, it had more years in school with more professionally trained personnel and more scientifically selected textbooks than the WWII men, yet it could not read, write, count, speak or think as well as the earlier, less-schooled contingent.

A third American war began in the mid-1960s. By its end in 1973 the number of men found non-inductable by reason of inability to read safety instructions, interpret road signs, decipher orders, and so on—the number found illiterate in other words—had reached 27 percent of the total pool. Vietnam-era young men had been schooled in the 1950s and the 1960s—much better schooled than either of the two earlier groups—but the 4 percent illiteracy of 1941 which had transmuted into the 19 percent illiteracy of 1952 had now grown into the 27 percent illiteracy of 1970. Not only had the fraction of competent readers dropped to 73 percent but a substantial chunk of even those were only *barely* adequate; they could not keep abreast of developments by reading a newspaper, they could not read for pleasure, they could not sustain a thought or an argument, they could not write well enough to manage their own affairs without assistance. [8]

Literacy rates among the general population also declined sharply during this same period. In 1940, the literacy rate throughout America was 96 percent for whites and 80 percent for blacks. Notice that unlike today, four of five black people were literate, despite segregated schools, Jim Crow laws, and massive discrimination against them. After the 1940s, adult literacy rapidly deteriorated.

By the 1990s, surveys by the National Adult Literacy and National Assessment of Educational Progress organizations showed that 17 percent of whites and 40 percent of blacks could not read at all. In short, illiteracy had doubled among blacks and quadrupled among whites. Yet, by the 1990s, public schools spent three to four times more tax money on education (adjusted for inflation) than they did in the 1940s when the literacy rate for both blacks and whites was much higher. [9]

In 1993, the Educational Testing Service published the results of its 1992 adult literacy survey in America (the newest 2003 survey will be published sometime in 2004). The survey used a 26,000-member representative sample of 190 million Americans over sixteen years old who had attended public school for an average of 12.4 years. John Taylor Gatto listed the following results of this literacy survey in *The Underground History of American Education*:

Forty-two million Americans over the age of sixteen can't read. Some of this group can't write their names on Social Security cards or fill in height, weight, and birth dates on application forms.

Fifty million Americans can't recognize printed words on a fourth or fifth-grade reading level. Consequently, they can't write simple messages or letters.

Fifty-five to sixty million are limited to sixth-, seventh-, and eighth-grade reading. A majority of this group could not figure out the price per ounce of peanut butter in a 20-ounce jar costing $1.99 when told they could round the answer off to a whole number.

Thirty million have ninth and tenth-grade reading proficiency. Neither this group nor any of the preceding groups could understand a simplified written explanation of the procedures used by attorneys and judges in selecting juries.

About 3.5 percent of the 26,000-member sample demonstrated literacy skills adequate to do traditional college study, a level reached by 30 percent of secondary students in 1940 and by 30 percent of secondary students in other developed countries today.

Ninety-six and a half percent of the American population is mediocre to illiterate where deciphering print is concerned. This is no commentary on their intelligence, but without the ability to take in primary information from print and to interpret it they are at the mercy of commentators who tell them what things mean.[10]

Some social analysts have blamed the sharp decline in literacy partly on race or genetics. The theory is that allegedly smart people marry other smart people, and allegedly not-so-smart people marry other not-so-smart people. Yet the huge drop in literacy between World War II and the Korean War happened in only a ten-year period. Genetics and evolution don't work that fast, so the genetic explanation can't be true.

Also, black literacy in the United States is about 56 percent, yet the black literacy rate in Jamaica is 98.5 percent, a figure considerably higher than white literacy rates in America.[11] Also, the shocking drop in literacy after World War II ravaged whites as well as minorities.

If genetics or heredity wasn't the problem, what caused the severe decline in adult literacy after the 1940s? One major change that has been easy to track and document is that since World War II, most public schools have converted to non-phonics reading instruction such as the "whole-language" or "look-say" method.[12] I will explain in detail in Chapter 3 why whole-language reading instruction is the culprit behind this shocking decline in literacy.

Children's literacy has also deteriorated badly, not just since World War II, but over the last 120 years. For example, reading exercises for *fifth*-grade students in the 1882 *Appleton School Reader* were based on selections from such authors as Mark Twain, Benjamin Franklin, Henry David Thoreau, John Bunyan, Daniel Webster, Samuel Johnson, Sir Walter Scott, Lewis Carroll, William Shakespeare, Oliver Wendell Holmes, Thomas Jefferson, and Ralph Waldo Emerson.[13]

In contrast, in 1995, a student-teacher for a fifth-grade class in Minneapolis wrote the following letter to the local newspaper:

> . . . I was told [that] children are not to be expected to spell the following words correctly: back, big, call, came, can, day, did, dog, down, get, good, if, in, is, it, have, he, home, like, little, man, morning, mother, my, night, off, out, over, people, play, ran, said, saw, she, some, soon, their, them, there, time, two, too, up, us, very, water, we, went, where, when, will, would, etc. Is this nuts? [14]

In 2002, the New York State Education Department's annual report on the latest reading and math scores for public school students found:

• 90 percent of middle schools failed to meet New York

State minimum standards for math and English exam scores.

• 65 percent of elementary schools flunked the minimum standards.

• 84 percent of high schools failed to meet the minimum state standards.

• More than half of New York City's black and hispanic elementary-school students failed the state's English and math exams. About 30 percent of white and asian-american students failed to achieve the minimum English test scores.

• The results for eighth grade students were even worse. Here, 75 percent of black and hispanic students flunked both the English and the math tests. About 50 percent of white and asian-american eighth graders failed the tests.[15]

These studies show that public schools are failing all groups of children, black, white, hispanic, poor, and middle-class. The New York State Education Department's annual report was a harsh indictment of our public schools. Unfortunately, this frightening illiteracy is not limited to New York students. Similar test results occur in public schools across the country. According to the 2002 national report card on reading by the National Assessment of Educational Progress (NAEP), 64 percent of our children are less than proficient in reading even after *twelve years* of public school.[16]

Dr. G. Reid Lyon, Branch Chief of the National Institute for Child Health and Human Development also talked about the terrible illiteracy problem in our schools when he said:

. . . You know if you look at where we are today, the bottom line is for a country like America to be leaving behind 38-40% of its youngsters in terms of not learning to read is unconscionable. What makes it equally or doubly unconscionable is if you disaggregate the data: 70% approximately of young African-American kids can't read. 70%! If you look at Hispanic kids, the figure is 65-70%![17]

Let's recap the decline of literacy in this country over the last 150 years. By the 1850s, *before* we had compulsory, government-controlled public schools, child and adult literacy rates averaged over 90 percent, making illiteracy rates less than 10 percent. Today, as shown by the New York State Education Department's annual report and other studies, student illiteracy rates in many public schools range from *30 to 70 percent*. This is an education horror story and betrayal of our children.

The Tragic Consequences of Illiteracy

It may seem obvious why literacy is so important in our technologically advanced society. However, many parents may not fully realize the emotional pain and life-long damage illiteracy can cause their children. Literacy, the ability to read well, is the *foundation* of children's education. If children can't read well, every subject they try to learn will frustrate them. If they can't read math, history, or science textbooks, if they stumble over the words, they will soon give up reading out of frustration. Asking children who are poor readers to study these subjects is like asking them to climb a rope with one arm.

Kids learn to read in their most formative years, which is why reading can profoundly affect their self-esteem. When children learn to read, they also start learning how to think abstractly, because words convey ideas and relationships between ideas. How well they read therefore affects children's feelings about their ability to learn. This in turn affects how kids feel about themselves generally—whether a child thinks he or she is stupid or bright. Children who struggle with reading often blame themselves and feel ashamed of themselves.[18]

As Donald L. Nathanson, M.D., Clinical Professor of Psychiatry and Human Behavior at Jefferson Medical College noted:

First reading itself, and then the whole education process, becomes so imbued with, stuffed with, amplified, magnified by shame that children can develop an aversion to everything that is education.[19]

Often, poor readers will struggle just to graduate from high school. They can lose general confidence in themselves and not try for college or a career. Their job opportunities can dry up. Their poor reading skills and low self-confidence can strangle their ability to earn money. They can struggle financially their whole lives. If they marry and have children, they can struggle even more. Life for illiterate adults can easily degenerate into misery, poverty, failure, and hopelessness. According to a 1992 study by the National Institute for Literacy, "43% of Americans with the lowest literacy skills live in poverty and 70% have no job or a part-time job. Only 5% of Americans with strong literacy skills live in poverty." [20]

As Dr. Grover Whitehurst, Assistant Secretary of the U.S. Department of Education, said, "Reading is absolutely fundamental. It's almost trite to say that. But in our society, the inability to be fluent consigns children to failure in school and consigns adults to the lowest strata of job and life opportunities." [21]

Illiteracy also perpetuates social injustice. It keeps many low-income black, hispanic, and other inner-city minorities in poverty. It perpetuates the cycle of failure in minority communities. It pushes many low-income minority children into drugs and crime because too often they don't see any other way out of their poverty. As David Boulton, organizational learning theorist and co-producer of the *Children of the Code* PBS Television Documentary Series, noted:

> Even if you cut the numbers in half, statistically, more children are at risk of suffering long-term life-harm from the consequences of not learning to read well than from parental abuse, accidents, and all known childhood diseases and disorders combined. Even if you cut the numbers in half, the national cost of reading related difficulties is greater that the cost of the wars on crime, drugs, and terror combined.[22]

That is what illiteracy can mean, what it does mean for millions of public-school children who can barely read. Does any parent want this kind of future for his or her children?

It Wasn't Always This Way

The public-school system in America has become a dismal failure. But education in many other times and cultures has been quite successful. The ancient Greeks, whose civilization was at its height around 550 B.C., founded Western civilization as we know it. The Athenian Greeks invented or perfected logic, drama, science, philosophy, astronomy, mathematics, literature, and much more. Yet ancient Athens *had no compulsory schools*.

Other than requiring two years of military training for young men that began at age eighteen, Athens let parents educate their children as they saw fit.[23] Parents either taught their children at home or sent them to voluntary schools where teachers and philosophers like Socrates, Plato, and Aristotle gave lectures to all who wanted to learn. These great teacher-philosophers did not need a license to teach, nor did they have tenure. The ancient Athenians had a free-market education system. The thought of compulsory, state-run schools and compulsory licensing would have been repulsive to them. The ancient Athenians respected parents' natural rights to direct the education of their children.

In contrast, Sparta, Athens's mortal enemy, created the first truly state-run, compulsory education system on record. Spartans lived and died for the city-state, and had to serve their rulers from birth until sixty years of age. Their society was a brutal military dictatorship in which male children literally belonged to the city, not to their parents. The Spartan military government took boys from their homes and parents at the age of seven and forced them to live in military-style barracks for the rest of their lives. Spartan men were life-long soldiers whose highest duty was to obey the commands of their leaders. It is no coincidence that Sparta had compulsory, state-run education.[24] If a society believes that children belong not to parents but to the government, then the state's rulers must control children's education by compulsion.

The citizens of the early Roman Republic enjoyed an education system similar to ancient Athens. It was voluntary, and parents paid tutors or schools directly. There was very little government interference, so a vibrant education free market of tutors, schools, and apprenticeships developed.

One aspect of Roman society that compromised their education system was that Roman parents wanted their children to learn knowledge that only Greek teachers could provide. However, most Greeks in Rome at the time were slaves.

As a result, the Greek teachers could not personally or financially benefit by their work. Often their morale was low and they were subject to harsh discipline. Unlike the free teachers in ancient Athens, Greek slave-teachers in Rome had little incentive to innovate or continually improve their skills. As a result, the quality of education stagnated.

Also, a majority of the Roman population was slaves, both from Greece and other areas Rome had conquered. Naturally, these slaves had no rights and no control over their children's education.

Things got worse after Julius Caesar was assassinated in 44 B.C. and Emperor Augustus took power. The quasi-democratic Republic turned into the dictatorial Roman Empire ruled by Emperors. To secure his power, each succeeding Emperor tightened his grip on education. They increasingly regulated education, suppressed teachers who spoke against the Emperor, and eventually required teachers of Greek and Latin rhetoric to be licensed and paid by the State. The quality of education in Rome then grew progressively worse.[25]

The parallels with the history of education in America are striking. Here too, when our schools were voluntary and parents paid teachers and schools directly, we had a high-quality, constantly improving education system. After state governments created compulsory public schools, education in America has been going down-hill ever since.

After Rome fell, Europe stagnated in the Middle Ages. During this time, the Roman Catholic Church had almost a complete monopoly on education with its church schools and monasteries, but these schools were also voluntary. However, because of this monopoly control, there was little progress or innovation in either scientific knowledge or the quality of education.

One bright spot during this time was in the Muslim world in their golden age between the eighth and eleventh centuries, when education and scientific knowledge blossomed. This happened because, as in ancient Athens, Muslim Sultans (rulers) interfered very little with education, tolerated religious dissent, and parents paid tutors or schools directly.

Jewish and Muslim teachers and scholars created a vibrant, innovative, free-market education system throughout the Muslim world. These great scholars also rediscovered the works of Aristotle and other ancient Greek thinkers and translated their works into Arabic and Latin. They also advanced knowledge in many fields such as astronomy, mathematics, and medicine.

The Muslims' brilliant, mostly free-market society helped awaken Europe from its slumber in the Middle Ages. European scholars rediscovered the science and knowledge of the ancient Greeks when they came into contact with the Muslim world in Spain, in the Crusades, and later through Italy.[26]

This two-thousand-year-old tradition of mostly voluntary, parent-directed education came to America from Renaissance Europe when colonists from England set up schools in the Massachusetts Bay and Jamestown, Virginia colonies in the 1650s. The education system in each colony varied. There were many small, private non-religious grammar schools and colleges, Quaker and Lutheran schools, fundamentalist and liberal Protestant schools, schools that taught the classics, and technical schools that taught children a trade. It was a vibrant and voluntary free-market education system that catered to children's needs and abilities and parents' budgets.[27]

Many towns had one-room schoolhouses that local residents or church members paid for. Many communities funded their schools through a combination of taxes and tuition from parents. There was voluntary, tax-supported public schooling in Boston since 1635, but these public schools enrolled only a small fraction of the student population by the 1790s. Most parents taught their children reading, arithmetic, and Bible studies at home. Throughout the thirteen colonies, parents controlled and paid for their children's education, and formal schooling in a town or church-sponsored school was voluntary.

Many children also learned a trade through apprenticeship, a respected tradition that had been around for hundreds of years. Parents often apprenticed their boys (girls mostly stayed at home) to a local tradesman or professional, like a clerk, blacksmith, or lawyer. The boy would work only for room and board, and the tradesman would teach the child his trade. George Washington learned his surveying skills as an apprentice. John Adams, our second president, apprenticed with a practicing lawyer in Boston. Apprenticing was a common way for an ambitious young man to learn a trade or profession in colonial times. Sadly, this unique and valuable learning method has almost disappeared today.

Benjamin Franklin, a brilliant writer, businessman, diplomat, and scientist, was a self-made man and mostly self-taught. Although Franklin's father was a candlemaker, he was intelligent and well-read. He taught Ben and his other children how to read, a skill that Ben took to quickly. Young Benjamin attended a local grammar school at age eight but stayed there hardly a year. His father sent him to another "writing and arithmetic" school, but Ben failed in arithmetic there. As a result, his father then removed him from this formal school, and at ten years old Ben went to work for his father. [28]

However, Benjamin didn't like the candle-making business, so his father introduced him to other trades to see if he liked any of them, which he didn't. At age twelve, Franklin's father apprenticed him to his older brother James, a printer in Boston. Unfortunately, Ben didn't get along with his brother, so at age sixteen Ben left Boston and walked to Philadelphia to seek his fortune. In Philadelphia, he eventually opened his own printing business and became successful.

Franklin loved books and read voraciously. He taught himself to read and write well, studied arithmetic, and even taught himself French, all from books his father gave him. He read contemporary and near-contemporary authors, such as John Bunyan, Cotton Mather, and Daniel Defoe, as well as Plutarch and other classical writers that most college students today find difficult reading. [29]

Franklin's education by poor but literate parents, as well as his later self-education, was not the exception at this time—it was the norm. George Washington went to school briefly at eleven years old. He didn't like school much—he preferred to spend his time dancing and horseback riding. His grammar school, where he learned geometry, trigonometry, and surveying, required young Washington to know how to read, write, and do basic arithmetic *before* it admitted him.

George attended school for exactly two years. During this time, he taught himself practical skills he could use when he started to work, such as how to write legal forms for commerce, including leases, patents, bills of exchange, and tobacco receipts. He also studied geography and astronomy on his own, and by eighteen years old had devoured novels by Henry Fielding, Tobias Smollett, Daniel Defoe, and classical Roman works like Seneca's *Morals*, Julius Caesar's *Commentaries*, and the *Histories* of Tacitus. These are difficult books most college students today have never heard of, much less read. Years later, after serving as military commander-in-chief in the Revolutionary War, Washington became a self-taught architect and designed his magnificent home at Mount Vernon.[30] Yet, many historians consider Washington the *least* well-read among the Founding Fathers.

Like most of the other Founding Fathers, including Samuel Adams, Thomas Jefferson, and James Madison, most average colonial Americans spent few years, if any, in formal grammar schools of the day, yet they knew how to read and write well. Most local grammar schools expected parents to teach their children to read and write before they started school. Most colonial parents apparently had no trouble teaching their children these skills.

At least ten of our presidents were home-schooled. James Madison's mother taught him to read and write. John Quincy Adams was educated at home until he was twelve years old. At age fourteen, he entered Harvard. Abraham Lincoln, except for fifty weeks in a grammar school, learned at home from books he borrowed. He learned law by reading law books, and became an apprentice to a practicing lawyer in Illinois.

Other great Americans were similarly educated. John Rutledge, a chief justice of the Supreme Court, was taught at home by his father until he was eleven years old. Patrick Henry, one of our great Founding Fathers and the governor of colonial Virginia, learned English grammar, the Bible, history, French, Latin, Greek, and the classics from his father.

Abigail Adams, Martha Washington, and Florence Nightingale were all taught at home by their mothers or fathers. John Jay was one of the authors of the Federalist Papers, a chief Justice of the Supreme Court, and a governor of New York. His mother taught him reading, grammar, and Latin before he was eight years old. John Marshall, our first Supreme Court Chief Justice, was home-schooled by his father until age fourteen. Robert E. Lee, Thomas "Stonewall" Jackson, George Patton, and Douglas MacArthur were also educated at home. Booker T. Washington, helped by his mother, taught himself to read by using Noah Webster's *Blue Back Speller*.

Thomas Edison's public school expelled him at age seven because his teacher thought he was feeble-minded. Edison, one of our greatest inventors, had only three months of formal schooling. After Thomas left school, his mother taught him the basics at home over the next three years. Under his mother's care and instruction, young Edison thrived. If Thomas Edison was alive today as that child of seven, school authorities would probably stick him in special-education classes. Poor Thomas would waste his precious mind and be bored to death until they released him from school at age sixteen.

Many of our greatest writers and artists, such as Mark Twain, Agatha Christie, Pearl S. Buck, Charles Dickens, and George Bernard Shaw, were also home-schooled or self-taught. Irving Berlin quit school in the second grade and taught himself to be a musician. Photographer Ansel Adams and architect Frank Lloyd Wright's parents taught them the basics at home. Joseph Pulitzer, the great newspaper publisher who created the Pulitzer Prize, was home-schooled. [31]

This is only a partial list of great Americans who were home-schooled or never saw the inside of a public school. Most of the famous and accomplished Americans children study about in their history books were either educated by their parents or mostly self-taught. These famous Americans' achievements prove that to succeed in life, a child does not have to attend a compulsory public school.

How Did Government
Take Control of Education?

If literacy and academic standards were so high before the 1850s, why did we let state governments take control of education? What happened?

Briefly, the story is as follows. In the 1840s, American intellectuals and education theorists such as Horace Mann adopted the German educational theory that children belong to the government, not their parents. In 1717, King Frederick William I of Prussia (today's Germany) set up Europe's first national, government-controlled school system. Mann and a small group of influential American education activists visited Prussia to examine their schools and came home praising them. They admired how the Prussian system gave their education bureaucrats complete control over children's minds and education and molded children into obedient citizens. The Prussian school philosophy was expounded in 1917 by Franz de Hovre:

The prime function of German education is that it is

based on a national principle . . . . A fundamental feature
of German education: education to the State, education
for the State, education by the State. The Volksschule is
a direct result of a national principle aimed at national
unity. The State is the supreme end in view. [32]

The German philosopher Johann Fichte, one of the key
contributors to the Prussian school system, said that, "schools
must fashion the person, and fashion him in such a way that
he simply cannot will otherwise than what you wish him to
will." [33]

It is no coincidence that the Nazis gained power in Germany. For two hundred years before the 1930s, German schools
had indoctrinated children with the idea that absolute obedience to the government was their highest duty, and that the
individual had no rights and did not matter.

Mann and his colleagues studied the Prussian schools
and then pushed to impose the same system here. How could
they do this in America, where education was voluntary and
most children learned at home? Simple. They vigorously lobbied state legislatures to create government-controlled public
schools. State politicians of the day listened to these educationists' arguments and created the first state-run school system in
Massachusetts in 1852. Over the next fifty years, with Massachusetts as the spearhead, all states in the union created similar
public-school systems.

However, Mann and his followers soon realized that American public schools would not be effective and all-controlling
as they were in Prussia if parents could refuse to send their
children to school. So the next step was to push for compulsory-attendance laws that forced parents to send their children
to these schools. By 1900, most states had such laws.

Compulsory public schools did not succeed without a fight.
Many angry parents realized that these schools violated their
liberty and parental rights, and did not willingly hand their
children over to school officials. In Massachusetts, almost 80
percent of the voters resisted compulsory education. In 1880,

Massachusetts had to send its state militia to "persuade" the parents of Barnstable, on Cape Cod, to give up their children to the state schoolmasters.[34]

Mann and his group of education activists were also part of a larger group of influential Protestant leaders in America who pushed hard to create public schools. What did they hope to accomplish? According to author John Taylor Gatto:

> A small number of very passionate American ideological leaders visited Prussia in the first half of the 19th century; fell in love with the order, obedience, and efficiency of its education system; and campaigned relentlessly thereafter to bring the Prussian vision to these shores. Prussia's ultimate goal was to unify Germany; the Americans' was to mold hordes of immigrant Catholics to a national consensus based on a northern European cultural model. To do that, children would have to be removed from their parents and from inappropriate cultural influences. [35]

In colonial America, learning the three Rs was initially left to parents and churches. In the first half of the nineteenth century, millions of Catholic immigrants from Ireland and eastern Europe came to America. These immigrants threatened New England's Calvinist Protestant culture.

Public-school activists like Mann saw compulsory education as a way to achieve a uniform culture among an increasingly heterogeneous people. These Protestant leaders realized they could use compulsory public schools to influence immigrant children to accept Protestant values and ideology. American Catholics responded by creating a network of private schools.

Mann and other public-school promoters imported three main ideas from the authoritarian Prussian schools:

> The first was that the purpose of state schooling was not intellectual training but the conditioning of children to obedience, subordination, and collective life. Thus

memorization outranked thinking. Second, whole ideas were broken into fragmented subjects and school days were divided into fixed periods, so that self-motivation to learn would be muted by ceaseless interruptions. Third, the state was posited as the true parent of children.[36]

Mann and his followers thought these ideas represented a scientific approach to education. Yet there were no scientific studies at the time to show how children learned, or that the Prussian system they promoted did in fact help children to learn.

Now think about our public schools today. They mirror exactly the three Prussian education principles noted above. First, public schools promote collective learning and conformity to authority. Compulsory-attendance laws force children to attend school. Students sit in barracks-like classrooms, twenty to thirty students to a class. Students have to obey school rules and study the core subjects teachers and principals tell them to study. Individualized instruction is rare.

Second, the school day is divided into fifty-minute periods, and during each period children learn a different subject. At the sound of the bell, like Pavlov's dogs, students go to their next class. Each class is totally disconnected from every other class. Students are not allowed to concentrate on one subject for more than the fifty-minute period. Learning becomes disconnected and superficial. Students have to read and memorize material from dumbed-down textbooks and then regurgitate this material on tests. Students get few if any courses in logic, thinking, creative problem solving, integrating knowledge on different subjects, or anything the ancient Greeks would call true education. They rarely learn any subjects they can personally relate to. Is it any wonder that public-school classes bore so many children?

Third, public schools increasingly usurp parents' job of raising and educating their children and teaching them moral values. Schools now give children psychological counseling,

sex education, food-lunch programs, values-clarification programs, and many other tasks parents used to handle. School
authorities have expanded their mission and now seek to mold
the "whole" child. Increasingly, schools are now part priest,
nutritionist, social worker, psychologist, and family counselor.

Drugs and Violence in the Schools

Public schools not only fail to educate our children, they
can also be natural breeding grounds for drugs and violence.
Children are packed into classrooms with twenty or more other immature children or teenagers, all the same age. The peer
pressure in school becomes socialization, pushing many children into using drugs and alcohol.

Young boys and girls have raging hormones and budding
sexuality, and male teenage testosterone levels are high. Teenagers are in the half-child, half-adult stage of life and often lack
judgment and are emotionally immature. Pack twenty teenagers together into classrooms for six to eight hours a day, and
you have a mixture that can lead to trouble. It's inevitable that
violence will break out—it's built into the system.

Also, even the most conscientious teacher is usually too busy
and overworked to give children the individual attention they
need. Critics of home-schooling often say that home-schoolers
don't get proper socialization, an argument I will answer in a
later chapter. But so-called socialization in public schools is
often cruel and violent. Bullying, peer pressure, racial cliques,
sexual tensions, and competition for the teacher's approval all
create a stressful, sometimes violent environment.

Compulsory-attendance laws also contribute to violence in
the schools. In most states, these laws force children to stay in
school until they are sixteen years old or graduate high school.
Teenagers who hate school or are aggressive or potentially violent sociopaths, can't leave. As a result, they often take out their
hatred and aggression on other students. Those children who
want to learn are forced to endure bullying and violence by

these troubled teens.

Also, the law is on the side of violent or disruptive students who are classified as "disabled." In 1975, Congress passed the Individuals with Disabilities Education Act (IDEA). Based on this legislation, in 1988 the Supreme Court ruled that schools could not remove disruptive disabled children from classrooms without a parent's consent. If parents don't consent, teachers are out of luck. Disabled children who are socially impaired, can't get along with other kids, or sometimes turn violent, therefore fall under this category. Of course, this adds yet another layer of potentially violent children who teachers can't remove from class. [37]

Violence in public schools can literally kill your child. In the 2000-2001 school year, students were victims of about *1.9 million* nonfatal violent crimes such as rape, assault, and robbery. [38] This figure equals about 9,000 violent incidents every school day throughout America, or about one every three seconds.

Public schools are also a drug pusher's heaven. Thousands of teenagers smoke, drink beer, and try marijuana or hard drugs because of intense peer-pressure. Schools put hundreds of children together in one big building or courtyard. Mix in overworked or indifferent teachers who have little time or desire to supervise children's extracurricular activities. That's why drug pushers circle schoolyards like vultures. Where else can they find groups of vulnerable victims all herded together for their convenience? Is it any wonder that drug and alcohol use is a major problem in public schools?

In the 2001-2002 school year, 34.9 percent of tenth-grade students surveyed said they had smoked cigarettes within the past year. Fifty-one and two tenths percent said they had drunk beer, and 33.4 percent said they got bombed on that beer. Also, 29.8 percent of the same tenth-grade students said they had smoked marijuana within the past year, and 78.7 percent of these marijuana users said they got "bombed or very high" on it. [39]

When children are home-schooled, parents can advise and

watch over their kids. At home, there is no peer pressure to try drugs, as there is in public schools. Drug pushers don't hover around private residences.

Parents should therefore ask themselves: Do my children belong in violent, drug-infested public schools that can barely teach my kids to read? In Chapter 2, we will examine other ways public schools threaten your children.

2

Anti-Parent, Anti-Judeo-Christian, and Anti-American Values in Public-School Classrooms

Compulsory public schools are anti-parent, by their nature, despite school officials' calls for more parental involvement and cooperation. Public schools are government institutions that seek to control our children's values as well as their education. Because parents have always (rightly) believed that these important tasks are their responsibility, totalitarian societies such as the former Soviet Union usually regard parents as competitors for control of children's minds and values. Unfortunately, the same applies to our government-owned-and-operated public schools. Below we will examine some of the ways public schools are anti-parent.

Compulsory-Attendance Laws

Compulsory-attendance laws are school authorities' first assault on parental rights. These laws are a form of prison sentence for children—they force almost forty-five million chil-

31

dren to sit in often boring classes six to eight hours a day for eight to twelve years. Compulsory-attendance laws force parents to hand over their children to state education employees called teachers, principals, and administrators, whose good-will and competence parents must take on faith. Compulsory-attendance laws show contempt for parents' rights because they are based on the notion that state governments own our children's minds and time for twelve years, and that parents should have little say in the matter.

In effect, these laws allow state education officials to legally kidnap millions of children, allegedly to benefit the children by giving them an education. "Kidnap" may seem like a harsh word, yet wouldn't you apply that word to someone who took your child by force against your will or your child's will?

Unfortunately, most parents voluntarily send their kids to the local public school. These parents believe they are doing the right thing or have no alternative, so they might not believe that school authorities kidnap their kids. However, millions of other parents are so disgusted with public schools that they either homeschool their kids or send them to private schools.

Every year, school authorities and social service agencies harass or threaten hundreds of home-schooling parents who remove their children from public school. If parents refuse to send their children to the local public school, and do not follow a state's home-schooling regulations, school authorities can file child abuse or neglect charges against parents. They can then call in social service agencies that threaten parents with jail or threaten to take away their children and put them in foster homes.

These threats are not empty. Over the past thirty years, school authorities across the country have arrested some home-schooling parents and forced their terrified children into foster homes. School authorities are dead serious about defending compulsory-attendance laws because public schools' existence depends on these laws. The Home School Legal Defense Association (HSLDA) claims to represent "approximately 365 home-schooling families a year who are wrongly charged of some form of child abuse or neglect" because they chose not to comply with compulsory-attendance laws.[1]

School authorities' harassment of home-schoolers reveals the nasty compulsion underlying our public schools. Many school officials believe they have the right to force parents to send their children to public school. They get angry at home-schooling parents who defy their authority, which is one reason why they harass these parents.

The Pacific Justice Institute wrote about increasing political intimidation of home-schooling parents in California in one of its press releases:

> The California Senate is presently considering a bill that could greatly intimidate homeschoolers and other parents in California. SB 950, which is sponsored by Senator Alarcon, would add habitual truancy to the definition of child abuse in Welfare and Institutions Code Section 300.

The same press release quoted Brad Dacus, then president of the Pacific Justice Institute:

> This provision enables a child to be immediately taken from their family and put into the juvenile court system with no prior opportunity for parents to make their case. Under present law, truancy is addressed through the school district, where parents are entitled to make a defense before any action is taken against the child or family.
>
> Those who would potentially lose their children as a result of this bill would include homeschoolers wrongfully accused of truancy or any child who has up to five unexcused absences. Such unexcused absences usually include family vacations outside scheduled school vacation days. This dangerous bill creates an unnecessary fear that parents will have their children taken with no due process whatsoever.[2]

Compulsory-attendence laws give local governments the power to control children's education, and to punish parents who dare to presume they have the right to educate their children at home. As always, the school authorities' final argument is a gun—if parents don't comply with these laws, police can enter their home and take their children from them by force.

Sexual Corruption of Children in Public Schools

One of parents' most important duties is to protect their children from harmful sexual values and behaviors. Yet many public schools force potentially harmful, sometimes shockingly explicit sex education on their students. Most of the time, parents have no control over the content of these classes. Occasionally a group of parents finds out about a particularly obnoxious sex-education class and protests to the principal or local school board. The class may be dropped, only to be replaced by another class that teaches equally objectionable material.

Many school authorities insist that children need comprehensive sex education from kindergarten through high school. They believe parents can't be trusted with this task because parents allegedly have shameful feelings about sex or "outdated" moral or sexual values. School authorities, claiming they know best regarding sex education, usurp the parents' role, allegedly for the good of the children. School authorities' cavalier attitude towards parents on this issue shows their anti-parent bias and their contempt for parents' right to control the values their children are taught.

Many sex-education classes indoctrinate children with sexual values that can cause them irreparable harm. According to Christopher J. Klicka, author of *The Right Choice, Home Schooling*, many sex-education textbooks used in public schools throughout the country teach that any kind of sex is acceptable, including adultery, homosexuality, masturbation, and premarital sex. In effect, these textbooks preach that kids should engage in any kind of sex that they feel comfortable with. [3]

Horror stories about sex-education classes and flagrant violations of parents' rights confront us from around the country. Here are just a few of those stories:

• On March 19, 1996, a public school in East Stroudsburg, Pennsylvania made 59 sixth-grade girls submit to a genital examination as part of a routine physical. The school did not ask for parental consent. During the exam, school officials blocked the exit doors and refused to let the crying and pleading young girls call their parents.[4]

• In Stephens County, Georgia, parents were shocked to discover that their fourteen and fifteen-year-old daughters had been driven to a birth control clinic by a public-school staff member without their knowledge. The county clinic administered AIDS tests and Pap smears to the girls and gave them birth control pills and condoms. The school denied parents access to the test results and defended its actions on the grounds that the counselor believed that she was doing what was best for the girls.[5]

• The Pacific Justice Institute filed a lawsuit on behalf of parents against the Novato [California] Unified School District for authorizing pro-homosexual presentations without any prior notice or consent. According to the Pacific Justice Institute Press Release, "The presentations entitled 'Cootie Shots,' exposed elementary-school children as young as seven years old with skits containing gay and lesbian overtures. The presentations were followed by question and answer sessions about what constitutes 'normal' families, and acceptance of those who choose the homosexual lifestyle."[6]

• Carol (last name withheld for privacy), a schoolteacher, couldn't believe what she was being asked to teach in her sex-education class. The curriculum forced her to show second-graders pictures of nude boys and girls and ask them to name body parts. School authorities told Carol and her fellow elementary-school teachers that there were no absolute moral rules, so she shouldn't be concerned about what she had to teach the children.[7]

• In Pittsburgh, Pennsylvania, parents became furious about a comprehensive survey given to elementary-school children in the Gateway School District. The five-to-ten-year-old students were asked questions regarding "forced sex, the torture of animals, the use of guns, and setting fires." Many of the children were so upset by these questions that they became physically ill, started bed-wetting, or began having nightmares. By the time these problems were brought to light, the survey had already been given to over 1,500 children in the Pittsburgh area.[8]

• A Massachusetts Department of Education employee described the pleasures of homosexual sex to a group of high school students at a state-sponsored workshop on March 25, [2000] at Tufts [University], this way: "Fisting [forcing one's entire hand into another person's rectum or vagina] often gets a bad rap. . . . [It's] an experience of letting somebody into your body that you want to be that close and intimate with . . . [and] to put you into an exploratory mode."[9]

• On March 25, [2000] the Massachusetts Department of Education, the Governor's Commission For Gay and Lesbian Youth, and GLSEN [Gay and Lesbian and Straight Education Network] co-sponsored a statewide conference at Tufts University called "Teach-Out." Among the goals were to build more GSAs [Gay/Straight Alliance clubs] in Massachusetts and expand homosexual teaching into the lower grades. Scores of gay-friendly teachers and administrators attended. They received state "professional development credits." Teenagers and children as young as twelve were encouraged to come from around the state, and many were bused in from their home districts. Homosexual activists from across the country were also there."[10]

• A mother was shocked and outraged when she discovered that her son had to read a novel about teenage gay pornography for his English class. The woman had enrolled her son in Newton South High School's summer program to help prepare him for the English portion of the Massachusetts State Standardized Test. Little did she know that her son's teacher had recently bragged in a *Boston Globe* newspaper article how he was quietly introducing 'gay, lesbian, bisexual, and transgender' subjects into his academic high school classes.

"In this class, the teacher passed out a copy of *The Perks of Being a Wallflower* by Stephen Chbosky to each child as the class's required reading assignment, with instructions to write an essay on the book when they finished it."

"The book is aimed at teenagers, and is told from a teenage boy's perspective. The book contains explicit references and discussion regarding: Sexual acts between teenagers, male masturbation, oral-genital sex, a great deal of profanity, male homosexual acts between teenage boys, including kissing, seduction, 'having a crush,' and anal sex, illegal drug use, homosexual acts between men and boys, sex between a boy and a dog, and female masturbation using an object."[11]

• In Newton, Massachusetts, the school forced ninth-grade girls in the health classes to go to a drug store and buy condoms and practice putting them on a banana.[12]

I apologize to the reader for the long list of graphic horror stories. Unfortunately, the examples I listed barely touch what goes on in sex-education classes throughout the country.

When parents who find out about such classes vehemently object, school authorities often arrogantly dismiss parents' complaints. A Michigan state Senate committee studying the problem of parental consent in public schools, found:

> The treatment of parents with the temerity to object to sex education curricula also reflects a more general attitude toward the role of parents in public education today. "There is a pervasive attitude among many administrators and health educators," the Michigan Senate committee found, "that they know best what children need. They communicate to parents that they are the professionals and the parents are unschooled amateurs." Too often, the committee found that parents were treated as if they were an "incidental biological appendage in the raising of their children."[13]

Parents should *not* trust school officials on this issue. They should make sure their local public schools are not exposing their children to such shocking sex-education material.

Public Schools Turn a Deaf Ear To Parents' Complaints

School authorities continually claim they want more parent cooperation and participation in their children's education. They complain when parents don't show up for parent-teacher conferences or push their children to do their homework. Yet this constant cry for parent cooperation is often a smoke-screen pretense to make parents think they have some control over their children's education. In most cases, parents have no such control. Teachers and principals may placate parents or ask for their cooperation, but they rarely make the important changes parents ask for.

For example, most parents want their children to learn to do basic arithmetic without using calculators as a crutch. A poll by *Public Agenda* found that 86 percent of parents want students to learn arithmetic by hand before they use calculators. However, the math-teaching policy for most public schools today is that

all children beginning in kindergarten have access to calculators at all times to do math problems.[14]

Most school districts make important teaching-method or
curriculum decisions in secret, without parents' knowledge or
approval. A parent's only recourse is to complain to principals
or school authorities after the authorities have dictated their
curriculum or teaching methods and the parent sees the damage to her children. Unfortunately, such complaints are often
futile.

Jerry Moore has a web site dealing with education issues,
called *Jerry Moore's School Talk*, where parents can write in their
complaints about public schools. On April 9, 2000, Mr. Moore
wrote:

> I recently talked with a parent who is disgusted with
> the way the district makes decisions. She claimed, with
> some validity, that committees meet and decide impor-
> tant issues without the public knowing about when and
> where the meetings are held. In effect, she said, the deci-
> sions are being made in secret. She also said that if the
> school is going to continue this practice, the least it can
> do is survey parents for their opinions before making
> decisions.[15]

Unfortunately, this parent, like most others, didn't realize that school authorities don't want her opinion. Too often,
school authorities ignore parents suggestions or complaints
because they truly believe they are the experts and parents are
just annoying amateurs. Many school officials believe parents
should not have any real input in their children's education.
That is one reason why school authorities hold their committee meetings in secret.

Another reason is that school authorities fear that parents
will complain about certain classes and curriculum subjects.
For instance, as we noted in the graphic examples above, many
public schools have introduced homosexuality propaganda
into sex-education classes. When parents find out about these

classes, they frequently complain to the school principal and local politicians. As a result of these complaints, many states have passed Parent-Notification Laws. These laws require schools to notify parents about possibly objectionable classes, and give parents the right to withdraw or "opt-out" their children from these classes. These laws haven't worked. One parent complained:

> The current "notification" law has been a terrible failure. It is cumbersome, vague, not fully inclusive, and unenforceable. It was supposed to protect parents and children from graphic sexuality and homosexuality in the schools, but simply hasn't worked. . . . The current law is very narrow in scope . . . . It forces parents to opt-out their children. Parents often have to go through a cumbersome bureaucratic process and fill out forms to remove their kids from the class. This can be intimidating and confusing. . . . Many school districts simply ignore the law. When pressed by parents, they'll often say they forgot or there was a glitch in getting the notifications out. . . . The Department of Education does not enforce the law.[16]

These examples show that many school officials do not comply with state laws that would protect children from graphic homosexual material in sex-education classes. Here again we see an example of school authorities' arrogant contempt of parents' rights.

Turning Children into Spies against Their Parents

Some public schools try to turn children against their parents with scary classroom stories or lessons about child abuse. Public-school authorities have increasingly decided that *they* are children's first line of defense against alleged child abuse.

This new attitude falls under what is now known as a "protective behavior" curriculum. The assumptions behind this curriculum are that every child needs to be warned about and prepared for possible dangers of verbal, physical, and sexual abuse because every child is a potential victim, not only of strangers but *of his or her own family*.

Increasingly, school authorities instruct teachers to ask children questions about their parents' behavior and actions toward them at home. The questions amount to asking kids to spy on their parents and report incidents that make them feel "uncomfortable." Some school authorities use such tales by children to investigate or file charges of child abuse against parents who often did no more than yell at their children or spank them lightly.

In effect, to allegedly protect children, school authorities now consider *all* parents as potential abusers, invade the privacy of parents' homes, and turn children against their parents. Often, children are disturbed and emotionally traumatized by the insinuations school authorities put into their heads. The following incident described by Charles J. Sykes, in his book *Dumbing Down Our Kids*, illustrates this disturbing anti-parent campaign by public schools across the country:

> I first became aware of the protective behaviors curriculum when a mother called me to tell me of an experience she had with her daughter. Her child, an elementary schoolgirl, had come home in tears. When she saw that her mother was home and waiting for her, she rushed to her in relief. "I wasn't sure you'd be here," she told her mother. Her mother reassured her that she would always be there for her. In school that day, her daughter told her, her class had discussed "bad" touching including spanking.
>
> In the course of the discussion, children had been encouraged to share with the teachers and classmates whether they had ever been touched in that way and the girl had said that her mother had spanked her. The

children were also told that people who engaged in bad touching would be taken away and put in jail. For the rest of the school day the girl was terrified that her mother who had spanked her would now be taken away and locked up for her bad touching.[17]

In 1992, the school board in Kettle Moraine School District in southeastern Wisconsin, adopted a 164-page "protective behaviors" program for kindergarten through fifth-grade students. The program explicitly teaches children to fear sexual abuse from their parents and other family members, and coaches the children on reporting such incidents to school officials. This program is not an isolated incident from one public school. Most public schools now teach children about the dangers of sexual abuse from adults, including their parents.[18]

School authorities often verbally abuse parents who complain about "protective behaviors" curricula, calling them "back-to-basics" or "pro-family" people who belong to conservative religious groups. Most parents would consider being pro-family a good thing, not an insult.[19] However, remember that school authorities, like authoritarian governments, often consider parents their natural enemy or competitor. From the authorities' point of view, being pro-family implies being *against* school authorities who think they are protecting children by having them report their parents' allegedly unacceptable behavior..

Paul Craig Roberts' article in *Capitalism* magazine, "The U.S. Child and Family Services Gestapo Targets Parents," describes how some schools now get children to spy on and fear their parents:

> In many schools, teachers ask young children if parents touch their private parts, spank them, or scream at them (psychological abuse). Children are asked, "When you misbehave, how are you punished?"[20]
>
> Parents are slowly learning the hard way that raising a child the way they were raised can be a crime. If

you want to avoid ruin, understand that child advocates have succeeded in convincing school teachers, doctors, your neighbors—just about anyone who sees your child—that three out of four parents are child abusers. . . . Child advocates have put in place a system of reporting on parents that is more intrusive than the systems used by communists and National Socialists [Nazis].[21]

This anti-parent agenda is not limited to sex-education classes or getting kids to spy on their parents. For example, teachers in a values-clarification program in Oregon asked third graders if any of them ever wanted to beat up their parents. Fourth graders in a "talented and gifted" program were shown a movie in which children were actually fighting with their parents. In a Tucson high-school health class, teachers asked students how many of them hated their parents. These classes insert what one Tucson parent called a "wedge of doubt, distrust and disrespect" between children and their parents.

Many school authorities don't want parents to know what the schools are teaching their children. In some schools, teachers explicitly instruct students not to tell their parents what is discussed in class.[22]

Federal law prohibits public schools from asking children for highly personal information without parents' permission, yet many public schools blatantly disregard this law. In 1995, syndicated columnist Debra J. Saunders found that in Petaluma, California, a mandatory high-school course called Human Interaction had parents up in arms. The course included take-home and in-class worksheets asking such questions as whether students should be able to discuss in class how much money their parents made and whether any of the students' parents or other close relatives had a history of alcoholism or mental illness.[23]

In light of the public-school system's anti-parent agenda, parents should question their children periodically whether their teachers ask them personal questions about themselves or their family, and what kinds of questions the teachers ask.

Americans pay taxes for public schools to teach children to read, not to spy on or fear their parents.

Anti-Judeo-Christian Bias

The Assault on Values

Is there anything wrong with lying, cheating, stealing, shoplifting, taking drugs, premarital sex, insulting your parents, pornography, irresponsibility, or getting pregnant? Not according to the values taught to children in many public schools today.

From the earliest times in America, teachers believed that schools should teach moral values. What good is a child who knows when Columbus discovered America but can't tell right from wrong? The most popular reading instruction books in the nineteenth century were the *McGuffy's Readers*, which taught children to read through stories of increasing complexity. Each story also taught children a moral lesson about values such as honesty, hard work, integrity, perseverance, compassion, respect for others' rights, and individual responsibility. Up to the 1930s, most schools in America reinforced the Judeo-Christian values most parents taught their children at home.

Today, many school authorities seem to have contempt for religion and traditional moral values. Public schools now push anti-American, anti-Judeo-Christian, politically correct values on their students. They force children to endure years of "values clarification" classes which teach children that moral values are subjective and meaningless. These classes teach kids that whatever feels good at the moment or whatever the group considers acceptable is a "good" value.

Most parents, when asked in surveys, say they want schools to teach their children such traditional Western values as honesty, hard work, integrity, justice, self-control, responsibility, respect for parents, and fidelity in marriage. Unfortunately, those values are not what most public schools teach.

Values-clarification programs often pretend to teach children real values to pacify parents, but textbooks used in values-clarification classes often censor or distort traditional family and religious values. Author Christopher J. Klicka cites a study on these textbooks conducted by Dr. Paul Vitz and funded by the National Institute of Education:

[Vitz] found an unsettling censorship of nearly all religious events in history textbooks. . . . Vitz discovered that traditional family values, and many conservative positions, have been reliably excluded from children's textbooks. . . . Vitz also found, after reviewing forty social studies textbooks used in the public school for grades one through four, that no mention is made even once of "marriage," "wedding," "husband," or "wife." A "family" is commonly defined [in these books] as a group of people.

Families are routinely depicted without a father, without a mother, or [as] a couple without children. Marriage is never mentioned as the foundation of the family and yet these books are supposed to be textbooks which introduce the child to an understanding of contemporary American society. There is no doubt, as Vitz explains, that these textbooks clearly foster the notion of family without marriage.[24]

Values clarification differs radically from traditional moral codes because it claims that children do not need established values to make moral choices. Values clarification teachers don't care which values children choose because in their view all values are subjective. The right value, they assert, depends on the situation and the individual—a value is good if it "works" for a particular child at a particular time.

To many values clarification teachers, cheating, lying, stealing, or assaulting another student are not bad acts in themselves. Such actions are just "unfortunate" choices that students make, depending on circumstances and personality traits, out of many alternative moral choices. Abiding by the Ten Commandments is merely one such option.

Values clarification classes deliberately teach children to be nonjudgmental about moral values. Sykes writes:

> Such nonjudgmentalism is a feature of the approach known as values clarification, in which, as William Kirk Kilpatrick [author of *Why Johnny Can't Tell Right From Wrong*] writes, classroom discussions are turned into "bull sessions where opinions go back and forth but conclusions are never reached." In such classes, the teacher resembles nothing so much as a talk show host presiding over classes "where the merits of wife swapping, cannibalism, and teaching children to masturbate are recommended topics for debate." This approach dominates classes in human growth and development where sexuality is described in mechanical and functional terms and moral choices presented as morally neutral options, and in "drug education programs in which drugs are scarcely mentioned except to say that taking them is a personal choice."[25]

Here are some examples of how values clarification programs affect our children:

> A 1988 study of more than 2000 Rhode Island students in grades six through nine found that two-thirds of the boys and half of the girls thought that "it was acceptable for a man to force sex on a woman" if they had been dating six months or more. A write-in survey of 126,000 teenagers found that 25 to 40 percent of teens see nothing wrong with cheating on exams, stealing from employers, or keeping money that wasn't theirs. A seventeen-year-old high school senior explained: "A lot of it is a gray area. It's everybody doing their own thing."[26]
>
> A 1992 survey by the Josephone Institute for Ethics of nearly 7000 high school and college students, most

of them from middle and upper-middle-class backgrounds, found the equivalent of "a hole in the moral ozone among America's youth."

A third of high school students and 16 percent of college students said they have shoplifted in the last year. Nearly the same number . . . said they have stolen from their parents or relatives at least once.

One in eight college students admitted to committing an act of fraud, including borrowing money they did not intend to repay, and lying on financial aid or insurance forms. A third of high school and college students said they would lie to get a job. One in six said they have already done so at least once. More than 60 percent of high school students said they had cheated at least once on an exam. Forty percent of the high school students who participated in this survey admitted that they "were not completely honest" on at least one or two questions, meaning that they may have lied on a survey about lying.[27]

These results indicate an ethical meltdown. Many public schools teach children that only self-gratification and their feelings of the moment matter, that there are no moral absolutes, and that "they need whatever they want, and deserve whatever they need."[28] Admittedly, some parents are to blame for not teaching their children good ethical values, but values-clarification programs are an assault on the time-tested values most parents teach their children.

Since ancient times, all societies have known that certain acts are inherently wrong and immoral. This knowledge became embedded in a cultural or religious moral code which recognized that human beings must respect each other's person and property. Judaism and Christianity, for example, teach that lying, stealing, or murdering another human being is wrong, not only because these acts are prohibited by the Ten Commandments, but because they are inherently unjust to other human beings.

With rare exceptions, such as killing in self-defense, the morality of these basic values seldom depends on the situation or the individual. All of us are born with the same rights to life, liberty, and property. Respect for each other's rights and person simply reflects this fact of life.

Because values-clarification programs teach children that all values are subjective, they corrupt children at the deepest level. If all values are subjective, there is no moral difference between mercy and murder, honesty and theft, sexual consent and rape, loyalty and treachery, or fidelity and adultery.

In a world where anything goes, children are turned into amoral creatures who will do anything to satisfy their momentary desires. Yet these are the insidious moral values that public schools now preach.

It is possible that school authorities teach values clarification because they personally want a non-judgmental world. Many school employees or administrators don't like having their work judged by parents or outside, independent authorities. In a non-judgmental, values-clarification world, they would not have to endure such 'insults' to their integrity or intelligence. Is it any wonder that they teach our children not to judge others, and that all values are subjective?

Pagan Religions in the Public Schools

Many public schools now teach children anti-Judeo-Christian beliefs and pagan religions, and try to mold children's minds through the latest techniques in behavioral psychology. Here are some examples of how schools now use pagan beliefs as brainwashing techniques in classrooms across America, from Berit Kjos's book, *Brave New Schools*:

> "Come to the medicine wheel!" the teacher's cheery voice beckoned the Iowa fourth graders to a fun Native American ritual. "And wear your medicine bags."
> Jonathan grabbed his little brown pouch and hur-

ried to his place. His favorite teacher made school so exciting! She brought Indian beliefs about nature into all the subjects: science, history, art, reading. She even helped the class start the Medicine Wheel Publishing Company to make writing more fun.

She taught Jonathan to make his own medicine bag, a deerskin pouch filled with special things, such as a red stone that symbolized his place on the medicine wheel astrology chart. This magic pouch would empower him in times of need, such as when taking tests. Jonathan wanted to show it to his parents, but his teacher said no. He didn't know why.

Sitting cross-legged in the circle, the class sang a song to honor the earth: "The Earth is our Mother. We're taking care of her. . . . Hey younga, ho." Then the teacher read an Indian myth from the popular classroom book, *Keepers of the Earth*. It told about a beautiful spirit woman who came to save a starving tribe of Sioux Indians. This mystical savior brought sage to purify the people, and she showed them how to use the sacred pipe, a symbol of "the unity of all things" for guidance and prayer to the Great Spirit.[29]

When Rachel Holm, a Minnesota mother, visited Mounds Park All-Nations School, she found magic dream-catchers in every classroom, mystical drawings of a spiritualized earth, and a ring of stones in the schoolyard for medicine wheel ceremonies. She heard politically correct assumptions about the evils of Western culture and the goodness of pagan spirituality. How can public schools promote Native American rituals but censure Christianity? she wondered.[30]

What's wrong with these apparently innocuous classes, aside from the issue of separation of religion and schools? The kids were having fun as they learned, so what could be wrong? Plenty. By teaching pagan religions, public schools throughout the country are filling impressionable young minds with group think, multiculturalism, Earth worship, astrology, polytheism (belief in many gods), and pantheism (belief in spirit gods that exist in trees, rocks, and water). The God of Moses is out in our public schools, and Earth worship is in.

Teachers in public schools across the country now stress feelings and mystical experiences, not facts and reason or critical reading and thinking. Their behavior-modification techniques indoctrinate children with emotion-driven group think and anti-Western, anti-Judeo-Christian values.

In classrooms throughout the country, Judeo-Christian beliefs are cast aside or ridiculed. Multicultural studies, environmental propaganda, and arts education classes now indoctrinate children with New-Age religious beliefs.

Public schools sometimes put these pagan or new-age religions into their curriculum without parents' knowledge. In January, 2003, a group of parents sued a Sacramento Unified School District because certain teachers at their local elementary school were aggressively and secretly teaching anthroposophy, a religion that combines traditional Western religion with astrology and New-Age religion. Pacific Justice Institute lawyers representing the parents indicated that many other public schools in California are now adding New Age and Eastern religions, including Islam, to their curricula. [31]

What follows is only a small sample of the flood of pagan spiritual sessions taking place in classrooms throughout the country:

1. *Altered states of consciousness*: Teaching students to alter their consciousness through centering exercises, guided imagery, and visualizations has become standard practice in self-esteem, multicultural, and arts programs. They often encourage contact with spirit guides.[32]

2. *Dreams and visions*: After studying a pagan myth, students are often asked to imagine or visualize a dream or vision, then describe it in a journal or lesson assignment.[33]

3. *Astrology*: Countless teachers across the country re-

quire students to document their daily horoscopes. Others help students discover their powers and personalities through Aztec calendars and Chinese horoscopes.[34]

4. *Other forms of divination*: Through palmistry, I Ching, tarot cards and horoscopes, students learn to experience other cultures and tap into secret sources of wisdom. Students in Texas were told to create a vision in their minds and "describe in your best soothsayer tones the details of your vision."[35]

5. *Spiritism*: While pagan myths and crafts show students how to contact ancestral, nature, and other spirits, classroom rituals actually *invoke their presence*. California third-graders had to alter their consciousness through guided imagery, invoke or "see" their personal animal spirits, write about their experience . . . and create their own magical medicine shields to represent their spirit helper.[36]

6. *Magic, spells, and sorcery*: Many parents consider magic and spell-casting too bizarre and alien to pose a threat, yet gullible students from coast to coast are learning the ancient formulas and occult techniques.[37]

7. *Occult charms and symbols*: Dreamcatchers, Zuni fetishes, crystals, and power signs like the quartered circle and Hindu mandala are only a few of the empowering charms and symbols fascinating students today.[38]

8. *Solstice rites*: After seating themselves "according to their astrological signs," Oregon students who traded Christmas for a Winter Solstice celebration watched the "sun god" and "moon goddess" enter the auditorium to the beating of drums and chanting. "Animal spirits" . . . . . followed.[39]

9. *Human sacrifice*: Students are given lessons on death education with assignments like the "Fallout Shelter." Other lessons advocate the cultural endorsement of abortion and euthanasia as a way to prepare the new generation to accept many new forms of human sacrifice, such as the notion of sacrificing oneself for the

"common good."[40]

10. *Sacred sex*: Students get lessons about pagan societies' appreciation for the "unifying power of promiscuity." By studying these pagan notions on sexuality, children get the idea that promiscuity is normal and acceptable. [41]

11. *Serpent worship*: Many ancient or primitive cultures throughout history have worshipped snakes, which have symbolized occult power, wisdom, and rebirth. Public-school multicultural history classes that celebrate these primitive societies can idealize cultures that worshipped serpents.[42]

Dreams, visions, magic, spells, sorcery, astrology, spirit worship, divination, solstice rites, human sacrifice, sacred sex, and altered states of consciousness? Is this what our children should be learning? Should schools turn children into Earth- and spirit-worshipers? Should parents pay property taxes for public schools that promote pagan religions that can affect their children's ability to tell facts from spirit dreams?

Teaching pagan beliefs and religions can harm children. Author Aldus Huxley wrote about 'new-think' indoctrination in *Brave New World*, his frightening novel about a future totalitarian society. In his book, school authorities molded children's minds so that as adults, they lost their ability to think critically.[43]

Indoctrinating children with pagan beliefs in our public schools could have a similar effect. If a child believes he or she can turn into a bird or pass a math test by rubbing a voodoo necklace, then facts, reason, hard work, perseverence, and critical thinking go out the window.

School authorities would say that they are simply trying to get children to appreciate other cultures and religions. Pagan religious ceremonies can be strange and colorful and young children can be entranced by them. However, teachers can keep children busy with art, nature and museum trips, and dozens of other interesting activities. With all these other choices available, should public schools entertain children with pagan religions if by doing so they could harm children's grasp of reality?

Emotionally Shocking
Children To Teach Warped Values

Many public schools have classes that desensitize children to moral values and even cause them to question the value of life itself. According to syndicated columnist and author Thomas Sowell:

> The techniques of brainwashing developed in totalitarian countries are routinely used in psychological conditioning programs imposed on American school children. These include emotional shock and desensitization, psychological isolation from sources of support [i.e., parents], stripping away defenses, manipulative cross-examination of the individual's underlying moral values, and inducing acceptance of alternative values by psychological rather than rational means.[44]

Here are examples of how some teacher-facilitators emotionally shock and desensitize children. A California teacher gave her tenth-grade students the following written assignment:

> You're going to consult an oracle. It will tell you that you're going to kill your best friend. This is destined to happen, and there is absolutely no way out. You will commit this murder. What will you do before this event occurs? Describe how you felt leading up to it. How did you actually kill your best friend?
>
> Ashley, one of the students, felt uneasy about this assignment, and told her mother about it. Her mother called the English teacher the next day and asked her to

change her daughter's assignment. Her mother didn't like the idea of telling her daughter to write a story about murdering her best friend. Here's how the confrontation [between teacher and parent] went after this.[45]

"Certainly Ashley knows the difference between fantasy and reality," said Ms. S [the teacher] . . , with a touch of sarcasm.

"Of course she does . . [said Ashley's mother]. But when you ask someone to imagine how she would go about murdering a friend, you could stir up nightmarish feelings."

"I have been giving the same assignment for years," answered Ms. S. Then she added the standard argument that parents across the country have learned to expect: "No one has ever complained about this before."

"That's a shame," responded the mother. "It seems to me that parents should be appalled!"

"If I give Ashley a different assignment she will be made to feel foolish."

"Are you saying that she will either get an F or be made to feel foolish? Is this a no-win situation for her?"

The teacher didn't answer, but the next day she carried out her threat. Staring straight at Ashley, she spoke to the entire class: "Of course you know the difference between fantasy and reality. And certainly you are capable of writing an assignment without becoming emotionally involved."[46]

Fortunately, Ashley stuck to her guns and followed her mother's advice. She wrote an essay on a different assignment. But the teacher brainwashed and psychologically coerced the other children into writing this essay. This is not a unique assignment. Every day, teacher-facilitators routinely shock millions of children around the country with similar exercises on topics ranging from suicide, euthanasia, and homosexual or occult practices, to who the children would kick out of a lifeboat if there wasn't room for everyone.

In many of these stories, one lesson hammered home is that a group of people has the right to sacrifice some of its members for the good of the group. This lesson is probably not a coincidence because public schools are funded and controlled by state and Federal governments. To create an authoritarian society in America, children must learn to go along with the group and its leaders. When children's reading and critical thinking skills are crippled, they find it harder to question or disobey their rulers. This call for sacrifice for the good of the group or "society," as the group is called in our nation, is what fascist, socialist, and communist societies constantly preach.

In keeping with this idea of the collective good being more important than individual rights, many high schools now force students to do so-called volunteer work to graduate. After the Civil War, Congress passed the Thirteenth Amendment to the Constitution, which outlawed involuntary servitude. Yet many high schools around the country now force students to do mandatory community service to get a diploma. Of course it is good when teenagers help others in their community, voluntarily. However, when school authorities *force* children to "serve" others, this is blatant, deeply un-American, involuntary servitude.

Some public schools prepare younger children for such service through manipulative cross-examination and brainwashing techniques. Berit Kjos, in his book *Brave New Schools*, cites this example:

A familiar tale told to first-graders in Pennsylvania shows what happens when old stories are squeezed into the mold of the new paradigm. We all know the story of the Little Red Hen who wanted some bread to eat. She asked some of her barnyard friends to help make it. But the cat, the dog, and the goat all said no. Finally she did all the work herself. However, when the bread was done, her unwilling friends came to help her eat it.

"Won't you share with us?" they begged.

"No," she answered. "Since you didn't help, you don't get anything."

In the context of the old paradigm, the moral of the story is: You get what you work for. But the new paradigm point is different. Listen to the kinds of questions the first grade teacher asked her class: "Why was the Little Red Hen so stingy? Isn't it only right that everyone gets to eat? Why should she share what she had with some who had none?"[47]

Notice the insidious message in these questions. They make children believe that no one has a right to keep what they work for if the group wants it. The message teaches that there is no such thing as individual rights, property rights, or the right to keep what you earn. It teaches that it is immoral to oppose the group who wants to loot what you worked for. Such behavior-modification techniques indoctrinate children with group conformity and sacrifice to the group. Is this what public schools should be teaching our children?

Unfortunately, I've hardly touched on the brainwashing that public schools daily commit against innocent children. Three excellent books cover this subject in detail, *Brave New Schools* by Berit Kjos (Harvest House, 1995), *Dumbing Down Our Kids* by Charles J. Sykes (St. Martin's/Griffin, 1995), and *Why Johnny Can't Tell Right From Wrong* by William Kilpatrick (Touchstone Books, 1992). These books are eye-opening, and frightening, but they are must reading for every parent.

Multiculturalism:
Anti-American Values in
Public-School Classrooms

Like the classes in pagan religions mentioned earlier in this chapter, multiculturalism classes also sound innocuous. Parents believe that such classes teach their children to respect and understand other cultures, which sounds like a worthwhile goal. That's what many school authorities intend parents to believe. Instead, multiculturalism classes sell the "oneness" of all peoples and cultures. They teach that no culture or set of beliefs is better than another.

The problem is that some cultural beliefs *are* worse than others. Many societies or governments around the world are tyrannical and strangle their people's freedom. Some countries have corrupt dictators or religious dictatorships that violate women's basic human rights and turn them into second-class citizens. These societies or governments do not value or protect personal, economic, and political freedom as we do.

For example, Americans don't slash the faces of women who wear makeup, or stone women to death who have committed adultery. State or local governments in America don't shut down newspapers whose editorials they don't like. In America, a person accused of a crime is presumed innocent until proven guilty, and has the right to a trial by jury. In tyrannical societies around the world, people don't enjoy such rights. Therefore, to say that all cultures are equally good for their people is to claim that there is no difference between liberty and tyranny, between a free country and societies or governments that oppress men and women in their daily lives. All cultures are *not* equal in this regard.

Supposedly nonjudgmental multiculturalism classes refuse to acknowledge that many non-Western cultures are brutal, or that they suppress personal liberty. These classes also attack Americans' alleged arrogance in thinking that our values are better than those of less freedom-loving cultures.

These classes often attack such American values as individualism, individual rights, economic freedom, and women's equality before the law, through stories, slanted textbook material, and other brainwashing techniques. Apparently praise for America is now regarded as criticism of other cultures. "We can't teach that only America is good," said one tenth-grader who had moved from India to Florida in 1993. "That would hurt my feelings."[48] No, we can't teach that only America is good, but we don't have to teach that only America is *bad*.

Alarmed parents in every state are reporting their experiences with their children's multicultural lessons. One parent stated:

> When I looked at the video about Columbus, I was very upset. It began with a teacher grabbing a purse from a student's desk and saying, "This is my purse. I didn't steal Samantha's purse. I discovered this purse." Columbus was presented as an antihero who sought gold and slaves, brought genocide to the indigenous [natives], and should be ridiculed. It never mentioned that the supposedly peace-loving Carob Indians owned slaves and would fatten, castrate, and eat male babies as cannibalistic rituals. True, the European immigrants did exploit Indians, but there are two sides to the story . . . .[49]

Actually, Columbus set sail to find a route to the East Indies to buy spices. He did not sail into the unknown Atlantic Ocean to enslave native cultures. He didn't even know these cultures existed. Columbus and the explorers who followed him kept searching for a way around the new continents they discovered so they could sail West to China, India, and the Spice Islands. Unfortunately, when the Spanish explorers discovered gold and silver in South America, human greed kicked in with a vengeance, but their behavior does not make the contributions of Europeans and Americans to world civilization any less valuable.

This Columbus controversy is just one example of how multiculturalism classes and history textbooks distort history and promote anti-American values. Many public schools across America use the *National Standards For United States History* (developed by the National Center for History in the Schools) as a curriculum guide for American history and multiculturalism instruction. These *National Standards* often one-sidedly paint American and Western civilization as the bad guys, and non-Western or native-American cultures as innocent victims of European or American greed and corruption.[50]

It is certainly true that European explorers and settlers tragically spread smallpox and other diseases among Native populations, often decimating whole tribes. Europeans also conquered and dispossessed Indian tribes from their ancient lands. Lastly, Europeans imported slaves into the American colonies, and it finally took a devastating Civil War to end this horrible institution in America. However, these facts are not the whole truth, and therefore one-sided.

The same *National Standards for United States History* fails to give the whole picture. Noted history scholar and author, Thomas Sowell points out that at the time Europeans discovered and settled America, slavery had been a common institution in most human societies for thousands of years. The ancient Egyptians, Greeks, and Romans enslaved thousands of men, women, and children of every race and color from the countries they conquered.

When Columbus first discovered the North American continent, slavery was still very much alive in cultures and continents around the world. In Africa, slavery had been common for thousands of years. Warring tribes typically killed the men and enslaved the women and children of other tribes they conquered. Some African tribes even helped Europeans catch slaves from neighboring tribes. For hundreds of years, Arab countries sent slave caravans south to attack tribes in central Africa and bring slaves back through the Sahara desert. Before Columbus came to America, as in Africa, Native-American and Caribbean island tribes constantly warred with each other and took each other's women and children as slaves. Nearly twenty years after blacks were freed in our Civil War, white people were still being sold as slaves in the Turkish Ottoman Empire.[51]

Throughout history, including among American native tribes, stronger or more aggressive cultures invaded and enslaved weaker or less technologically advanced cultures. Slavery and dispossessing native populations from their lands is an age-old story, the story of human cruelty and inhumanity.

In the American Revolution, the colonies were fighting for their lives against the British, so they had to pull together or be defeated. After American colonists won the war, at the Constitutional Convention in 1787, Southern colonies insisted that slavery be allowed to continue. If all the colonies did not reach a compromise on this issue, they would have disintegrated into weak separate States and be vulnerable to renewed British attacks. That was the context of the slavery issue at the time.

It is certainly true that many of our Founding Fathers owned slaves, even though they hated the institution of slavery. However, if it wasn't for men like Washington and Jefferson, there would be no United States, a country founded on the historically startling idea that all men are created equal. It was the *power of that idea* that finally led to the abolition of slavery in America and equal rights for women.

Yet these kinds of facts and context are left out of our multiculturalism classes and American-history textbooks. As a result, many public schools give our children lessons on why they should disrespect American ideals and heroes.

After reading this chapter, concerned parents may want to ask themselves these questions: Do I really know what my local public school is teaching my children? Should I subject my children to brainwashing and political propaganda? Should I turn over my children to schools that preach anti-parent, anti-Judeo-Christian, and anti-American values? Should I expose my children to schools that put shocking sexual material into their so-called sex-education classes? Do I pay school taxes for teachers to frighten my children with stories of child abuse, and turn my children into spies against me? Is the alleged convenience of sending my children to the local public school worth this threat to my children's minds and values?

In the next chapter, we will explore why public schools fail our children, year after year, and why they are beyond repair.

3

Why Are Public Schools So Bad?

In Chapter 1, we examined the frightening failure of our public schools. The question I pose in this chapter is, "why?" Why do teachers, principals, and administrators preside over a school system that can't seem to teach our children to read? Why are millions of students illiterate after twelve years of sitting in public-school classrooms? Why doesn't the system improve?

Destructive and Incompetent Teaching Methods

To succeed in school and later in life, most students must become proficient in the three well-known basics: reading, writing, and arithmetic. Of these three, the most important is reading, the fundamental skill a child needs to learn almost all other subjects or to study any subject in greater depth. Children who read well can easily explore science, geometry, history, or anything else that intrigues them.

Poor reading skills can cripple children's minds, impair their ability to learn, and cause them continual frustration in school. This frustration can make them hate reading and want to give up on learning. Since reading is so important, it is essential that educators teach children to read with a proven and effective reading method.

Whole-Language Reading Instruction

Since reading is such a fundamental skill, let's look at how public schools teach children to read. Many schools today teach reading by the whole-language (or "look-say") method, rather than phonics. The phonics system, which for centuries was the primary method parents used to teach their kids to read, is rooted in the basic structure of the English language. Every word in English can be spelled with only twenty-six letters and pronounced by using these letters alone or combinations of these letters (like th and sh). A child has only to learn the alphabet and the related letter sounds to begin putting words together.

With the phonics method, most children can learn to read in a relatively short time. This is confirmed by John Taylor Gatto, who taught English and reading for twenty-six years in some of the worst public schools in New York City. The New York Department of Education awarded him New York City Teacher-of-the-Year in 1990. In his book, *Dumbing Us Down*, Mr. Gatto writes, "No, the truth is that reading, writing, and arithmetic only take about one hundred hours to transmit as long as the audience is eager and willing to learn."[1]

Let me repeat this. Mr. Gatto, an award-winning English teacher for twenty-six years, learned that it only takes about a hundred hours to teach a willing child to read, write, and do basic arithmetic. If this is so, what are public schools doing with our children for *twelve years* while they turn them into functional illiterates?

Learning to read is like learning to drive a car or master any other complex skill. If we drive a car, the skill of driving seems effortless. Our eyes, hands, and feet work together seamlessly and automatically, without conscious thought. But to get to this skill level, we first had to learn driving basics. If your father taught you to drive, he drilled you on these basics. He taught you how to turn the steering wheel, where the gas and brake pedals were, how to stay in your lane, about turn signals and stop signs, using mirrors, keeping to speed limits, and looking ahead while you drive. These basics took time and practice to learn. Yet those of us who have been driving for many years take these basics for granted. We drive automatically and competently.

Reading is a complex skill like driving. Children have to learn the basics before they can learn to read well. Once children learn these skills, they can eventually read complex books like *War and Peace.*

What are these skills? To read, one must recognize thousands of words. Since all English words are built from only twenty-six letters, the huge task of recognizing letters and their sounds and putting them together to form words becomes greatly simplified. An English-speaking child can sound out the letters and then put the sounds together to read the word.

I do not wish to over-simplify the complexity of our rich English language, however. Like other western languages, English has its peculiarities. For example, many vowels have more than one sound, and many sounds can be spelled more than one way. Also, reading a word is not the same as comprehending its meaning, and understanding a series of words is not the same as understanding the meaning of a sentence or paragraph. These are more complex skills that a child learns later. However, even with these complexities, English is far easier to learn than Chinese or Japanese, where children have to memorize thousands of word pictures rather than twenty-six letters and their sounds.

Reading is difficult at first, but, once learned, the process becomes automatic and unconscious. When we can read quickly without sounding out every letter of every word, all the knowledge of the world opens to us. However, like learning to drive a car, if we don't learn the basic skills, we don't learn to read, or we read poorly.

Enter public-school education theorists and school administrators who think otherwise. Don't adults read without sounding out every letter of every word, they ask? So why teach children phonics? Why put children through the alleged boredom, drudgery, and hard work of learning letter sounds? How can reading be joyful if literature becomes drills? If children memorize whole words instead of putting together letter sounds, all this pain will be gone. Rather than teaching kids the alphabet and how to sound out M-O-T-H-E-R, teach them to recognize the word MOTHER and other whole words in a book, like Chinese word-pictures or ancient Egyptian hieroglyphics. Have the child read simple books that repeat each word over and over, so that they come to recognize the word. Do this for each word, whole-language advocates claim, and the child will learn to read.

Author and education researcher Charles J. Sykes describes whole-language reading instruction in one first-grade classroom:

Reading instruction begins with "pre-reading strategies" in which "children predict what the story is about by looking at the title and the pictures. Background knowledge is activated to get the children thinking about the reading topic." Then they read the story. If a child does not recognize a word, they are told to "look for clues."

The whole-language curriculum gave specific suggestions that children: "Look at the pictures," ask "What would make sense?" "Look for patterns," "Look for clues," and "Skip the word and read ahead and then go back to the word." Finally, if all this fails, parents/teachers are told, "Tell the child the word"....Nowhere is the child told to "sound it out."[2]

When kids couldn't figure out a word, educationists gave these further suggestions: "Ask a friend, skip the word, substitute another meaningful word."

Look at the pictures. Skip the word. Ask a friend. Is

this reading? [3]

On the surface, these instructions sound like the teachers are very attentive and caring in their reading lessons. Common sense tells us that children would benefit by such seemingly attentive instruction. Yet, in reality, these whole-language reading "strategies" put children through reading torture by making them have to *guess* what a word is rather than *reading* it (sounding it out with phonics).

To understand what a torture this can be for children just learning to read, imagine if you (as an adult) had to go through these convoluted reading guessing games every time you read the daily newspaper. Imagine the hours upon hours it would take you to read a *single article* in the paper if you had to use complicated guessing strategies for every word you were reading.

Most people would agree with Sykes that these whole-language reading strategies are not reading. They are at best emergency measures for figuring out words above the child's reading level. School authorities claim that because whole-language instruction does not need alphabet drills and phonics, it is joyful and meaningful. However, children will hardly be inspired to love reading if they have to read books that contain only a few simple words they can recognize. Children would be as frustrated reading such a book as an American adult would be who had to read a book written in Russian.

As Sykes points out:

The classic example of the repetition used to bolster the look-say method [whole-language reading] was the mind-numbingly inane *Dick and Jane* series of books. In 1930, the *Dick and Jane* primer taught a total of 68 different words in 39 pages of text; by 1950, the pre-primer had grown to 172 pages, but the number of words had been cut to 58. By 1950, children were being soaked with the banality of readers that repeated the word "look" 110 times, the word "oh" 138 times, and the word "see" dragged grasping into the text 176 times. Eventually, children learned to recognize the words.[4]

This mind-numbing reading method is joyful and meaningful to children? Is it any wonder that kids get bored in class and see reading as a frustrating chore?

Whole-language supporters also claim that their method stresses meaning and context, not basics. It tells kids to read by guessing, looking for clues, and discussing the words with other children in a group. These tactics allegedly make reading holistic, intuitive, child-centered, and self-esteem-enhancing.[5] But whole-language instruction, though it doesn't involve phonics drills, does require dreary, continuous memorization. Teachers force children to read the same words over and over again so they memorize them, rather than sound out the letters to decipher the word. This method is like training a monkey to recognize the word "stick' or "banana" by repeating it endlessly.

Here's an analogy that might put whole-language instruction in a better perspective. When you teach children to swim, you do so by gradual steps. You have them practice arm and leg motions and proper breathing while they stand in the shallow end of the pool. You show them how to float, how to kick their legs, how to stroke their arms, and how to coordinate their arms and legs with their breathing. Gradually, as they get the mechanics down and lose their fear, you let them try a few stokes in water slightly over their heads. Finally, after they prove their ability, you let them swim in the deep end of the pool.

Now imagine a swimming instructor who teaches kids to swim by the "whole-body" swimming method. This instructor claims that teaching children the mechanics of swimming by gradual steps is boring and stressful, that it doesn't consider the "whole" child or make swimming "joyful, meaningful, holistic, intuitive, child-centered, and self-esteem-enhancing." So this instructor's method is to throw a child into the deep end of the pool the first time out, and let the child figure out how to swim by "just doing it." If the child thrashes his arms around wildly, let him "guess" what the proper arm and leg motions are. Let him learn by "immersing himself" in the experience. While he is sinking, the terrified child can always scream for help to the instructor who is getting ready to throw another kid into the pool. This is the equivalent of the whole-language reading method.

G. Reid Lyon, PhD, is one of the nation's leading experts on how children learn to read. He is chief of the Child Development and Behavior Branch within the National Institute of Child Health and Human Development (which is part of the National Institutes of Health). He is responsible for research programs in reading development, reading disorders, learning disabilities, and other related language disorders. He periodically reports his findings to the White House, Congress, and other U.S. Agencies.

In an interview published in *School Reform News*, Dr Lyon explained in detail why children need phonics to learn to read, and why whole-language instruction doesn't work:

> First of all, [when you read] you are going to scan and fixate on the letters of the text and, even though you're an expert reader and do it very quickly, the eye movements that we study tell us that the eye does move across every word. People don't skim, but the eye actually fixates on most words and, as quickly as that happens, you also translate those visual symbols into sound.
>
> Surprisingly, and in contrast to what conventional wisdom has suggested in the past, expert readers do *not* use the surrounding context to figure out a word they've never seen before. The strategy of choice for expert readers is to actually fixate on that word and decode it to sound using phonics. That's an important finding because for the past 20 to 30 years, a number of teaching methods have been developed on the assumption that you don't need to learn how to decode letters to sound or speech to sound—that is, you don't need to learn phonics.

These methods say you use the holistic or surrounding context to predict unknown words, but we have found that's clearly not the case. No more than 20 percent of words in the text can be predicted from the surrounding context. If we insert a word you've never seen before—a nonsense word—you will decode it.

It's literally impossible for a reader to memorize the visual configuration of every word. That's why our alphabetic language with 26 letters that correspond to about 40 to 44 sounds provides the reader with enormous capability to crack open words they haven't seen before. You don't have to memorize every word.

We now have a very clear understanding that reading is not a natural process. If it were, we wouldn't have so many youngsters having difficulty learning to read, and we also would have more cultures on this planet with a written language as well as an oral language. A number of building blocks have to be mastered as one comes to the written word. A major prerequisite for learning to read an alphabetic language like English is to understand that the words we use in our speech are actually composed of individual sounds. While that may seem like common sense, it's very difficult for some children and adults to get that. As I speak, the words coming out of my mouth are obviously composed of different sound elements, but your ear never hears them.

The individual sounds are called phonemes, which beginning readers learn before proceeding to text. But those squiggly lines on the page really don't mean anything until the brain hooks them to sounds and then links those sounds together to form words. As youngsters are learning to read, they'll use this phoneme awareness to develop what's called the alphabetic principle, which is an understanding that the print in front of you is, in fact, linked to various sounds.

As a child's coming along, he's never seen the word "bag" before, and what he has to learn is that the "b" written symbol goes with a sound like "b" and the "a" goes with a sound like "a" and so forth, and that's how a child learns to decode the sound.

Apparently, in its purest form, whole language is a philosophy that argues against deconstructing anything into its parts. It argues for a holistic look at all academic content, not just reading. A whole language philosophy would suggest that teaching children phonemes and how those sounds link to letters is fragmenting the language. Their proposal would be that reading is, in fact, a natural process, and that children learn to read by reading. *That's simply not the case* [italics added].

Reading is anything but natural. It's a fairly new skill in evolution, relative to oral language, and it is contrived. Why 26 letters? Why 44 sounds? Other alphabets have more or less sounds or more or less letters. Much as we may not like it, reading is initially a technical skill, and it requires a learning of a number of fundamentals to do it well.[5]

As common sense would predict from Dr. Lyon's analysis, whole-language instruction turns millions of children into functional illiterates. Despite hundreds of hours spent memorizing the same words again and again, children are lost when they try to read a new book with different words or read more advanced material. They don't recognize the new words they never memorized from previous *Dick and Jane* books (or similar books they use today). Children get frustrated trying to read new material and spending hours with whole-language guessing games. Not trained in phonics, they can't sound out the letters in the new words to read them. This has serious consequences.

According to Sykes:

At the end of a couple of semesters, a child with the mastery of phonetics [phonics] could read an estimated 24,000 words. Look-say [whole-language reading] requires children to memorize whole words, much like the Chinese learn individual ideograms. Thus, they learn by reading the same words over and over again. Instead of a potential vocabulary of thousands of words, children are able to read only a few hundred. [6]

The state of California gave us a direct and unique test-comparison between the phonics and whole-language reading methods. Before 1987, California still used remnants of the phonics method to teach children to read.

In 1987, California schools dropped phonics instruction almost completely. The schools embraced a literature-based approach to reading that de-emphasized phonics. Children would be spared the "drudgery" of having to learn the dreary rules and mechanics of reading. Instead, kids would learn to read by immersing themselves in the wonders of literature through the whole-language method.

One survey found that 87 percent of the reading teachers in California used the new techniques, and fewer than one in ten teachers emphasized phonics instruction in their classes. This statewide switch to whole-language instruction turned California's public schools into a full-scale test of phonics versus whole-language theories.[7]

By 1993, six years into the phonics-less curriculum, a national reading survey conducted by the Educational Testing Service found that California's fourth-graders' reading skills had plummeted. They ranked forty-ninth and tied with students from Mississippi for dead last in their reading abilities compared with students throughout the country. Even when California's non-immigrant white fourth-graders were considered separately, they still finished in the bottom fifth of the fifty states in the test. [8]

What happened after political pressure forced California educators to teach phonics again in the 2001-2002 school year? To the California school authorities' surprise, reading scores started to rise sharply. They rose sharply even in overcrowded Los Angeles schools, where one quarter of the teachers did not have formal teaching credentials.[9]

Clearly, whole-language instruction is a prescription for disaster, and is the main culprit behind our children's appalling illiteracy and plummeting reading skills. According to a 1994 Educational Testing Service report, half the nation's college graduates could not read a bus schedule and only 35 percent of graduates from four-year colleges could consistently write a brief letter about a company's billing error. Another study found that this massive illiteracy has caused businesses to lose $40 billion in revenue a year to set up remedial reading classes for new employees who just graduated from high school. Whole-language instruction is a primary reason why 30 percent of Americans are functionally illiterate.[10]

Yet, in the face of such a literacy disaster for American children, many school authorities deny or rationalize the results of whole-language instruction. Why do they continue to teach this reading method to children? What do they gain? There is always a reason for seemingly irrational behavior, and school authorities have many.

One of the top education advisors to then California governor Pete Wilson, explained why California school administrators kept whole-language instruction: "Our state's educational leaders decided it was terribly insulting for kids to have to learn number tables or how to spell words, so we ended up with math books without arithmetic, and literature books without reading."[11] Yes, you read the quotation correctly. California's school authorities thought that teaching children the basics insults them. When we learn any skill, we have to learn the basics—that's reality. So reality also insults children?

Another reason teachers use whole-language instruction is that their so-called teacher colleges never taught them the phonics method. Most teachers are reasonably intelligent people who can teach subjects they know themselves. Teachers who weren't taught the phonics method will naturally feel inadequate to teach it to their students. However, few teacher colleges or university education programs bother with phonics today.

Phonics and drills require a teacher-centered approach, including lesson plans that produce real results, and constant testing to evaluate students' progress. In contrast, whole-language instruction is student-centered, and an easy way out for ill-trained teachers who never learned the phonics method. With whole-language instruction, students often sit around in circles and talk about their feelings, or simply listen passively to their teacher read a book aloud, and try to follow the words as best they can.

Phonics and drills can be a drudge in public schools, if they are taught at all, because overworked or ill-trained teachers don't have the time or skill to make them otherwise. Yet, learning basic reading skills doesn't have to be a chore. Young children eagerly learn the alphabet and letter sounds at home, with the right stimulus. Interesting and creative how-to-read and phonics books, learn-to-read computer software for young children, and learning channels on cable TV can make learning letters and phonetic sounds a delight for children. Also, young children learn to read faster when parents read to them and link reading to other activities kids may enjoy, such as cooking, playing with toys, or shopping at the supermarket with Mom or Dad.

School authorities also claim that drills and phonics are unfair to children because they can cause them stress and threaten their self-esteem. Some children might feel this way, but the vast majority of young children love learning. Real self-esteem comes from achievement, and achievement needs tasks, content, and increasingly complex skills children learn with the help of their parents. Real achievement gives most kids joy, not stress, as long as children are interested in what they are learning. Also, what lesson is more important for kids to learn than rewards come from effort and perseverance?

It is not phonics or drills per se, or any other lessons children learn that can stress them or hurt their self-esteem. Rather, it is the teaching methods and testing and grading systems in public schools that turn kids off to reading and learning. Infants and very young children embrace learning with a passion, which is why they learn so fast. Yet, as teacher and author John Holt observed, by the time these same children have progressed to the fifth grade in school, most are listless, bored, apathetic, and often fearful in class.

Public-school children are pressured to get the "right" answer, and are sometimes hurt or humiliated by teachers or other students when they get the wrong answers or bad grades on tests. The kids are also stressed because in school they compare themselves to other students in the class rather than learning and enjoying the material for its own sake. Also, children often have no interest in the subjects they have to study in class, which makes it harder for them to concentrate on the material and please the teacher. As a result, many children withdraw from reading and learning out of self-defense or boredom. Learning then becomes a game of getting the "right" answer for the teacher, or not answering at all to avoid pain and humiliation.

Learning any new skill or subject can give children joy if this learning isn't tied to fear, boredom, or humiliation, as it often is in public schools. Public schools are under enormous pressure to test and grade students to prove that they are earning the tax dollars we give them, and to ward off parents' complaints. So this constant pressure on kids from tests and grading can make children fearful and turn them off learning. We will see later in Chapters 8 and 9 that home-schooling, Internet schools, and other education options parents have, can reduce or eliminate the stress that public schools create and make children eager to learn.

School authorities also condemn the phonics method for deep-rooted philosophical reasons. Sykes explains:

> . . . But in its purer forms, "whole-language" is not merely an instructional technique, it is an overarching philosophy of education. Its advocates believe that children learn "naturally," that children learn best when "learning is kept whole, meaningful, interesting and functional," and that this is more likely to happen when

children make their own choices as part of a "community of learners" in a noncompetitive environment.

Not surprisingly, this is not a place where drills in phonics or an emphasis on the mechanics of reading is likely to be stressed. Nor is there much room for stressing that there are right and wrong ways of spelling or writing in this brave new world in which children monitor themselves, take chances, express their feelings, and look at pictures in books. Whole language, riffs one enthusiast, is "child-centered, experiential, reflective, authentic, holistic, social, collaborative, democratic, cognitive, developmental, constructivist and challenging."[12]

Do you remember the dangerous "whole-body" swimming method I described earlier? Here we have it as a reading method.

This reading philosophy is deeply rooted in the public-school psyche. That is one reason why, despite the overwhelming evidence against whole-language instruction, many public schools still use this method. If a teaching method is only a current fad, it might change. In contrast, school authorities that are deeply committed to their philosophy of education, find it exceedingly hard to change.

Whole-language supporters who can't refute their critics' arguments or deny the glaring evidence of their own failure, sometimes attack their opponents the way children do—by calling them names. They label concerned parents who push phonics instruction as extremist Christian Rightists, rabid haters of public schools, or educational simpletons who can't understand the alleged complexity of modern learning theories.

When school authorities dismiss parents by claiming they don't understand the "complexity" of whole-language instruction, they try to make parents feel ignorant to quell their complaints. Even worse, school authorities' claim of complexity is simply not true. If anything, whole-language instruction is simpler to teach than phonics. The phonics system asks children to learn letters, sounds, and sound combinations. Whole-language instruction simply forces students to memorize the same words over and over again, like a parrot. Also, if teaching children to read is so allegedly complex, why is it that over a million parents now teach their children to read quite competently at home with learn-to-read books and phonics programs?

School authorities delude themselves into thinking they are education gurus with special skills no parent can possess. Home-schooling parents' success humiliates many public-school apologists, and refutes the claim that teaching children to read is too complex a job for allegedly amateur parents.

Let reality be the judge of whole-language instruction in public schools. As noted earlier, children who learn to read by the phonics method quickly outpace whole-language readers. Also, the California experiment described above closes the book on this issue.

Whole-language instruction turns reading into a frustrating chore. When children find it hard to read, their love of learning withers and their self-esteem and self-confidence drop sharply. Later in life, they can find it hard to get a decent job or function in society. Their ambition and their world shrink as their minds contract.

If you want to see a gripping drama about what illiteracy can do to a person, you should see the wonderful 1990 movie, *Stanley and Iris*, with Robert De Niro and Jane Fonda. De Niro gives a powerful performance as Stanley, a man whose life is filled with misery, degradation, loss of ambition, and humiliation because he can't read.

Stanley can't drive a car because he can't fill out the Motor Vehicle Department application or read street signs on the driving test. He can't have a checking account because he can't fill out deposit slips or balance his checkbook. He has to put his aging father in a welfare old-age home because, not being able to read, he can only take menial jobs and make very little money. He suffers constant, daily humiliation because he always has to ask other people's help to read the simplest form or application. He can't read a newspaper or magazine. He has few friends because he is embarrassed if other people find out he can't read. He rarely dates women because he feels like a total failure, so he can never have a loving wife or children. His illiteracy cripples his self-respect. His one chance at life is being ruined because he can't read, in a society that makes reading a fundamental skill needed to succeed or even survive.

The movie shows how Stanley transforms his life through his heroic effort to learn to read. He does this with the help of a factory worker named Iris (Fonda), who teaches Stanley to read with the phonics method.

The degree to which children can't read is the degree to which their lives can mimic Stanley's. It is appalling to think of the millions of Stanley's our public schools turn out. In effect, whole-language reading instruction is an education crime against our children.

Invented Spelling

As part of the whole-language philosophy, many public schools now teach what they call "invented" or "creative" spelling. Under this theory of spelling, teachers tell children that there is no one correct way to spell a word, that kids can invent whatever spelling they like. It takes time and effort to correct spelling errors, and many public schools no longer bother. Also, many school officials now believe it is not important to teach correct spelling because a child will "eventually" learn to spell correctly. Sykes provides the following real-life examples of invented spelling in our public schools:

> Joan W. and Beverly J. [last names omitted for privacy] are not experts. They just didn't understand why their children weren't learning to write, spell, or read very well. They didn't understand why their children kept coming home with sloppy papers filled with spelling mistakes and bad grammar and why teachers never cor-

rected them or demanded better work. Mrs. W. couldn't fathom why her child's teacher would write a "Wow!" and award a check-plus (for above average work) to a paper that read:

"I'm goin to has majik skates. Im goin to go to disenalen. Im goin to bin my mom and dad and brusr and sisd. We r go to se mickey mouse."

On another assignment where the children were told to write about why, where, and how they would run away from home without their parents knowing about it, here's what one child wrote: "I would run awar because by mom and Dad don't love me. I would run away with my brother to the musan in mlewsky. We will use are packpacks and put all are close in it. We will take a lot of mony with us so we can go on the bus to the musam. We will stay there for a tlong timne so my mom and dad know they did not love us."[13]

Not only is this child's spelling atrocious and the teacher's "Wow" grade damaging to the child, but the lesson itself is insidious. Should teachers be giving writing assignments to children about how and why they should run away from home?

Spelling affects people's lives. A person who doesn't spell words correctly can't communicate effectively with employees, supervisors, customers, patients, clients, business associates, contractors, or parents. He or she can't be sure of the exact meaning of misspelled words in a contract, mortgage, medical consent form, or other crucial documents or instructions. Invented spelling also makes a bad impression on employers and college admissions officers. Yet many public schools no longer think spelling is important enough to spend time on during the school day.

New Math

Just as public schools let children invent their own spelling, they now promote creative math in the "new math" curriculum. Yet if any discipline requires accuracy and clear thought, it is math. Numbers should not be subject to interpretation and invention. Five times four will always equal twenty, no matter how a child feels about it.

Most parents think that their children should learn arithmetic the old-fashioned way—by memorizing the multiplication tables and learning how to add, subtract, divide, and multiply without the aid of a calculator. Yet many school authorities don't agree with this idea. They don't want to bore children with the alleged drudgery of multiplication tables and by-hand math calculations. Why waste time with this, say principals and administrators, when we have cheap handheld calculators? So most public schools now let students use calculators from the earliest grades, and skimp on teaching children the basics of arithmetic. "In the new math class," a 1994 *Los Angeles Times* article reports, "work sheets and drills at the chalkboard are out. So is an emphasis on complicated paper-and-pencil computations such as long division."[14]

A Feb., 2003 article in The *New York Sun* examined New York City public schools' new math curriculum (called Everyday Math):

> Everyday Mathematics requires massive fixes at the most basic level. The program does not teach the standard procedure at all for subtraction and division, and offers a hopelessly confusing potpourri of methods for all the four elementary operations (addition, subtraction, multiplication, and division). The program has pedagogical features (notably, rapidly jumping around over different topics without staying focused long enough for pupils to achieve mastery) that appear to make it all but unworkable as intended. It introduces calculators as early as kindergarten and this will contribute to the failure of many pupils to acquire proper facility with numbers and operations.[15]

School authorities also encourage teachers to turn math into a debating society, another way to get children to socialize and get along with the group. Teachers let children debate solutions to simple math problems among themselves. Instead of giving children simple and easy-to-understand rules for adding, say 3 + 3, teachers tell students to work the problem out among themselves until they come to an agreement on the "correct" answer.

> In one class, the authors of the *Arithmetic Teacher* article enthuse, children approached the problem of 75 divided by 5 by adding 5 + 5 + 5 + 5 + 5 + 5 until the total comes close to 75. The teachers seemed especially impressed by the creativity of the students who counted this out *on their fingers*.[16]

Why do public schools teach this new math? Education theorists claim that new math teaches children *how* to learn instead of what to learn. They insist that this method encourages children to enjoy and "value" mathematics and become more confident problem solvers.

New-math's philosophy is therefore similar to whole-language beliefs. Like whole-language teachers, new-math instructors insist that children put the cart before the horse, that they do math problems without first learning math basics. Children in whole-language classes are pushed into reading without first learning how to sound out letters and words. In new math classes, children who have not been taught how to add, subtract, or multiply are given real math problems to solve. New-math apologists have the odd idea that children will "somehow" learn basic skills along the way as they struggle to solve the problems.[17]

With philosophies and teaching methods like these, it's no wonder that children's math skills keep deteriorating and that our kids have become increasingly math deficient. American children now consistently lag behind students from other countries in their math abilities.

In California, which often leads the country in new-math teaching methods, the math deficiency of public-school students is particularly noticeable. The National Center for Education Statistics, in its *National Assessment of Educational Progress* for 2003, rated the math skills of fourth and eighth-grade California students in the bottom 10 percent of the participating states.[18]

Weak skills and low test scores are not the only problems these teaching methods create. Math educators now put less emphasis on right and wrong answers. Because many schools no longer require students to learn the basics, many teachers no longer require exact answers on math tests. These teaching methods hurt students' math skills, but they benefit teachers, principals, and schools. When students don't have to be concerned with right answers, teachers can grade tests arbitrarily and test scores can go up. High test scores make math teachers and their schools look good to parents, while their children become math illiterates.[19]

To illustrate why it is crucial to come up with the one correct answer in math, imagine yourself on a Boeing 747, thirty thousand feet in the air, flying from New York to Miami. Suppose your pilot and copilot are new-math trained high-school graduates plotting their course to Miami, and this is the discussion between them: Frank the pilot says, "I think our course heading is twenty-eight degrees latitude by forty-six degrees longitude. See, the latitude figures seem to add up to around twenty-eight, and the longitude numbers seem to add up to about forty-six." His copilot, Bill, disagrees. "But Frank, I feel that your numbers aren't right. It seems to me that the latitude is about thirty-four and the longitude could be almost forty-one. Let's discuss this a while and see if we can come up with some figures we can both agree on. Gee, I'm sorry we left our calculators at home." Meanwhile, your plane gets lost over the Atlantic, never to be heard from again.

Just as precise spelling and clear writing are needed to communicate ideas, precise math is needed to calculate exact quantities. New-math's bizarre teaching methods can frustrate kids and turn them off math. If they get frustrated, they will end up hating math. That can strangle their desire or confidence to major in the science, computer, or technology fields, which today offer great career opportunities. New-math is not just another failed education theory by public-school authorities. It can wreck your children's math self-confidence, and hurt their ambition and opportunities in life. The new math is yet another example of how public schools are betraying our children.

Dumbing-Down the Textbooks

Oddly enough, one reason public-school authorities use the incompetent teaching methods we've examined up to now is that these authorities want to protect children's self-esteem. Failure hurts anyone's self-esteem, at least temporarily, so many school authorities have decided that no child should be hurt by failing.

One way they accomplish this goal is to use whole-language readers in the primary grades, and dumbed-down textbooks in math, English, history, and science for older students. When schools reduce textbooks to easy reading levels, most students pass their tests, get good grades, and please their parents. This makes everyone happy, but the children still can't read very well.

Today's students read material such as the following passage from an eighth-grade reader titled *Hilda: The Hen Who Wouldn't Give Up*, cited by researcher Gary Hull: "Hilda was very excited. Her aunt had just hatched five baby chicks. Hilda couldn't wait to see them, but her aunt lived five miles away. How was Hilda going to get there? It was much too far away."[20] This is a passage from a text for thirteen-year-olds. Notice not only the simple reading level here, but the almost-infantile content level. In this country a hundred years ago, thirteen-year-old students read complex books that college-level students read today.

Math textbooks are also simplified. Addison-Wesley's textbook *Secondary Math: An Integrated Approach* promotes the 'team math' technique. According to Gary Hull, Ph.D., author of the book *Caution: Textbooks Are Hazardous To Your Child's Mind In Math, History and Literature*, this technique encourages students to distrust their own minds and rely on the collective opinions of their fellow students to solve math problems. He notes: "The 'team-math' approach employs a technique called 'jigsawing,' where Susie, Johnny and Sally each get one part of the problem to work on. Then the group agrees, by arbitrary consensus, on an overall solution."[21]

This technique is dumbing-down by group-think. It tells students that they can't solve a math problem by themselves— students have to consult fellow members of their math team, then vote on the correct answer (like my imaginary pilots voted for the correct navigation course).

History textbooks also get dumbed down. Hull quotes the director of the American Textbook Council saying that history texts "have lost a lot of literary quality as we've replaced the core text with pictures, white space, and all sorts of glossy graphics." Hull comments:

These textbooks are gutted of any substantial presentation of history as a sequence of causally interrelated events. Pages are now filled with colorful visuals not to support the narrative, but to replace it. The student is supposed to learn by pictures, not by words. This method of teaching makes the development of a child's conceptual faculty impossible.[22]

A textbook representative employed by Harcourt's textbook subdivision told a reporter for the *Seattle Times* in 1996,

"Absolutely they've been dumbed down. I think what we've heard a lot of, throughout the country, is that there needed to be an image of American students doing well. In order for us to show them as being smarter, let's dummy down what we're teaching them. You'll appear to be smarter, even though you're not."[23]

Why do public schools dumb-down the textbooks? First, most public schools today and for the last fifty years have emphasized the whole-language (or look-say) reading method over phonics. They also use group learning, self-esteem protecting, and other failed teaching methods. As a result, the average student's reading ability has been severely damaged. Students who are victims of the whole-language method find it difficult to read words they haven't seen before. Textbooks therefore have to be written in simple words that poor readers can recognize.

Second, public schools group students by age, not ability. Since all children differ in their abilities, there are always slower-learning students in every class. Out of good intentions, school authorities often gear reading instruction for an entire class to the level of the slowest learners. So textbooks were dumbed-down to accommodate these students. This is a classic case of the usual unintended consequences caused by well-intentioned but bad government policies.[24]

Dumbed-Down Tests
and Grade Inflation

Many public schools dumb-down the tests students take and inflate students' grades. Often, the school's goal is to fool parents into believing their children are doing better than they are. If parents think their kids are doing fine, they don't complain to teachers, principals, or their local school board.

If public schools teach whole-language reading, invented spelling, and new math, and use dumbed-down textbooks in all subjects, it's inevitable that students will do poorly on standardized tests like the SAT (Scholastic Aptitude Test). To compensate for students' poor academic abilities, school authorities often dumb-down in-class tests and inflate students' grades. According to Sykes:

More than two-thirds of American eighth-graders say that they get mostly A's and B's. According to the [American] College Board, the percentage of students reporting that they had an average grade of A rose from 28 percent to 32 percent between 1987 and 1994. At the same time, their average SAT scores fell by 6 to 15 points. . . . Giving out ever-increasing grades for ever-more mediocre work reflects the collapse of standards throughout the educational system.[25]

John Jacob Cannell, a West Virginia doctor, was confused about some of his teenage patients. He saw a parade of teenage pregnancy, depression, delinquency, and drug abuse. Many of these troubled teenagers seemed to lag far behind their peers in reading and other basic academic skills. When Cannell spoke to local public-school officials, they told him that these troubled teenagers had scored well on the school's standardized tests. Yet, independent tests found that many of these teenagers were sitting in seventh-grade classrooms and had only third-grade academic skills. Realizing that something was wrong with the public-school grading system, Cannell did an extensive research study on testing procedures throughout the country. Here's what he found:

- Not a single one of the fifty states reported that its students scored below average at the elementary level on their total battery of scores.[26] More than two-thirds of American students—70 percent—were being told that they were 'above average' based on the test scores.[27]
- More than 90 percent of American school districts claimed to be performing above average. Cannell's study found that some of the poorest, most desperate school districts in the nation are able to pacify the press, parents, and school boards by testing 'above the national norm' on one of these commercial 'Lake Wobegon' [dumbed-down] achievement tests. Among those claiming to be 'above average,' he [Cannell] found, were

Trenton and East Orange, New Jersey, Boston, St. Louis, Kansas City, East St. Louis, and New York City—all districts notorious for the breakdown in their schools. In many of those cities, years of misleading and Pollyanish claims of academic above-averageness had staved off critics, accountability, and reform, while many of the schools themselves went from wretched to hopeless.[28]

If you compare these deceptive test results with the literacy statistics in Chapter 1, where we saw literacy rates of 50 percent or less in many public schools today, you see that public schools have become snake-oil salesmen. They con parents into thinking the schools are selling a good education, when what they really sell is educational failure. Sykes comments on Cannell's findings:

> Given the high stakes, the pressures on schools to cheat on their testing may have proven irresistible to some. After Cannell published his study, he received letters from across the country detailing various testing ruses. "Some teachers openly admitted cheating," he wrote. "Others were concerned that if they didn't cheat, they would look bad compared to the teachers who did. All the teachers complained that cheating is encouraged by school administrators."[29]

As we would expect, the educational establishment bitterly attacked Cannell's study because it openly exposed their test-grade rigging. However, the U.S. Department of Education ultimately upheld Cannell's report when it concluded that "we generally concur with the central finding of Dr. Cannell's report."[30] So it seems that state education departments and school districts across the country were lying to parents about their children's real academic abilities.

Myron Lieberman, educational consultant and author of *Public Education: An Autopsy*, found that investigation of Cannell's charges confirmed that public schools had inflated average test scores in the following ways:

1. Poor students were excluded or discouraged from taking the tests.
2. Teachers assigned tests as homework or taught test items in class.
3. Test security was minimal or even nonexistent.
4. Students were allowed more time than prescribed by test regulations
5. Unrealistic, highly improbable improvements from test to test were not audited or investigated.
6. Teachers and administrators were not punished for flagrant violations of test procedures.
7. Test results were reported in ways that exaggerated achievement levels.[31]

In a frantic scramble to hide their failure, school officials descend one step lower on the cheating scale. When many students fail their tests or get low grades, some public-school officials blame the test. Or, they simply *redefine* test failures as "success" and mediocre test grades as "above average." It's as if a delusional person insists that his bar of lead is really gold.

Many school authorities sincerely believe that teachers hurt students' feelings with low test scores. So, instead of changing their teaching methods or asking students to work harder, they simply inflate the test scores.[32]

The Wisconsin Department of Education found that many of its students were failing the state's GED test. The test was designed so that seven out of ten students would pass, but only about 52 percent were passing. Sykes comments:

The state's educrats could have undertaken a study of the state's curriculum and standards; or they could have exhorted aspirants to the GED to prepare more thoroughly, which might have had the effect of improving the GED's already shaky reputation. Instead, they decided to simply lower the passing score by 20 points retroactively. Hundreds of applicants who had failed the test in previous years were now awarded diplomas. The state's superintendent of public instruction vehemently denied that he was "dumbing-down" the test: he was merely readjusting the scores, he explained.

A representative of one of the state's teachers union explained that the issue was not about academic quality, but about "fairness." She was not referring to the unfairness of low academic achievement, but to the unfairness of tests that measure achievement.[33]

Many public-school officials feel intense pressure to alter test results and redefine failure as success to fool parents and politicians. Such educational fraud means that parents *cannot* and *should not* trust any claims by teachers or school authorities about their children's alleged academic abilities.

A fifth-grade teacher in Chicago said the following to Jonathan Kozol, author of *Savage Inequalities: Children In America's Schools*:

It's all a game . . . Keep [the kids] in class for seven years and give them a diploma if they make it to eighth grade. They can't read, but give them the diploma. The parents don't know what's going on. They're satisfied.[34]

Andrew J. Coulson, in his brilliant book, *Market Education: The Unknown History*, sites another example of how public schools deliberately lie to parents about their children's academic abilities:

Consistently greeted by A's and B's on their children's report cards, the parents of Zavala Elementary School had been *lulled into complacency* [italics added], believing that both the school and its students were performing well. In fact, Zavala was one of the worst schools in the district, and its students ranked near the bottom on statewide standardized tests. When a new principal took over the helm and requested that the statewide scores be read out at a PTA meeting, parents were dismayed by their children's abysmal showing, and furious with teachers and school officials for misleading them with inflated grades.[35]

The *No Child Left Behind Act* of 2001 is making this problem of cheating, low academic standards, and public schools lying to parents, even worse. Under this Act, the Department of Education now requires students to pass standardized tests. Failing schools will lose federal funding and other perks if their students consistently turn in a bad performance on these tests.

Holding schools and teachers accountable, and expecting students to demonstrate what they've learned, sounds like a good idea. But this Act means that badly-taught students, victims of dumbed-down texts and bad teaching methods like whole-language instruction, now have to pass difficult standardized tests they are not ready for. As a result, millions of students may fail these tests, not because they are dumb, but because the schools never taught them to read properly or solve a math problem without a calculator. Millions of high-school students with low reading and math skills now risk not graduating from high school until they pass these tests.

It is important that parents know the unvarnished truth about their children's real academic abilities. However, many parents are now frantic because they see their children's failing grades on these new tests. As a result, they complain to school boards that they do *not* want their children taking these tests or not graduating from high school because of low test scores. To protect their children, many parents are now *demanding* dumbed-down tests to make sure that their kids graduate from high school and go to college.

The *No Child Left Behind Act* is now forcing many parents to condone schools that dumb-down their tests and standards, instead of blaming these schools for their children's failure to learn. This is another unintended consequence of government programs that try to fix problems that a government-controlled school system created in the first place.

State lawmakers in New York, Wisconsin, Massachusetts, and other states have yielded to parents' pressure on this issue. School authorities in these states have scrapped or watered-down high-stakes graduation tests. [36]

In Wisconsin, state legislators backed off plans to require high-school graduation tests because of strong opposition by parents from affluent suburbs. One parent group calling itself "Advocates for Education" argued that high-stakes testing would not be fair to children and would hurt educational quality in the schools. Critics of the graduation tests were worried that the tests would put too much pressure on the children. Suburban parents lobbied parent-teacher organizations, and state legislators eventually scrapped the graduation test before a single high-school student had taken it.

Similarly, New York and Massachusetts officials yielded to pressure by parents to set low passing grades for their new graduation tests. In Virginia and Arizona, state boards of education have backed away from graduation tests that were too tough for even the so-called better schools. Only 7 percent of schools in Virginia met new achievement standards, and 9 out of 10 sophomores in Arizona schools failed a new math test. [37]

In New York City, school authorities estimated that over 30 percent of the city's 11th-graders would not be eligible to graduate if the English language standard that will take effect next year was being applied today. Diane Ravitch of the Brookings Institute in Washington is a longtime analyst of New York's public-school system She estimated that in some neighborhoods, less than 5 percent of high-school seniors would qualify to graduate under the new standards. [38]

Parents, particularly those with younger children, should take heed. You don't want to end up with high-school kids who may not graduate because they can't pass the new tests. As we've seen, you certainly can't trust your public school's assessment of your children's academic abilities. You should therefore consider having your children's math and reading skills evaluated by an independent *outside* company (I list many of these companies in the Resources section).

After getting this evaluation, if your children's math and reading abilities are far below what your local public school led you to believe, you might then consider finding education alternatives *outside* the public schools (which I discuss at length in Chapters 8, 9, and the Resources section).

Faking the Drop-Out Rates

Another way school authorities deceive parents is by inflating high-school graduation rates and underestimating drop-out rates. The New York Department of Education claimed that the high-school graduation rate in 1998 was 75 percent. A study by the Manhattan Institute for Policy Research estimated the graduate rate in 2001 to be 65 percent.[39]

According to a study done by California Parents for Education Choice (CPEC), in 1998 the California Department of Education(CDE) reported that the "official" high-school drop-out rate for 1998 was 3.3 percent. What the CDE didn't report to the press was that they used a one-year drop-out rate, rather than a drop-out rate that measured how many students left high-school over a *four-year* period.

CPEC successfully lobbied the California state Board of Education in 1998 to force the CDE to disclose high-school graduation rates. These graduation rates are a more accurate measure of how many students dropped out in the four years between the 9th and 12th grades in high-school. When these figures were revealed, it turned out that the 1999-2003 statewide drop-out rate was a 29.2 percent, *not* 3.3 percent. For the same time period, the Los Angeles Unified School District had an appalling drop-out rate of 53 percent.[40] Jay Greene, a Senior Fellow at the Manhattan Institute for Policy Research, points out that these inflated graduation rates and underestimated drop-out rates are a problem with public schools across the country.

School authorities have many ways to fudge the numbers.

Public schools can deceive parents because no one audits their drop-out or graduation-rate reports. Schools don't have the resources or incentive to find out why individual students dropped out of school. They don't know whether a child's family simply moved away, or whether the child dropped out for good or dropped out later in another school. In such cases, it's much easier for the school to simply eliminate such students from their calculations under the heading of "unknown."[41]

Public schools have a vested interest in grossly underestimating drop-out rates and overestimating graduation rates. If the true figures came out, parents and legislators who support the system might call for drastic reform measures, and school principals and administrators might be fired or schools shut down. Also, state and federal tax money schools receive is pegged to actual attendance. When schools have low attendance or high drop-out rates they get less tax money and government subsidies.[42]

These fudged drop-out and graduation-rate numbers are just another way public schools try to cover up their on-going failure. They are another example of why parents *should not trust* any facts or statistics school authorities tell them. School authorities need to defend their system. Their jobs, pensions, and power are at stake. That makes any claims they make about students' progress or academic abilities immediately suspect.

Automatic or "Social" Promotion

To protect children's self-esteem or deflect complaints by parents, many public schools today automatically advance failing students to the next grade level. In other schools, a student is left back a maximum of one year, then promoted again regardless of his or her academic skills.[43]

The *No Child Left Behind Act* tries to solve this problem. The federal government is pressuring public schools to set minimum standards that each student must pass before advancing to the next grade. Missouri, California, New York, and other states have also passed new laws that create stricter promotion standards.[44]

However, in spite of these new laws, many states still have semi-automatic advancement based on the student's overall performance. Many schools consider a student's portfolio of work, attendance record, or other mitigating factors. Based on these factors, the school may advance students to the next grade, even though they do poorly on their tests or read at a previous grade level.[45]

When students who should be failing, automatically advance to the next grade from elementary school through high school, the problem keeps getting worse. By graduation day, some students who get diplomas are straight-A illiterates whose high grades disguise their near-illiteracy. In effect, these students receive a counterfeit diploma that is nothing more than a twelve-year attendance record.

What does automatic promotion teach children? Many students set their standards no higher than what their teachers or schools expect of them. Automatic promotion lets students coast along with little or no effort, knowing they will advance to the next grade even if they never study or do their homework, or even if they receive low grades on their tests. Automatic promotion also tells kids they can succeed in life without effort or perseverance, and that mediocrity and laziness are acceptable. It tragically sets children up to fail later in life when they apply for college or a job. These are not lessons that schools should be teaching our children.

The Cheaters

Because many children can't pass their tests, even tests that are deliberately dumbed-down, an increasing number of principals and teachers are helping their students cheat on tests, or inventing meaningless grading systems. This is another way that school authorities fool parents into thinking that their child's school does a good job.

In 1992, the scholarly journal *Educational Measurement: Issues and Practice* published the results of a national survey about teacher cheating. Janie Hall and Paul Kleine, the authors of the report, asked 2256 public-school teachers, principals, superintendents, and testing supervisors if their colleagues cheated on tests. Forty-four percent of those questioned answered yes. Also, 55 percent of the teachers surveyed said they were aware that many of their fellow teachers changed students' answers, taught specific parts of tests prior to the tests, and gave students hints during tests.[46]

In December 1999, a special investigation of New York City schools revealed that two principals and dozens of teachers and assistant teachers were helping students cheat on standardized math and reading tests:

> New York City school officials are again struggling with accusations of cheating, which some educators say is the downside of raising academic standards. In the Big Apple, that downside was exposed in painful detail when a 17-month investigation revealed that teachers and administrators helped city students cheat on standardized tests by giving them questions in advance and even marking answer sheets for them, investigators said. Fifty-two school employees in the nation's largest school system are accused of taking part in crude cheating schemes designed to improve elementary and middle school students' performance on tests, according to Edward Stancik, special investigator for the New York City schools.
>
> Meanwhile, in New York City, Stancik reported that he found teachers in 32 schools have been helping students cheat for at least three years. The fallout of inflated scores, Stancik said, is that "children don't get the help they need, parents don't know how well or poorly their students are doing, and the public doesn't know which schools are functioning well."[47]

New York City schools are not the only players in this cheating game. Similar scandals or allegations involving public-school teachers and principals have been reported in Ohio, Georgia, Texas, Arizona, and Massachusetts. Wherever there is pressure for public schools to show good results, cheating raises its ugly head.

Unfortunately, the measures school authorities take to prevent future scandals are usually ineffective. In New York City, the Board of Education formed committees to investigate the problem, and some administrators were fired.

However, real change can't happen *because the system didn't change*. Concerned parents will continue to pressure teachers and principals to make sure their children pass, and some teachers and principals will succumb to this pressure because they fear for their jobs or school funding if their students fail. The pressure to cheat is built into the system because many public schools can't teach kids to read well enough to pass even dumbed-down tests, no less the new standardized tests.

Cheating lets parents, teachers, and principals fake reality and pretend that the schools are doing their job. Of course, when cheated high-school graduates take their college entrance exams or start their college studies, reality hits them square in the face. That's when the real struggle begins. But public schools have to play this cheating game to ward off criticism and keep their funding. Thus, the vicious cycle continues, victimizing millions of children.

Outcome-Based Education

Another reason public schools fail our children is because many schools use an insidious teaching method called Outcome-Based Education (OBE). On the surface, the term "outcome-based" would make a typical parent believe that the program stresses real academic "outcomes" or achievement in math, reading, writing, and other skills. But, as we will soon see, like many other terms school authorities use to describe their teaching methods, the phrase "outcome-based" is a smoke screen to hide the program's real goals. Sykes describes a typical OBE program:

"Diane [last name withheld for privacy] wanted to be a supportive parent. She was involved in her children's education and even worked as a volunteer at Eastside Elementary School in her community of Sun Prairie, Wisconsin. Using slogans such as 'All Students Can Learn' (an idea that Diane liked), Eastside had implemented a new philosophy of education called Outcome Based Education which insists that students be given as much time as they need (or want) to learn the subject matter. In her daughter's fourth-grade class, [Diane] found that every time a project or report came due in language, math, social studies, or science, half to two-thirds of the class did not have the work done. Even so, there was no penalty or loss of credit for late assignments.

In Outcome Based Education, she was told, no student ever fails. Every student must be given as much time as needed to meet the outcome goals. That also meant that if sloppy, incomplete, or poorly done assignments were handed in, students were not graded down, because they could always be redone. In practice, that meant that the only thing students had to do was keep up with the lowest achiever in the class, because outcome-based classrooms did not move on until all students met the goal. The students, not the teacher, set the pace.

[Diane] found that half of the fourth graders at Eastside could not tell time or count change. But there was no sense of urgency in correcting the situation. Students were allowed to take tests over and over again until they got a passing grade. As a result, students at Eastside were three-and-a-half months behind students in the same grade at private schools in her area. If the children's school seemed uninterested in academic achievement, Diane found the school remarkably interested in her children's attitudes and feelings.

Fourth-grade students spent an entire unit (four to five weeks) studying Wisconsin's Indians. But at the end, there was no test. The teacher explained, "There was too much material to test and, anyway, the main reason for this unit is to be sure the students develop the proper attitudes toward Indians." The new philosophy also was reflected in the school's new grading system. Starting with first graders, students no longer receive A's, B's, and C's on their report cards. Instead they are given "C," "S," or "N." "C" stands for "consistently," "S" for "sometimes," "N" for "Not Yet."

"These grades," [Diane] pointed out, "could not be more ambiguous. They mean nothing. Does 'sometimes' mean twice a day, once a week, three times a month? Is 'not yet' implying that this is an expected goal this quarter, or have we not been introduced to this, or is the teacher frustrated beyond reason with a child's refusal to try and 'not yet' doing anything? 'Not yet' could mean any of these things. These 'report cards' did not report anything." The lessons the children were learning, she concluded, were "procrastination, the ability to do any quality work without consequences, lack of responsibility, and the acceptance of mediocrity."[48]

A Virginia teacher and mother had a similar experience with Outcome-Based Education:

Cheri [last name omitted for privacy] was the 1988 Stafford County (Virginia) Teacher of the Year and in 1991 she was a finalist for the Agnes Meyer Outstanding Teacher Award sponsored by the *Washington Post*. After her family relocated, her daughter Tiffany was enrolled in schools that had begun implementing Outcome Based Education. A seventh grader, Tiffany had been an eager student, but shortly after she started at her new school, she began to beg to stay home.

"The work was far too easy," Cheri recalls, "but what was worse was that any display of intelligence was ridiculed in a cruel and demeaning way by many of the other students. Hard work and self-discipline are looked down upon, and status is often achieved by non-performance. The prevailing attitude among many students is 'Why study? They can't fail me so who cares?' What sort of work ethic is this producing in these children? No one fails, regardless of how little they do. Instead, they receive 'incompletes,' which can be made up at any time. The kids have the system figured out. When there is a football game or show on TV the night before a test, a common comment is: 'Why study? I'll just take the test and fail it. I can always take the retest later."[49]

OBE facilitators are told to protect children's feelings. Often, an entire class is held back until the slowest students understand the previously covered material. Average or faster-learning students, chained to the slower learners, are bored to death in their classes. The feelings of the slower-learning kids arc protected, at the expense of the precious time of all the other students.

Here are the life-lessons OBE teaches children—laziness, dishonesty, irresponsibility, and procrastination. OBE teaches that learning is a con game and that content, knowledge, and reading skills are irrelevant, as long as a student's outcome is to feel good and get along with others. In short, OBE programs can be a menace to your children.

Also, the outcomes that OBE teacher-facilitators push don't relate to content and real academic skills at all. Instead, they relate to a laundry list of odd or vague non-academic skills and emotional states. Sykes provides the following examples:

One of Minnesota's original outcomes called for the "integration of physical, emotional, and spiritual wellness." Kentucky's state educational goals include such

"valued outcomes" as "Listening," which officials defined as students "construct meaning from messages
communicated in a variety of ways for a variety of purposes through listening." This was distinguished from
"Observing," which they defined as "students construct
meanings from messages communicated in a variety of
ways for a variety of purposes through observing."

Other goals included: "Interpersonal Relationships," in which "students observe, analyze, and interpret human behaviors to acquire a better understanding
of self, others, and human relationships"; "Consumer-
ism": "Students demonstrate effective decision-making
and evaluate consumer skills"; "Mental and Emotional
Wellness": "Students demonstrate positive strategies
for achieving and maintaining mental and emotional
wellness"; "Positive self-concept": "Students demonstrate positive growth in self-concept through appropriate tasks or projects"; "Adaptability and flexibility":
"Students demonstrate the ability to be adaptable and
flexible through appropriate tasks or projects"; "Multicultural and World View": "Students demonstrate an
understanding of, appreciation of, and sensitivity to a
multicultural and world view"; and "Ethical View":
"Students demonstrate the ability to make decisions
based on ethical values."[50]

Math and reading skills are often on the bottom of school
officials' list of outcomes, if these skills are mentioned at all.
Parents should ask themselves if they want their children going to public schools that waste their kids' time with the kinds
of outcomes that Sykes listed above, rather than teaching their
children how to read and write.

The outcomes many public schools push also indoctrinate
children with moral or ethical values that many parents might
object to. A crucial issue is therefore what or *whose* ethical values will children be subjected to? Unfortunately, much of the
public-school establishment is liberal, anti-religion, and pro-

big government in their views. So school curriculum developers often create outcomes that reflect these views.

In *Dumbing Down Our Kids*, Sykes points out that, for example, Pennsylvania school officials were so enthusiastic about their OBE program that they created fifty-one separate outcomes. Most of the outcomes concerned values, feelings, or attitudes, such as:

All students relate in writing, speech, or other media, the history and nature of various forms of prejudice to current problems facing communities and nations, including the United States. All students make environmentally sound decisions in their personal and civic lives.[51]

The primary goal of many OBE programs is not to improve children's academic skills, but to teach them politically-correct attitudes. Sykes gives this example from Milwaukee schools:

In Milwaukee, where the average grade point average of high-school students hovers around a 'D,' the district's department of Curriculum and Instruction developed ten goals and performance indicators for students. The number one goal and indicator for Milwaukee Public Schools did not deal with math, reading, or even . . . readiness to work. Instead, goal one read: Students will project anti-racist, anti-biased attitudes through their participation in a multi-lingual, multi-ethnic, culturally diverse curriculum. (Note: students *will* project the requisite attitudes. Not *study* or *understand*, or even *learn about*. They will project the mandated attitudes. What happens if they don't?).[52]

These "mandated attitudes" are OBE's real goals and outcomes. OBE usually brushes aside reading, writing, and math skills as unimportant. Instead, OBE pushes a psycho-babble mix of social, political, interpersonal, and getting-to-understand-different-cultures values.

Public schools cripple children's ability to read and do basic math. They dumb down their tests, textbooks, and curriculum. They commit educational fraud against parents by hiding their failure and incompetence with rigged test scores and report cards. They indoctinate children with politically-correct "outcomes" that have little to do with learning basic academic skills.

If a private school did these things, you would quickly take your child out of the school and file civil charges against the owner. Yet public schools have been getting away with these educational crimes for decades. As the next chapter will show, these problems are even worse for low-income minority children and their parents.

4

Low-Income Minority Children: The Most Abused Victims of Public Schools

Low-income minority parents and their children are enduring victims of public schools. For over fifty years, these parents have pleaded with education authorities to give their children a decent education. Yet, if anything, the drugs, violence, and illiteracy in the schools seem to get worse every year.

In Chapter 1, we examined the frightening literacy statistics that show how badly public schools fail our children. Those statistics show that public schools injure low-income minority children most of all. These children consistently suffer math and reading skills substantially below the already low skills of white public-school students. According to the *National Assessment of Educational Progress*, 58 percent of low-income 4th graders cannot read and 61 percent of low-income 8th graders cannot multiply two-digit numbers.[1]

High-school graduation rates also tell the same story. The Manhattan Institute For Policy Research, in their September, 2003 report, found that only 51 percent of all black students and 52 percent of all hispanic students graduate. Also, only 20 percent of all black students and 16 percent of all hispanic students leave high school ready for college. In contrast, the graduation rate was 72 percent for white students and 79 percent for asian students. The college readiness for white students was 37 percent, and 38 percent for asian students.[2]

These are not just appalling statistics. They represent millions of bright, eager children whose minds and futures are crippled by public schools.

One reason inner-city schools fail low-income minority children is because many education officials seem to have racist attitudes toward these children's ability to learn. School authorities sometimes treat these kids as if they were mentally deficient or incapable of learning. As Chapter 3 revealed, many public schools now inflate grades and test scores to hide their failure to educate our children. In inner-city schools, this grade inflation is even worse. Teachers try to protect these children's self-esteem by giving them test and class grades completely inconsistent with their true academic abilities.

In 1990, three academics, Harold Stevenson, Chuansheng Chen, and David Uttal did a study of the attitudes and academic achievement of black, white, and hispanic children in Chicago. They found a disturbing gap between what parents thought their children were learning and the children's actual performance. Teachers in high-poverty schools had given A's to students for work that would have earned them C's or D's in affluent suburban schools.

In the study, black mothers of Chicago elementary-school students rated their children's skills and abilities quite high and thought their kids were doing well in reading and math. The children thought the same thing. The kids told the researchers that they were working hard in their studies and doing well.

Unfortunately, the researchers found that the parents' and children's self-evaluations of their math and reading skills were way above their actual achievement levels. There was a big gap between their optimistic self-evaluations and their dismal academic performance on independent tests. It seems that the public schools were giving these children a false idea of their academic skill levels. In other words, these children were heading towards failure and no one bothered to tell them. [3]

Real confidence comes from hard work, perseverance, facing and accepting academic challenges, and overcoming failures. The pseudo-self-esteem that school authorities promote is the opposite of real confidence. Many teachers and principals with good intentions try to shelter minority children from reality, hard work, and the possibility of failure. This implies that they believe low-income minority students are mentally inferior and therefore need to be sheltered. Los Angeles math teacher Jaime Escalante stated:

> Our schools today . . . tend to look upon disadvantaged minority students as though they were on the verge of a mental breakdown, to be protected from any undue stress. . . . Ideas like this are not just false. They are the kiss of death for minority youth and, if allowed to proliferate, will significantly stall the advancement of minorities.[4]

Public-school education in general is third-rate, to say the least. When school authorities believe that low-income minority children can't learn, their education deteriorates even more. Teachers won't expect much from these children, and kids usually live up to exactly what adults expect of them. Hence the appalling illiteracy and drop-out rates in inner-city schools.

The day of reckoning comes when these kids graduate. Because the schools failed miserably to give these children good reading and math skills, they often end up with no job, a dead-end job, or low-paying jobs. So this well-intentioned policy of protecting these children's self-esteem simply perpetuates the vicious cycle of failure and poverty for low-income minority families.

Moreover, this notion that low-income black or hispanic minority students are mentally inferior or unteachable is totally false. Studies show that these students learn well and succeed in the relatively few public schools that stress academic basics, enforce discipline, and demand hard work from their students.

In Chattanooga, Tennessee, there are six public schools that follow Mortimer Adler's "Paideia" curriculum. This curriculum is a disciplined and strictly traditional approach to teaching, with no electives or self-esteem courses. It has high standards for all students, whether rich, poor, black, or white. The schools demand hard work, dedication, and honor-student results from all students, and most students live up to those expectations.

Mohegan Elementary School is located in the South Bronx, one of the worst neighborhoods in the nation. Mohegan is one of several dozen schools that have adopted a curriculum known as the "Core Knowledge" plan. This structured curriculum was developed by E. D. Hirsch, Jr. and teaches core subjects such as history, literature, science, mathematics, and the arts. Hirsch's curriculum emphasizes content of learning, in contrast to public schools' vaguely worded "goals" that focus on "learning skills."

Hirsch's curriculum is unique for low-income minority schools because it doesn't condescend to its students. It does not assume poor or minority kids can't learn. Instead, it assumes all children can learn, and demands hard work and dedication from its students. As usual, most students live up to these high expectations.[5] Unfortunately, Mohegan Elementary and the six Chattanooga schools are rare exceptions in an otherwise bleak inner-city public-school system.

Another reason that public schools continually fail low-income minority children and their parents is because of the way public schools are funded. Public schools in many states get their funds from local property taxes. Higher-income suburban neighborhoods with more expensive homes raise more property taxes to pay for their schools. Poor inner-city school districts with lower property values usually get less tax money for their schools. More money does not necessarily mean better education, but it does pay for better school facilities for the children.

In the past five years, many states have passed funding-equalization legislation that switched education funding from property taxes to state income taxes. These new laws have dramatically reduced the big gaps in funding between inner-city and suburban schools, but have done little to improve education in low-income minority areas.

Homeowners in states that fund schools from property taxes are willing to pay higher taxes to insure better schools. That's because better quality schools not only help their children, but also raise property values in the neighborhood. One way suburban neighborhoods compete with each other is by the quality and reputation of their schools. Homes in areas that have quality schools usually have higher market values. Homeowners therefore have a direct financial interest in the quality of schools in their neighborhood, so are willing to pay higher school taxes to achieve that end.

In contrast, taxpayers who don't have school-age children and live in states that pay for schools from general taxes, resist tax increases for education. Also, many states now have multi-billion-dollar deficits. These states are finding themselves strapped for money to fund public schools through general taxes. As a result, inner-city schools in funding-equalized states are not getting the increased funding they hoped for, and are still educational disaster areas. [6]

Even more serious than any lack of money is the violence in inner-city public schools, where a child may be raped, bullied, or confronted by knife-carrying students or roving drug dealers. Millions of black or hispanic kids either drop out early, or serve a twelve-year education prison sentence with sometimes violent classmates, drug dealers, and often ill-trained or inexperienced teachers. In ghetto schools, part day-care center, part child prison, these kids often lose their future and sometimes their lives.

Not surprisingly, many public schools in low-income minority areas have severe discipline problems in the classroom. It takes only a few violent or hardcore troublemakers in each class to make it impossible for teachers to maintain discipline or teach the other students who want to learn. This problem is far worse than most parents realize. Carl Sommer, former New York City school teacher and author of *Schools in Crisis: Training for Success or Failure?* worked as a substitute teacher to investigate this problem. Here's what he found:

> To discover what was happening inside New York City schools, I taught as a substitute teacher for 28 days in 27 different schools in some of the best and worst schools in the city. Some classes were orderly, but in that short time I observed students climbing on desks, tables and cabinets; throwing paper airplanes and balls in classrooms; running around the rooms and halls; yelling, fighting, and knocking over chairs and desks. While substituting, I have been threatened, been cursed, had my foot stamped on, seen a teacher assaulted, and stopped numerous fights.[7]

Sommers also confirmed the serious discipline problem in public schools across the country from an unlikely source—teacher responses to an Ann Landers (newspaper columnist) letter:

> Ann Landers printed a letter from an Iowa teacher who resigned because she was "sick of being called foul names, sick of hearing students use four-letter words, fed up on garbage and fights in the halls, and the 'you-can't-make-me' attitude."[8]

Ann Landers responded to this letter by saying that she thought the problem couldn't be as bad as this teacher described. Teachers across the country wrote back to Ann Landers, commenting that they thought Landers was . . . "completely out of touch" . . . and "living in Disneyland" because of her mild assessment of the discipline problem in public schools.[9]

Sommers listed other responses to Lander's comment from teachers across the country:

Bryan, Texas: "Most teachers are so worn out trying to maintain discipline that they have no time or energy for teaching. Kids who want to learn are being ripped off."

Royal Oak, Michigan: "The public would not believe what goes on in the average classroom. Anyone who goes into teaching today should have his head examined."

Memphis, Tennessee: "I've taught school for 25 years. These last five years have been the worst. Everything that isn't nailed down disappears. The language in the halls and classrooms is unprintable."

Chicago: "I am a teacher who is also ready to quit. I have a nervous stomach from the fist-fighting in my classes. A student pulled a knife on me last week. Three teachers in our school were assaulted last month. It's a nightmare!"[10]

These incidents occurred in 1984. The problem is at least as bad if not worse today, especially in low-income inner-city neighborhoods. In January, 2004, New York City Mayor Michael R. Bloomberg announced a new initiative to curb the violence in twelve of the city's worst public schools.[11] The initiative created a task force of 150 police officers who will help impose order in these schools. The violence has become so bad that New York City police will roam the halls of these schools to keep the peace. This is just one recent example of how violence has escalated in inner-city public schools.

Fifty years ago, public schools had more leeway to expel students. Today, because of the fear of legal or physical retaliation (or accusations of racism if the student is nonwhite), a principal will rarely expel even the most violent or disruptive student.

The exception to this is the new "zero tolerance" rules many schools have adopted, where students found carrying drugs or weapons (or even toy guns) are sometimes expelled for a relatively short period of time. Also, many inner-city schools are now sending the worst troublemakers to special charter or private schools for drop-outs or potential drop-outs, if and when space is available for these students.

Compulsory-attendance laws compound the violence problem, forcing all children, including most of the troublemakers, to stay in school until age sixteen (age requirements vary from state to state, usually from 14 to 18 years old). As a result, these violent or disruptive students make it harder for teachers to teach those students who want to learn.

Another problem of particular concern to minority parents is the lack of qualified teachers in many inner-city schools. Teacher-union rules usually give teachers with seniority the right to transfer to a school of their choice.[12] Many experienced inner-city teachers take advantage of this rule and transfer to suburban schools. Inner-city schools are left with ill-trained or inexperienced teachers, or with teachers who aren't familiar with the subject they're assigned to teach.

White teachers also flee inner-city schools for other reasons besides the violence. Cultural differences often contribute to this exodus. Many white teachers can't understand or empathize with black and hispanic cultures, so they find it frustrating to teach in these schools.

Teacher and principal tenure privileges also hurt low-income minority children. Many teachers are competent and dedicated. However, if a teacher is poorly trained, incompetent, inexperienced, doesn't care about her job or the kids, ignores minority parents' complaints, or doubts her students' ability to learn, parents can't get rid of her. Tenure employment rules make it expensive and time-consuming to fire poorly trained or incompetent teachers or principals. So these teachers and principals stay on the job or just get transferred to another school.

A 1999 *New York Daily News* article revealed just how bad the problem of ill-trained or uncertified teachers has become in New York's inner-city schools:

The city's lowest-performing schools are staffed with high numbers of teachers who have not met the state's minimum teaching standards. These uncertified teach-

ers are concentrated in poor and minority neighborhoods in schools that have scored poorly on reading
tests. In some, more than half the teachers are uncertified. At the same time, schools in more affluent communities are staffed almost entirely by certified teachers, and their [students'] reading scores are generally
higher.[13]

In effect, inner-city schools usually get the worst-trained,
least-experienced teachers. Ill-trained or incompetent teachers
necessarily makes the children's education even worse.

Don't Depend On Government Solutions

Today, many parents pin their hopes for better schools
on government-sponsored alternatives like vouchers, charter
schools, Supreme Court decisions, or the *No Child Left Behind
Act* that Congress passed in 2001. I'm sorry to say that these
are mostly false hopes. If parents wait for these alternatives to
finally give their children a decent education, they will be waiting for a very long time. Parents, don't hold your breath on
these options.

Vouchers

Vouchers, which give tax money to parents to pay for tuition
in private schools, sound good in theory. The problem is that
voucher programs are few and very far between. The Supreme
Court declared vouchers constitutional in 2002, but currently
only thirteen cities or states have created significant voucher
or education tax-credit programs. The following list briefly describes the restrictions and limitations of each program:
    • Arizona Tax Credit program — a married couple can claim
a maximum of $625 tax credit for contributions they make to
a private organization that gives voucher scholarships to stu-

dents.

• Cleveland voucher scholarships — The maximum voucher of $2700 is limited to families whose incomes are below 200 percent of the federal poverty level. Parents have to pay all tuition costs above the $2700 voucher they receive.

• Colorado voucher program — the maximum voucher is $5000. Unfortunately, in April, 2004 the Colorado state legislature killed this program.

• Florida A+ Opportunity voucher scholarship program — the maximum voucher in 2002-03 was $4537 for K--3rd grade, and $3370 for kids in 4th-8th grades. However, the vouchers are limited to schools that get an "F" grade rating for two out of four years from the Florida Department of Education. So far, very few schools have qualified for this program.

• Florida "McKay" voucher program — is limited to students with disabilities. The voucher pays either the public-school cost per student or the private school tuition, whichever is less.

• Florida Income-Tax Credit program — is restricted to low-income families whose children are eligible for the federal free or reduced-lunch program. Corporations get a tax credit for contributions they make to an organization that funds voucher scholarships.

• Illinois Tuition Tax Credit — families get a maximum tax credit of $500 for tuition in a private school. The family has to spend at least $2250 on education expenses to qualify for the $500 tax credit.

• Iowa Personal-Tax Credit program — families can get a maximum tax-credit refund of 25 percent of tuition costs, with a maximum tax refund of $250.

• Maine Town-Tuitioning program — this program is limited to students who live in small towns that have no public schools. The voucher amount is usually based on the receiving town's school tuition rate.

• Milwaukee (Wisconsin) voucher program — the program is limited to low-income Milwaukee families. The maximum voucher for the 2002-03 school year was $5783 or the private school's tuition, whichever is less. The program can't give vouchers to more than 15 percent of Milwaukee's public-school students.

• Minnesota Tax-Deduction and Tax-Credit program — all families can get a maximum tax deduction of $1625 for children in grades K-6, and $2500 for grades 7-12, for money they spend on their children's education. Families earning less than $37,500 can get a tax credit worth up to $2000 per family.

• Pennsylvania Tax Credit program — companies get tax credits for contributions to a private organization that funds vouchers. There is a $20 million scholarship cap on the entire program.

• Vermont Town-Tuitioning program — is limited to families in towns that don't have their own public schools, and applies mostly to high schools. The voucher amount is based on the state's average per-pupil cost for public schools.[14]

As you see, each voucher program has restrictions that limit its benefits to a relatively small number of children or a small amount of money. Some programs like Milwaukee's give generous voucher amounts, but others pay only part of the tuition costs. Many of the tax-credit programs, whether personal or corporate, also cover only a fraction of tuition costs.

Because there are so few voucher programs, and they all have various restrictions, voucher programs *barely scratch the surface*—they only help a tiny fraction of the approximately 45 million school children who suffer through public-school.

The education establishment, teacher unions, and most state and federal legislators in the Democratic party are against vouchers. Teacher unions fight voucher initiatives tooth and nail with lawsuits. When the unions take state voucher plans to court, these lawsuits can drag on for years. The voucher fight is going to be a long, bitter, ongoing legal battle between parents, states, and the teacher unions.

One reason public-school employees fear vouchers is because they fear competition from private schools. Real competition from an education free market threatens their jobs, security, and education monopoly over most of our children.

School authorities and public-school employees therefore have a vested interest in keeping public schools alive, no matter how bad the schools are, or how much this hurts millions of low-income minority (and non-minority) children.

Also, most states today are running huge budget deficits. As a result, states are cutting back on programs already on their books, so they can hardly afford expensive new voucher programs. California had close to a $13 billion budget deficit (which it "closed" by the typical tactic of borrowing the money with new state bonds), Texas a $10 billion deficit, and New York about an $8 billion deficit[15] (these deficit numbers keep fluctuating, depending on which politician is citing which new study, but the deficits are huge).

Teacher unions, school authorities, and state democratic legislators fight vouchers every step of the way. However, even if these groups stopped their opposition, religiously-affiliated and secular private schools simply do not have the room for all the students who would like to transfer out of public schools, either with state vouchers or private scholarships.

According to Nora Murphy, a spokeswoman for the Archdiocese of New York, private Catholic schools in New York could accommodate only 3000 new students. Yet, in September, 2002, 240,000 New York students in failing public schools qualified to transfer to a "better" public school under the *No Child Left Behind Act*. If all these students' parents instead got vouchers for private schools (if such a voucher program existed), you see the problem.[16]

Of course, if tomorrow the federal government created a nationwide voucher program that gave $5000 to each school child, a program that would cost almost $250 billion a year, then private-school entrepreneurs would certainly create more schools to fill the demand.

However, the federal government's deficit for 2003 was about $374 billion, and is expected to rise to about $500 billion in 2004.[17] With crushing deficits like these, and with state governments also burdened by multi-billion-dollar deficits, what is the chance that you will see a voucher program in your neighborhood any time soon? It might *not* be wise for parents to wait around for such a voucher miracle.

Another problem is that many existing voucher programs don't cover the full cost of tuition in a private school.[17] As I noted earlier, average tuition costs for religiously-affiliated schools runs about $3500 to $4000 a year. Non-religious private-school tuition costs range from $7000 to $14,000 and up, a year. So Cleveland's $2250 a year voucher is better than nothing, but Cleveland parents who get the vouchers still have to pay thousands of dollars a year to make up the difference.[18]

So even if a voucher program came to your neighborhood within the next ten years, it might not pay full tuition even for a Catholic or Protestant-affiliated school. Worse, do you want to wait around for a voucher program while your children stagnate in public schools?

For all the above reasons, parents who want to give their children a decent education *now*, cannot and should not depend on vouchers coming to their local neighborhood anytime soon. Parents, don't wait around for another twenty years while voucher advocates fight drawn-out lawsuits and fierce opposition by teacher unions, public-school bureaucrats, and the entrenched education establishment.

Don't pin your hopes on state governments with huge budget deficits to create vouchers for every child in your state. Don't risk your children's future on state and local politicians who get campaign contributions from teacher unions and consistently vote against voucher programs. Depending on government authorities to come to your rescue is an exercise in futility.

Charter schools

Charter schools are public schools that get state education funding but are governed by their own self-elected board of trustees. Charter schools are an attempt to introduce the free-market principles of local control and competition into the public-school system.

These schools can try new or innovative teaching methods, relatively free from smothering, bureaucratic rules and supervision by central boards of education. As a result, parents, teachers, and principals have more control over curriculum and teaching methods. Many school authorities don't like charter schools precisely because these schools give more control to parents and principals and take power away from these authorities.

The charter school movement has spread rapidly since 1991. As of the 2003-2004 school year, there were about 3000 charter schools open in 37 states and the District of Columbia, teaching over 750,000 students.[19]

Many local school districts fear charter schools because the schools drain tax money from regular public schools. When a school district loses a student to a charter school, most of the state tax money allocated to the student goes to the charter school. For example, Houston currently has 46 charter schools, and in the 2001-02 school year, the public schools lost about 13,000 students to charter schools, which cost the local school districts about $53.5 million in state tax revenues.[20]

Charter schools also embarrass local public schools. These schools often do a better job educating students than regular public schools, and for less money. For example, in the 1999-2000 school year, Ohio charter schools got $2300 less per pupil in tax funds than local public schools. Charter schools therefore spotlight regular public schools' failure to educate students with more tax money at their disposal.[21]

School authorities that are hostile to charter schools often harass these schools in many ways. They reduce the schools' funding, deny them access to school equipment or facilities, put new restrictions on existing charter schools, limit the number of new schools, or weaken charter-school laws.[22]

School authorities harass charter schools in other ways. They create convoluted application procedures or don't give new-school applicants enough time to process their applications. They also use city agencies, zoning boards, or fire departments to harass the schools with regulations. For example, the Washington DC school district involved a local charter school with an asbestos removal issue that forced the school to spend over $10 million in renovation costs. Local school districts have an arsenal of regulatory guns with which to harass charter schools or reduce their numbers.[23]

Teacher unions initially opposed charter schools. However, when charter schools became popular, the unions changed tactics. They now grudgingly give approval to charter schools, on certain conditions. They often push for district control over the schools, collective bargaining for charter-school teachers, or other restrictions.

Some teacher unions have renewed their open opposition to charter schools with their usual lawsuits. The Ohio Federation of Teachers filed a lawsuit that seeks to declare Ohio's charter school laws unconstitutional. Ohio's charter schools have been dragged into this lawsuit, thereby forcing them to waste valuable time, money, and resources on legal battles. Teacher unions use such lawsuits to try to stop or slow down the charter-school movement. Also, Washington state and some other states still have no charter-school laws partly because of strong opposition by teacher unions and other interest groups who oppose these schools.[24]

Partly as a result of this harassment by state education bureaucrats, local school districts, and teacher unions, there are not nearly enough charter schools to fill the demand. There is a constant waiting list for these schools, especially in low-income minority neighborhoods. In the 2001-02 school year, the average charter school enrolled about 242 students. About 69 percent of these schools had waiting lists averaging 166 students per school, or over half the school enrollment.[25]

The over 750,000 students currently enrolled in charter schools may seem like a lot, but that number represents little more than 1.7 percent of the approximately 45 million children who attend public school each year. Yet charter schools have now been around for over ten years. As with vouchers, how long will it take, if ever, for charter schools to come to your neighborhood? Thirty years? Parents should consider if they want to wait around this long while their children suffer through twelve years of public school.

Charter schools also present other problems. If you can't find a charter school close to home or don't want to wait for an opening, creating your own charter school is a major project. You have to talk to most of the parents in your neighborhood to find out which parents might be interested in a charter school. You then have to spend a lot of time convincing these parents to work with you to create the school, with no guarantee of success for your efforts.

Not only would you have to spend a great deal of time, but charter-school founders get no public funds to initially create the school. They only get state funding once the charter school is up and running. That means you or other founders of a new charter school would have to use your own personal funds to pay for school facilities, advertising, curriculum planning, equipment purchase, budgeting, hiring personnel, and adhering to complex charter-school regulations. These expenses impose a huge burden on average parents, which sharply limits the number of parents who are willing to spend this kind of money for a school that may not even succeed.

Another big roadblock for charter schools is that most states have a complicated application process. You have to fill out or supply page after page of information. Most states also have "accountability" clauses which require the students in your new school to meet and maintain certain academic achievement levels. If your students don't meet these requirements, the state can cut off your school's funding, or shut down the school.

Tragically, the charter-school movement has almost stopped growing because of all the obstacles and regulations politicians, school officials, and teacher unions now put in its way. Dr. Chester E. Finn, Jr., Senior Fellow at Stanford's Hoover Institution, writes about this problem:

> . . . I see an awful lot of folks bent on stopping the char-

ter movement dead in its tracks and I see them making considerable headway. I don't believe it exaggerates to say that a war is being waged against charter schools. It's a shooting war, a guerilla war and a war of attrition, all at once. . . . .

Attacks are coming from many directions. State officials have led some of them (e.g. in Texas, Indiana, New Jersey, Michigan). Local school systems spearhead others (e.g. California, Pennsylvania, Massachusetts). Teacher unions, having failed in legislative chambers to arrest the charter movement, are turning to the courtroom (in Ohio, Pennsylvania)—and are intimately involved with just about all the other attacks. Governors who claim to be pro-charter . . . are going along with newly restrictive legislation. Blue-ribbon panels convened to solve charter problems end up compounding them, as happened a few months back in Michigan."[26]

Even if you get a charter school up and running in spite of these obstacles, and the school meets the state's accountability requirements, you have another problem. You now have to work together with a large group of parents and charter-school officials (unless the school hires an outside private company to run the school). A charter school is usually run by a board of directors composed of parents, teachers, the principal, and others. This board, and parents in the school, now have to decide what curriculum and teaching methods they will use, and make many other decisions.

You now have to deal with about 240 other parents in the school and all the board members. Each parent or board member will often want different subjects or teaching methods in the school that benefit *their* kids. One parent's child likes music and hates math. Another child likes science and hates foreign languages. One parent thinks kids only need one year of arithmetic and another parent might want trigonometry and calculus taught to all students.

So to make the school work, *compromise* is the order of the day. Compromise means that, in the end, no parent or child is fully satisfied with the curriculum or teaching methods. A parent whose child loves music will be disappointed if the board doesn't vote for a music program. A parent whose child hates math will be disappointed if the school board decides to force all students to take three years of math. The compromises and dissatisfaction will be ongoing, and are built into the system.

So even though the general quality of education in a charter school will usually be better than a regular public school, the charter school still does not give parents real choice for a great education that caters to *their* child's special interests, talents, strengths, or weaknesses.

Supreme Court Decisions

Since the civil rights movement began in the early 1960s, two generations of low-income minority parents have been waiting for reform by the white-dominated education establishment. They have waited for the miracle that would liberate their children from failed, segregated, drug- and violence-infested schools.

In 1954, the Supreme Court ruled in *Brown v. Board of Education* that segregated schools were illegal and must integrate. This ruling gave low-income minority parents great hope for the future. Yet, after 1954, Congress and civil rights groups spent another twenty years struggling to end school segregation throughout the country. During this time, schools bused minority students into white neighborhoods to insure integration. Ironically, public schools are now as segregated as ever, not through law, but through people's economic behavior and human nature.

Today's school segregation happens when concerned white and minority parents vote with their feet and their pocketbooks. All parents know that education is the foundation of their children's future, so white, black, and hispanic parents who have moved up the economic ladder flee to middle-class suburbs to find safer neighborhoods and better schools. The neighborhoods they leave behind become even poorer and more segregated.

This new form of segregation isn't limited to inner-city schools in the Northeast and Midwest. In the South, teachers are fleeing mostly black schools. A 2003 article in the *Christian Science Monitor* states:

> Across the region [the South], white, often middle-class teachers are leaving schools dominated by African-Americans almost as fast as they arrive. Many are moving to school districts with smaller populations of blacks, new studies show.
>
> In Georgia, the trend is as pronounced as anywhere: a new study from Georgia State University (GSU) in Atlanta says that 32 percent of white elementary school teachers left their posts at predominantly black schools in 2001—up from 18 percent in 1995. Moreover, they left well-to-do black districts at about the same rate as poorer ones. . . . Recent studies in Texas, California, and North Carolina reach the same conclusion.[27]

To make matters worse, antisegregation Supreme Court decisions of the 1950s and 1960s are now coming undone. A 2002 study conducted by Harvard University researchers shows that the Supreme Court now gives lower courts discretion to approve resegregation on a large scale, and this resegregation is underway.

In 1991, the Supreme Court ruled in *Board of Education of Oklahoma City v. Dowell* that a local school district that had complied with its integration court order for several years could now allow segregated neighborhood schools. In 1992, the Supreme Court, in its *Freeman v. Pitts* decision, authorized the piecemeal dismantling of school desegregation plans. In the 1995 *Jenkins* case, the Supreme Court rejected a lower court's attempt to keep the desegregation and magnet-school segregation remedy in the previous *Kansas City* case, unless the program showed actual benefits for African-American students. This decision sharply curtailed the reach and promise of the separate-but-equal *Milliken II* case.[28]

In other words, the Supreme Court has weakened its position on integration since 1991. Its recent decisions suggest that the Court believes that integration and equal education are no longer permanent rights. These decisions allow states to dismantle integration programs that fail to bring real academic improvements or end unequal education in segregated schools.

According to a study by the Civil Rights Project at Harvard University, 44 percent of black students in the South attended mostly white schools in 1988. By 2000, however, only 31 percent of black students went to schools where white students were the majority. The remaining 69 percent were still attending black-majority schools, meaning that schools in the South have become resegregated. The problem is even more acute in New York, where only 13.6 percent of black students and 13.3 percent of hispanic students attend majority-white public schools, but the average white child goes to a school where 80 percent of the students are white.[29]

Low-income minority children are going back to segregated schools created by urban flight and their families' lower average income. Low-income minority parents and children are now worse off than ever in terms of school segregation, with little hope that politicians or the Supreme Court will come to their rescue.

The *No Child Left Behind Act*

Many low-income minority parents are pinning their last hopes on the *No Child Left Behind Act* (NCLB) that Congress passed in 2001. This new federal law pushes local governments to classify public schools as "failing" if test scores for too many students fall below minimum standards. If their school falls onto this blacklist, students then have the right to transfer to a different public school with a better record, and get free tutoring from an approved list of outside tutors which their parents can choose from.

Can low-income minority parents depend on this new law to save their children? It hasn't turned out that way for several reasons. First, there aren't that many "better" schools in the public school system to transfer *to*. All public schools in a particular town, city, or state (depending on the jurisdiction) are controlled by the same central school authority. Yes, there are always a few "better" public schools, but these schools don't have nearly enough seats for all the students who qualify to transfer under the new law. For example, as we noted earlier, in New York, 240,000 students qualified for school-choice transfers in September of 2002. Yet only 1500 students found new seats in the better schools.[30]

New York City is *already* cutting back on the number of allowed transfers because of overcrowding at the better schools. In 2003, New York City officials said that 7000 students transferred to better schools. However, school authorities did not want to undermine the city's more successful schools and spend millions of dollars on busing and other expenses. So in 2004, the city will only allow about 1000 transfers. Even worse, the number of allowed transfers is being sharply reduced while the list of "failing" public schools in the city rose to 497, or more that 40 percent in 2003.[31]

We can assume that many other big cities across the country are under similar pressures. As a result, the school-transfer provision of the *No Child Left Behind Act* helps very few children and is almost useless.

Not only that, school authorities in many school districts have kept parents in the dark about their school being dumped on the new failing blacklist. A 2002 survey by the Albany-based, Foundation for Education Reform and Accountability found that *85 percent* of parents polled were not aware that their schools were now classified as failing. School authorities hadn't notified them.[32] Was this just an oversight by these schools, or maybe the schools didn't like the idea of losing tax funds if their students transferred out?

One of the NCLB Act's commendable goals is to give parents more school choice and inject a little competition into the system. However, the new law barely scratches the surface in this regard. If children from a failing school want to transfer to another school, they can only transfer to another *public* school that may have a better record.

Yet, parents first have to *find* a better public school in their neighborhood or within driving range, which from what we've learned about public schools is like trying to find the one good apple in a barrel of bad apples. Then, even if a parent found such a school, there will be long waiting lists to get in. So these provisions of the law introduce little real competition into the system.

The NCLB Act's private tutoring vouchers could theoretically be the most helpful part of this legislation. But here again, bureaucratic controls and school authorities' resistance to the program will probably defeat the possible benefits of these tutoring vouchers.

Schools classified as failing must first notify parents of their status. Next, they must tell parents about the tutoring program and give them a list of approved tutors. As I noted above, many public schools don't notify parents about the school's failing status. As a result, these same schools wouldn't notify parents about the tutoring programs.

Another restrictive provision of the NCLB law is that only students at schools that fail for a third year in a row are eligible for tutoring. So these students must suffer for *three years* before they are even eligible for this benefit. Also, we've already seen how easily schools manipulate student test scores to deceive parents and school boards. What will stop school officials from manipulating test scores to declassify themselves as a failing school by the third year, thereby denying students the right to tutors? [33]

Another problem is that city or state school authorities must spend the time and money to select "approved" tutors or tutoring companies. These are the *same school authorities* that set the standards for teacher licensing, so the instruction by tutors may not be much better than the kids are getting in regular classes.

The NCLB law also adds additional administrative burdens on schools. State education officials will have to supervise tutors to make sure they are doing a good job and not ripping off the taxpayer. School officials also have to help parents establish an agreement with the selected tutors that sets goals, payment terms, and a schedule of progress reports. Can overburdened school districts really take on these additional tasks when hundreds of thousands of students start qualifying for tutoring? [34]

Also, the NCLB law requires school districts to set aside 20 percent of funds they receive from the federal Title 1 program to help finance the new tutoring vouchers. The Title 1 law, enacted in 1965, provides federal funds for educating low-income students.[35]

In February, 2004, Harvard University's Civil Rights Project released the results of a study that examined the experiences of 11 school districts with the NCLB law. The study found that negotiating contracts and supervising the approved tutors put heavy administrative burdens on school districts. It also found that the 20 percent of Title 1 funds withheld for the tutoring program diverted these funds from the neediest schools.[36]

As a result, school districts are already complaining about the NCLB law's burdensome regulations and tax-transfer provisions. There is a saying, "you can bring a horse to water, but you can't make it drink." If school officials fear and resent many provisions of the NCLB law, they will find ways to evade the law. As we've seen, schools already do this by rigging test scores so the school stays out of the "failing" category, and by not notifying parents about their failing status or the tutoring programs.

Finally, even if a failing school notifies a parent that her children qualify for an approved tutor, her children *still* have to suffer through six to eight hours a day of public school for eight to twelve years. A public-school student in a failing school who gets a tutor is like a prison inmate who gets a little more food every day from the warden—they are both still in "prison."

If millions of students now qualify for help by approved tutors, *what does that say about the public schools* that make these children fail in the first place? It might be a better idea to simply close the public schools and pay tutors to educate all children with the tax money we save by shutting down the schools.

Past experience with federal education programs predicts that the NCLB Act will also fail low-income families. The federal government has spent over $120 billion on Title 1 programs for low-income students since 1965. Yet the literacy rates for these children today are appalling, and the achievement gap between low-income children and their peers has not closed.[37]

If the U.S. Department of Education wants to give real choice to parents, they should not be tinkering with a failed government-controlled school system that, by its very nature, strangles free choice and competition. For over three hundred years, Americans have been blessed with a system that gives them almost unlimited choices in their daily lives—*it's called the free market*. If parents could pay for their kids' education in a totally unregulated, fiercely competitive education free market, free from government controls, parents would have all the school choice in the world.

Yet too often, government officials have a bureaucratic mentality and distrust the free market, the same free market that brings them their cars, clothes, computers, electricity, and fresh food. The NCLB Act adds yet another layer of federal regulations to the already strangling layers of local and state-government regulations on education. If the federal government truly wants to give parents more school choice, they should be working to *remove* these local and state controls over education, not adding to them with their own regulations. That is like trying to cure a person dying of arsenic poisoning by giving him more arsenic. Naturally, government education officials can't understand the fact that government control of education is not the solution, it is the *problem*.

Over the past fifty years, federal, state, and city governments have spent hundreds of billions of dollars trying to "fix" the public schools. They have failed, time and again. As noted earlier, high-school drop-out rates in inner-city, low-income minority areas range from 30 percent to over 50 percent.

High-school drop-outs are far more likely to end up in prison during their lifetimes. A U.S. Bureau of Justice report estimates that approximately 47 percent of drug offenders and 75 percent of state prison inmates are high-school dropouts.[38] Dropouts are also about three times more likely than high-school graduates to end up on welfare.[39]

These are not just appalling statistics. These numbers represent *millions* of bright, eager low-income minority kids whose lives are likely to be ruined by public schools that fail them, and by officials who try to "fix" the schools with yet more government controls.

Trying to repair the public-school system is futile, precisely because it is a compulsory, government-controlled near-monopoly. Trying to fix this system with vouchers, charter schools, or new federal regulations is like trying to cure cancer with a band-aid.

For the reasons I outlined above, parents should *not* pin their hopes on *any* government-sponsored school-choice alternative. Vouchers, charter schools, and the *No Child Left Behind Act* are simply too little, too late, and too entangled by regulations. Also, powerful, entrenched special-interest groups in the public-school establishment benefit from parents' and children's subservience to the system, and will fight school-choice alternatives.

Low-income minority parents should *not* expect the public schools in their neighborhoods to improve. If you want to give your children a decent education and a chance at life, *you must take their future into your own hands, now*. It is useless to hope that the public-school system has the will or ability to reform itself. It is a waste of your time, and your children's precious time, to deal with, plead with, or complain to public-school authorities or employees who benefit by the system.

Instead, do as the citizen-slaves of communist East Berlin did when they fled to freedom in West Berlin—vote with your feet. Consider *writing-off* the public-school system. Consider taking your children *out* of these schools, permanently. You and your children remain victims of the public-school system only by your own consent. The power to withdraw your consent is a power that public-school authorities can't stop. *Withdraw your consent and refuse to be a victim any longer.*

There are many excellent, low-cost ways to give your kids a great education without public schools. One option is to organize your community resources to start local private schools in your neighborhood. Many local churches, especially in low-income minority areas, are already creating schools for neighborhood children. The Reverend Floyd Flake, former six-term U.S. Congressman and advocate for education reform, built the Allen African Methodist Episcopal Church in Queens, New York, into a congregation with nine thousand members. His church-sponsored school for local children has brought quality education to a blighted neighborhood. According to an article in *Headway Magazine*, more than 400 black congregations across the country have also started private schools in urban areas.[40]

There are *many* other education resources that low-income minority families can use to give their kids a quality, low-cost education. These resources include low-cost learn-to-read and learn-math books in libraries and bookstores, accredited Internet schools and tutors, computer learning software, and home-schooling. In Chapters 8, 9, and the Resources section, we will explore these options in detail.

In the next chapter, we will examine another great danger to both white and minority students—public schools across America now pressure millions of parents to give their children potentially dangerous, mind-altering drugs.

5

School Children Given
Mind-Altering Drugs

Public schools across America now pressure many parents
to give their children mind-altering drugs to control their children's behavior in class. The exact number of students taking
drugs like Ritalin is not precisely known. Dr. Lawrence Diller,
behavioral pediatrician and author of *Running on Ritalin: A
Physician Reflects on Children, Society, and Performance in a Pill,*
estimated that in the year 2000, about four million children
took daily doses of Ritalin.[1] He noted that nearly all the Ritalin was used to treat an alleged disease called ADHD (Attention Deficit Hyperactivity Disorder), and that Ritalin use had
jumped 700 percent since the 1990s.

Leonard Sax, a physician, psychologist, and author of "Ritalin, Better Living Through Chemistry," estimated that in the
year 2000, about six million American children, or about one
child in every eight, were taking Ritalin. He also noted that the
United States consumes about 85 percent of the world's consumption of this drug.[2]

In testimony before Congress in May, 2000, Terrance Woodworth, a deputy director of the U.S. Drug Enforcement Agency
(DEA), confirmed the vast use of Ritalin and other mind-altering drugs in our public schools. In his testimony, Woodworth
said:

127

The vast majority of all prescriptions for amphetamine [the drug in Adderall] and methylphenidate [known as Ritalin] (about 80 percent) are written for children diagnosed with ADHD. After sharp increases in the use of methylphenidate in the early 1990s, methylphenidate prescriptions have leveled off at about *11 million per year* [italics added] for the past four years. However, amphetamine prescriptions (primarily Adderall) have increased dramatically since 1996: from about 1.3 million to nearly six million.[3]

Whether the actual number of children taking Ritalin today is four million, six million, or eleven million, the statistics are horrifying. The real question is *why* are millions of school children given mind-altering drugs? Before we get to this question, we need to examine this so-called disease called ADHD for which drugs like Ritalin are prescribed.

Is ADHD a Real Disease?

As the testimony above indicates, the vast majority of Ritalin and Adderall is given to school children to treat an alleged disease called ADHD. Children who suffer from ADHD are said to be inattentive, impulsive, and hyperactive. They often get bored easily in class, squirm in their seats, are always on the go, or don't get along with other students or the teacher. In other words, children diagnosed with ADHD may simply be bright, normal kids, full of energy and bored out of their minds sitting in public-school classrooms.[4]

In his testimony to the Pennsylvania House Democratic Policy Committee, Bruce Wiseman, National President of the Citizens' Commission on Human Rights, stated that "thousands of children put on psychiatric drugs are simply 'smart.'" He quoted the late Sydney Walker, a psychiatrist and neurologist, as saying, "They're hyper not because their brains don't work right, but because they spend most of the day waiting for slower students to catch up with them. These students are bored to tears, and people who are bored fidget, wiggle, scratch, stretch, and (especially if they are boys) start looking for ways to get into trouble."[5]

Boredom is not the only reason children can exhibit symptoms of ADHD. Perfectly normal children who are over-active (have a lot of energy), rebellious, impulsive, day-dreamers, sensitive, undisciplined, bored easily (because they are bright), slow in learning, immature, troubled (for any number of reasons), learning disabled (dyslexia, for example), can also be inattentive, impulsive, or hyperactive.

Also, many factors outside the classroom can stress or emotionally affect children. Some of these factors are: not getting love, closeness, or attention from their parents; if a parent, friend, or sibling is sick or dies; if the parents are divorcing and there is anger, shouting, or conflict at home; domestic violence at home; sexual, physical, or emotional abuse by parents or siblings; inattention and neglect at home; personality clashes with parents or siblings; envy or cruelty directed at a child by classmates or by siblings at home, and many other factors.[6]

Also, many other medical conditions can cause children to mimic some or all of ADHD's symptoms. Some of these conditions are: Hypoglycemia (low blood sugar), allergies, learning disabilities, hyper or hypothyroidism, hearing and vision problems, mild to high lead levels, spinal problems, toxin exposures, carbon monoxide poisoning, metabolic disorders, genetic defects, sleeping disorders, post-traumatic subclinical seizure disorder, high mercury levels, iron deficiency, B-vitamin deficiencies (from poor diet), Tourette's syndrome, Sensory Integration Dysfunction, early-onset diabetes, heart disease, cardiac conditions, early-onset bipolar disorder, worms, viral and bacterial infections, malnutrition or improper diet, head injuries, lack of exercise, and many others.[7]

Because these medical conditions can cause some or all of ADHD's symptoms, it becomes next to impossible for any teacher, principal, or family doctor to claim with any certainty that a child has ADHD. To be certain, a doctor would have to *test* the child for all these other possible medical conditions. Since parents or doctors don't do this, every diagnosis of ADHD is suspect, to say the least.

Any of these medical conditions, normal personality variations, emotional problems, or outside-the-classroom stress-factors can disturb a child's attention, natural enthusiasm, or desire to learn in class, and make the child exhibit symptoms of ADHD. Yet, as psychiatrist Peter R. Breggin, author of *Talking Back To Ritalin*, and director of the International Center for the Study of Psychiatry and Psychology, notes, "These are the types of [normal] children who get diagnosed as suffering ADHD and who get subdued with stimulants and other medications."[8]

Many reputable authorities deny that ADHD even exists. According to Breggin,

> There are no objective diagnostic criteria for ADHD—no physical symptoms, no neurological signs, and no blood tests.[9]
>
> ADHD and Ritalin are American and Canadian medical fads. The U.S. uses 90 % of the world's Ritalin. . .there is no solid evidence that ADHD is a genuine disorder or disease of any kind . . . there is no proof of any physical abnormalities in the brains or bodies of children who are routinely labeled ADHD. They do not have known biochemical imbalances or 'crossed wires . . . ADHD is a controversial diagnosis with little or no scientific basis . . . A parent, teacher, or doctor can feel in good company when utterly dismissing the diagnosis and refusing to apply it to children.[10]

Many other medical professionals agree with Dr. Breggin. William Carey, a professor of pediatrics at the University of Pennsylvania concluded that:

> The behaviors associated with ADHD diagnosis reflect a continuum or spectrum of normal temperaments rath-

er than a disorder. He declared that ADHD "appears to be a set of normal behavioral variations" that lead to "dissonant environmental interactions." That is, when the varied but normal temperaments of children bring them into conflict with parents and teachers, the adults try to end the conflicts by diagnosing the children with ADHD.[11]

Some medical professionals, mental-health organizations, and government agencies claim that ADHD is a biologically-based and valid mental disease. In November, 1998, the National Institutes of Health (NIH) held its NIH Consensus Development conference on "The Diagnosis and Treatment of Attention Deficit Hyperactivity Disorder." At the conference, Dr. James Swanson, Ph.D., Professor of Pediatrics at the University of California, Irvine, was given the task of proving that there was a biological basis for ADHD. In his presentation, Swanson showed many brain-scan slides of children who allegedly had ADHD, and whose brain scans were different than normal children. According to Breggin, here's what happened next:

. . . Then a child neurologist in the audience raised a telling point. He noted that psychiatric drugs are potentially very toxic to a child's brain. Then he asked Swanson, "How many of the children with supposedly abnormal brains had been previously exposed to psychiatric drugs?" Swanson was forced to admit that all the children with "different" or "abnormal" brains in all the studies had been previously exposed to psychiatric drugs. The meaning was clear: Abnormalities that had been passed off as evidence of ADHD weren't necessarily connected to ADHD in any way, shape, or form. They were much more likely caused by exposure to psychiatric drugs. Then came the devastating follow-up question: "How could you withhold such vital information from your presentation?" Swanson made no direct reply.[12]

Swanson's failure to disclose that the children with abnormal brain scans had taken psychiatric drugs is part of what
Breggin calls the "Brain Scan Scam." Breggin notes that, "It is
part of a propaganda campaign aimed at the public and professionals . . . ." to convince the public that ADHD is a biologi-
cally-proven medical disease.[13] Breggin also noted the opinion
of the American Academy of Pediatrics on this issue:

> Despite its endorsement of the ADHD diagnosis, the
> American Academy of Pediatrics, like the NIH consen-
> sus development panel, found no convincing evidence
> that ADHD is biological in origin. The academy con-
> cluded that brain scans and similar studies "do not show
> reliable differences between children with ADHD and
> controls" and that they "do not discriminate reliably
> between children with and without this condition."[14]

To sum up, many medical and psychiatric authorities confirm that there is no conclusive scientific evidence to prove any
biological basis for ADHD symptoms. ADHD therefore seems
to be a fictitious disease. Before we discuss who profits by the
sale and use of mind-altering drugs for this fictitious disease,
let's look at some of the potential dangers of these drugs.

The Potential Dangers of
Mind-Altering Drugs

The DEA (U.S. Drug Enforcement Agency) has confirmed
that Ritalin and similar drugs can be potentially dangerous and
even lethal to children. In his testimony before Congress in
May, 2000, Terrance Woodworth, a deputy director of the DEA,
talked about the potential dangers of Ritalin and other mind-
altering drugs. In his testimony, Woodworth said:

> Of the many psychoactive substances proscribed to
> young children in the United States, only two controlled

substances are widely utilized by American physicians to treat children: methylphenidate (commonly known as Ritalin) and amphetamine (primarily Adderall and Dexedrine). Both are approved and used in the treatment of attention deficit hyperactivity disorder referred to as ADHD or ADD. Both of these substances are powerful stimulants that have been in Schedule II of the CSA [Controlled Substances Act] since 1971. Schedule II of the CSA *contains those substances that have the highest abuse potential and dependence profile* of all drugs that have medical utility [italics added].[15]

The DEA has assigned Ritalin to Schedule II of the CSA, the same schedule or list of drugs that includes cocaine, morphine, opium, and amphetamines. In other words, the DEA considers Ritalin to have the same potential for abuse as cocaine and amphetamines.

After an extensive review of the scientific data regarding methylphenidate (Ritalin), the DEA concluded the following about Ritalin's potential for abuse:

Like amphetamine and cocaine, abuse of methylphenidate can lead to marked tolerance and psychic dependence. The pattern of abuse is characterized by escalation of dose, frequent episodes binge use followed by severe depression, and an overpowering desire to continue the use of this drug despite medical and social consequences. The abuser may alter the mode of administration from oral use to snorting or intravenous injection to intensify the effects of the drug. Typical of other CNS [Central Nervous System] stimulants, high doses of methylphenidate often produce agitation, tremors, euphoria, tachycardia, palpitations and hypertension. Psychotic episodes, paranoid delusions, hallucinations and bizarre behavior characteristic of amphetamine-like psychomotor stimulant toxicity have all been associated with methylphenidate abuse. Severe medical consequences, *including death* [italics added], have been reported . . . Clearly, the literature indicates that addiction produced by methylphenidate abuse is neither benign nor rare in occurrence, and is more accurately described as producing severe dependence.[16]

The DEA further expressed its concern over literature that pro-Ritalin groups put out:

Of particular concern is that most of the ADHD literature prepared for public consumption by CHADD [Children and Adults With Attention Deficit Disorder] and other groups and available to parents, does not address the abuse potential or actual abuse of methylphenidate. Instead, methylphenidate (usually referred to as Ritalin by these groups) is routinely portrayed as a benign, mild substance that is not associated with abuse or serious side effects. In reality, however, there is an abundance of scientific literature which indicates that methylphenidate shares the same abuse potential as other Schedule II stimulants.[17]

The same DEA report also pointed out the potential conflict of interest between CHADD, an organization that promotes the use of Ritalin on school children, and Ritalin's manufacturer, Ciba Geigy (now Novartis), stating:

It has recently come to the attention of the DEA that Ciba-Geigy contributed $748,000 to CHADD from 1991 to 1994. The DEA has concerns that the depth of the financial relationship with the manufacturer was not well-known by the public.[18]

There have also been studies that show the similarity in effects on lab animals between Ritalin and cocaine. In these studies, lab animals that were given the choice to ingest cocaine or Ritalin made no distinction between the two.

When Ritalin is crushed and inhaled through the nose, it can have effects similar to cocaine. According to Dr. Leonard Sax, thousands of school children and one out of five college students now use Ritalin as a recreational drug. There is a black market in this drug in many public schools. Kids not only crush and sniff Ritalin, they steal for it and sell it to their classmates.[19]

Ritalin has also become a gateway drug. Children who take Ritalin for years are more likely to move on to harder drugs like cocaine.

Nadine Lambert, Ph.D., Professor and director of the School Psychology Program at the University of California, Berkeley, did a study of adults who took drug stimulants when they were children. Lambert found that these children were more likely to start smoking or using cocaine and to continue these habits into adulthood. She believes when children are given prescribed stimulants, their brains become sensitized to these drugs and this sensitization predisposes these children to cocaine abuse when they become young adults.[20] So one potential danger of giving children Ritalin is to make them more susceptible to trying harder drugs like cocaine, later in life.

Like any powerful drug, Ritalin can also have serious medical and psychological side-effects. While Ritalin (and similar drugs) can calm some extremely hyperactive or aggressive kids, it also has turned many normal, bright, but unruly children into manageable, "pacified" children. While helping some kids (however we define "help"), the drugs can cause serious harm to many others.

As Breggin states: "Ritalin and amphetamine have almost identical adverse effects on the brain, mind, and behavior, including the production of drug-induced behavioral disorders, psychosis, mania, drug abuse, and addiction." Breggin also asserts that these drugs "frequently cause the very same problems they are supposed to treat—inattention, hyperactivity, and impulsivity." [21]

Ritalin and similar drugs have another potentially serious side-effect. Stimulants constrict, flatten, or suppress a child's

mental activity and behavior, often making the child more obedient or compliant. This constellation of symptoms is related
to the depression produced in these children.[22]

In *Talking Back To Ritalin*, Breggin gives one child's personal experience with this drug: "Ritalin made me withdrawn.
Ritalin made me lifeless. My mother noticed a boy who was not
her son anymore. She took me off after two weeks."[23]

Breggin notes the following potential side-effects that have
been attributed to Ritalin and similar drugs:

• A large percentage of children on stimulants become
robotic, lethargic, depressed, or withdrawn.
• Ritalin can cause permanent neurological tics, including Tourette's syndrome.
• Ritalin can retard growth in children by disrupting
the cycles of growth hormone released by the pituitary
gland.
• Ritalin routinely causes gross malfunctions in the
brain of the child. There is research evidence from a
few controlled scientific studies that Ritalin can cause
shrinkage (atrophy) or other permanent physical abnormalities in the brain.
• Withdrawal from Ritalin can cause emotional suffering, including depression, exhaustion, and suicide. This
can make children seem psychiatrically disturbed and
lead mistakenly to increased doses of medication.
• Ritalin is addictive and can become a gateway drug to
other addictions. It is a common drug of abuse among
children and adults.[24]

This alarming list is supported by an extremely reputable
source, *The Physicians' Desk Reference*, which most doctors
use as their Bible for detailed information about prescription
drugs. The *Reference* lists the following common side effects
for Ritalin:

Nervousness and insomnia, hypersensitivity (including skin rash), urticaria, fever, arthralgia, exfoliative dermatitis, erythema multiforme with histopathological findings of necrotizing vasculitis, and thrombocytopenic purpurea; anorexia; nausea; dizziness; heart palpitations; headache; dyskinesia [jerky movements of hands or legs]; drowsiness; blood pressure and pulse changes, both up and down; tachycardia; angina; cardiac arrhythmia; abdominal pain; weight loss during prolonged therapy; reports of Tourette's syndrome and toxic psychosis; leukopenia and/or anemia; loss of appetite, and insomnia.[25]

The Reference cautions against using the drug for prolonged periods because chronic use can lead to drug dependence, abnormal behavior, and psychotic episodes. During drug withdrawal, severe depression can occur. Long-term follow-up is suggested if the patient exhibits basic personality changes.[26]

Another consequence of giving Ritalin to children is that many careless or overworked doctors then prescribe other mind-altering drugs to counter the potential side-effects of Ritalin. Instead of treating the problem, they treat the symptoms. Breggin describes this process for some of his private patients:

Despite public criticism, the prescription practices of many doctors throughout the nation have grown more aggressive and dangerous. In my private practice of psychiatry, where I work with adults and children, desperate parents often bring their children to me as a last resort. Their pediatrician, family doctor, or psychiatrist has suggested the addition of a fourth or fifth mind-altering drug to their child's treatment regimen. By this time, the child is being bounced around on an emotional roller coaster ride by the multiple medications.

Here is a pattern I have seen repeated a number of times in recent months. First the child is put on Ritalin or Adderall for minor school or family problems. When the stimulant causes insomnia, a sedating drug like

Klonopin or clonidine is added at night. When the drug combination makes the child depressed, an antidepressant like Prozac or Paxil is added. When the three drugs impair the child's emotional stability, making him aggressive and unpredictable for the first time, the parents are told their child's "bipolar" or "manic-depressive" disorder has "emerged." Now lithium or Depakote is added as a "mood stabilizer." When this medically negligent over-dosing with four drugs leads to bizarre behavior, the child is put on an "antipsychotic" such as Risperdal or Zyprexa . . . The "cocktail" of medications was guaranteed to ruin the child's mental life and eventually to leave lasting harmful effects. Yet this "polypharmacy" approach has become too commonplace.[27]

If torturing young children with cocktails of mind-altering drugs is not enough, some children have died from using Ritalin or similar drugs. Here is one parent's tragic story:

Our fourteen-year-old son Matthew died on March 21, 2000. The cause was determined to be from the long-term (age 7-14) use of Methylphenidate, a medication commonly known as Ritalin. The Certificate of Death under "due to" (or "because of") reads: "Death caused from Long Term Use of Methylphenidate (Ritalin)," according to Dr. D. [name withheld for privacy], the chief pathologist in Oakland County Michigan Hospital.

The chief pathologist in Oakland County Michigan, upon autopsy, said Matthew's heart showed clear signs of small vessel damage, the type caused by stimulant drugs like amphetamines. The medical examiners told me that a full-grown man's heart weighs about 350 grams and that Matthew's heart weight was about 402 grams. Matthew did not have a pre-existing heart disease or defect that we knew of . . . ."[28]

Between 1990 and 2000, the FDA MedWatch program

received notice of 186 deaths from methylphenidate. It's estimated that these numbers represent no more than 10 to 20 percent of the actual incidence of such deaths.[29] So these drugs are potentially lethal—they can snuff out the lives of innocent young children.

Here's another tragic story about a child who died from a psychoactive drug :

> Shaina [last name withheld for privacy] was a bright, energetic 10-year-old girl when she died in a pediatrician's office in . . . . February 2001. A little more than a half-hour earlier, she had collapsed in the school library. Shaina had a history of asthma and problems with her kidneys and urinary tract, but these problems weren't responsible for her tragic and unexpected death. A postmortem ruled that the child died from the toxic effects of Desipramine, a psychoactive drug she had been compelled to take after a school psychiatrist suggested she suffered from Attention Deficit Hyperactivity Disorder (ADHD).[30]

Besides the potentially deadly side-effects already described, some experts believe that these drugs can make kids violent, especially boys. Bruce Wiseman, national president of the Citizens' Commission on Human Rights, gave the following examples to support this argument.

Eric Harris, one of the teenage killers at Columbine High School, had been taking Luvox for obsessive-compulsive disorder. T. J. Solomon, the fifteen-year old boy who shot and wounded six fellow students at Heritage High School in Conyers, Georgia, had been taking Ritalin off and on for years. Shawn Cooper, a fifteen-year old in Notus, Idaho, was taking Ritalin for bipolar depression when he fired two shotgun rounds at classmates and teachers at his school. Kip Kinkel, the fifteen-year old boy who killed his parents and later killed two students and wounded twenty-two others at his Oregon high school, was on Ritalin and Prozac.[31]

Did these children's previous mental condition or emotional problems cause the violence, or did the drugs push these kids over the edge? Neither doctors nor school authorities know for sure.

These drugs can also make children feel bad about themselves. There are many accounts of teenagers who lie about taking their pills, and children who cry in doctors' offices and "cheek" the pill at home (hide it instead of swallowing it). Many children have made statements like the following about how taking these drugs makes them feel: "It takes over of me [sic]"; "it takes control;" "It numbed me;" "Taking it meant I was dumb;" "I feel rotten about taking pills; why me?;" "It makes me feel like a baby." "I don't know how to explain. I just don't want to take it any more."[32]

Why Are Children Given These Drugs?

Because disruptive children can make it impossible for teachers to teach, we can certainly understand their desire to "quiet" these children. Not only that, some violently disruptive or hyperactive kids seem to "benefit" by Ritalin in the short term. They quiet down enough so they can socialize better with other children, concentrate on their schoolwork, and learn better.

One teacher made the following comment that echoes many teachers' understandable frustrations in class, and why they get the urge to give Ritalin to unruly kids:

I'm of two minds regarding drug therapy. No question that it is overused, but as a teacher, I really hate those classes containing kids (and I teach high school) that are bouncing off the walls. They are disliked by the other students, and can render a class totally unmanageable . . . I don't like to see drugs tried until other remedies have been tried.[33]

Also, some parents at their wit's end with truly hyperactive, aggressive, or defiant young children, willingly cooperate with schools who want their kids to take Ritalin. Desperate, they often turn to Ritalin as a last resort, even though they would prefer not to drug their kids. Here's a few examples of some parents' nightmare, and why they turn to Ritalin:

> . . . One is that of a 4-year-old, Nicolas, who is clearly banging off the walls. His parents have chosen not to medicate him; instead the father quit his job and stays home to give him and their younger child more attention. Noelle, 12, a gifted gymnast who was flunking school and getting suspended for fighting, saw her symptoms improve with medication and now makes A's and B's. Alex, also 12, has a host of problems—he's overweight, depressed, failing in school and lonely. Antidepressants made him suicidal, but Adderall, one of the newer ADD medications, has helped. Robin, now 16, poses a case in which nothing has worked, and his family has basically cracked apart under the stress.[34]

Another parent writes:

> In the last few months before he left his school, Zachary turned into a very angry child. When I picked him up at school, he got into the car with a scowl on his face. He complained about every little thing. He picked on his little brothers. This was the beginning of the end for him. When Lisa took him to be evaluated, he threw such a fit that the psychologist couldn't even test him. She called Lisa to come pick him up and declared that he was "oppositionally defiant," which in layman's terms means, "This kid is a major asshole and you are going to suffer the rest of your life."
> Zachary is now at a public school and he takes 10 milligrams of Ritalin twice a day. He has not turned into a sheep, like I thought he would, nor has he lost his cre-

ative edge. He still stands at the end of our driveway, engaging in elaborate swordplay against imaginary foes with his stick and garbage can lid.

After four weeks, he has made friends, and he has stopped being so angry. Even though the Ritalin is out of his system by the time he gets home, he does his homework without banging on the walls or snapping pencils in half. His teacher declared him "a joy to work with." He goes to therapy twice a month, and he actually talks to the therapist. I hate to say it, but I believe that Ritalin is working for him.

I hate it because deep down I feel that if it weren't for school, Zachary wouldn't need this drug. I hate it because I read the articles and understand what is written between the lines about parents "relieved to blame a neurological glitch" or "seeking a quick fix." I hate it because I feel that our culture doesn't have room for wild men like Zachary, because I suspect that he is like the child one writer described as "an evolutionary remnant, a hunter personality trapped in a culture of desk jockeys."

But the fact is, Zachary isn't a caveman and his brain isn't functioning the way it's supposed to. This is made abundantly clear to me every time I spend more energy reeling Zachary in than I do on both of his two younger brothers put together. I hope that eventually I can develop the attitude a friend of mine has developed about her own son's ADHD."[35]

When parents are driven up the wall by children they cannot control, especially where both parents work, one can understand why they sometimes turn to Ritalin. But for every case like Zachary, there are many others where parents or teachers simply don't have the time, energy, or patience to deal with kids that are just willful, high-spirited, or independent, as so many children can be. Surely we don't have five million psychotic kids running around with ADHD, when thirty years ago few people even heard of this alleged disease.

Also, before we sympathize too much with these distraught parents, let's remember how potentially dangerous drugs like Ritalin can be, and that these drugs are classified by the DEA as being in the same family of stimulants as cocaine. In the short term, these drugs may help some children to calm down or concentrate. Over the long-term, children's minds and bodies can become addicted to these drugs and suffer serious harm.

We already noted that there is no conclusive scientific evidence to prove that ADHD is a real disease. Also, dozens of medical, personality, and home-environment stress factors can cause ADHD-like symptoms in children. So why are *millions* of school children given mind-altering drugs like Ritalin? To understand why, let's see how Ritalin use benefits public schools.

Public-school teaching is structured in such a way that it inevitably bores millions of normal, active children. These kids are stuck sitting in classrooms six to eight hours a day with twenty or more other kids. The teacher has to cover the curriculum, so she is pressured to teach all the kids the same material in the same way. Few teachers have the time or patience to know each child's unique personality, interests, strengths, or weaknesses, or give different instruction to each student.

Middle-school and high-school children often have to learn subjects they can't relate to, are not interested in, or that frustrate them, such as history, trigonometry, or foreign languages. As a result, many students get bored, watch the clock, and wait for the school day to end. Classroom "learning" usually consists of forcing students to read dumbed-down textbooks, memorizing facts from these textbooks, and then regurgitating these meaningless facts on dumbed-down tests. Students go from gym, to math, to chemistry, to English literature, to American history. Their day consists of disconnected lectures on disconnected subjects. Each class lasts only fifty minutes, so their train of thought breaks off at the sound of the bell.

Young children in elementary school have natural high energy, and each child has his or her own unique personality. Just being crammed into a classroom with twenty-five other children can be scary or annoying. Also, being told to learn certain tasks they may not care about by an adult they may not like, can annoy or frustrate many normal but emotionally immature children with a will of their own.

Overworked teachers are under a lot of pressure today. They must teach many students in their classes, cover the curriculum, test and grade the students, and prove to parents and the principal that their students are learning and doing well in their studies. Even worse, a teacher's job may now be threatened or she could be disciplined if her students do poorly on the new standardized tests. *The No Child Left Behind Act* puts pressure on teachers and principals to make sure students pass these tests because the school can lose funding or even close down if students' test grades don't measure up to minimum standards.

For all these reasons, over-worked teachers are under enormous pressure to maintain discipline in class so they can do their job. If some students are disruptive, don't pay attention, or cause trouble in class, the teacher must *do something* about these children to keep order. In the old days, teachers could discipline kids by smacking or restraining them. If a teacher tried this today, parents would quickly slap her and the school with a lawsuit, so that kind of discipline is now impossible. Also, as I mentioned earlier, compulsory-attendance laws now make it extremely difficult to expel a violent or disruptive student.

So how do school authorities solve this discipline problem? Too often, they pressure parents to give Ritalin to their children to "calm" the kids down or make them "focus" on their work. However, school authorities needed a way to justify using these mind-altering drugs on children. They found this "justification" by going along with the psychiatric establishment's claims about ADHD. They go along with the notion that millions of normal, active, or bored kids who might be having temporary medical, emotional, or other stress problems at home or in class, have an alleged mental illness called ADHD.

By claiming that normal but "disruptive" children have a

mental illness, school authorities feel justified in pressuring parents to give their kids Ritalin to "correct" the problem. Indeed, many well-intentioned teachers and principals have come to believe the ADHD rhetoric so strongly, that they sincerely believe they are helping children they think have ADHD.

Well-intentioned or not, schools also get many important benefits by taking the easy way out with Ritalin. School districts today are strapped for money because many states are running huge budget deficits. Schools can't spend the time, money, or effort it takes to find out what makes "problem" kids act out. They don't have the resources to give these children intensive, time-consuming psychological counseling, or test them for all the real medical conditions that might be causing the problem. So pressuring parents to give their normal but bored or unruly kids Ritalin to "quiet" them became the typical American quick-fix for solving complex problems.

In effect, school authorities now use drugs like Ritalin as chemical restraints to control children's behavior so they are passive and obedient. Nursing homes sometimes do the same thing—they give similar drugs to elderly patients who "act out," to keep them quiet. These drugs are a way of "pacifying" normal but bored or unruly school children. They are a way to mentally strap children to their desks so they "behave" as school authorities want them to behave.

How Schools Coerce Parents Into Giving Ritalin To Their Kids

Despite the potentially dangerous side-effects of Ritalin, school authorities now pressure parents to give Ritalin to their children. Naturally, most parents don't want to drug their kids. So how do schools pressure parents? They threaten to expel the child, hold the child back a grade, put the child into a special-education class, or threaten the parents with prosecution for child abuse.

Here's one parent's story:

Hello, my name is Bobby B. [last name withheld for privacy], and that little boy you see above [in a picture in the article] . . . is my pride and joy. The picture was taken on Halloween when he was 5 years old and he was already on Ritalin. He was put on Ritalin because the local school district informed us that if we did not put him on medication he would be removed from school. In fact his first year was a nightmare from the start.

Kindergarten is supposed to be fun and enjoyable for the child. However, Christopher had the teacher from hell and she made his life miserable. He could do nothing right and at the end of the school year she was going to flunk him out of her class . . . . Christopher's teacher thought he was nothing but trouble, too hyperactive, too hard to manage and she wanted nothing to do with him. This was the start of our own nightmare and our introduction to Ritalin and ADD. For the next 8 years our little boy was on this medication because without it he would not be allowed to continue in our public school system.

My wife volunteers at the school in the office area weekly, and she has told me of the hundreds of kids that are on Ritalin and other medication. They line up every day to get their medication in order for them to stay in school, and attempt to do their work in a drug-induced state.

About 12 months ago we were told to put Christopher on Adderall and that this medication would work better and would last longer. The side effects were the same, dehydration, loss of appetite, growth limitations and violent mood swings, and the fact is that no one knows what the long term effects on your children's health will be. We did as the Doctor advised and he has been on Adderall since.

Any time Christopher has a bad day in school, the teachers want to know if he took his medication for the day. You see, once a child is labeled ADD or hyperactive, it stays with them, and it's locked in the teachers' minds. Thus if the child has a problem, it must be that he/she did not take their medication. I am sure this goes on in public schools all over this country and parents like us have no choice or our choices are very limited. If you want your child to stay in school, Ritalin or Adderall is their solution to any and all behavioral problems.[36]

Here we have an example of school authorities not tolerating normal children who might be having a "bad day" or want to express their anger about something. As adults, we all have bad days and we all get angry occasionally. But because public schools are like mini-prisons that require "order" and "discipline" to function, children are expected to conform to the rules. They are not allowed to have bad days or express anger. Hence school authorities must pressure parents to give these children Ritalin to make the children passive in class.

Christopher's horror story is repeated again and again in public schools across the country. Here is another example:

Like thousands of children, 7-year-old Kyle [last name withheld for privacy] takes Ritalin for a diagnosis of attention deficit/hyperactivity disorder, or ADHD. And like thousands of parents, Michael and Jill worry about the drug's side effects, including sleeplessness and loss of appetite. But they keep their child on the medication, in part because they fear child welfare workers who will take him away if they don't.

Earlier this year, administrators from the . . . . school district called . . . . Child Protective Services, alleging child abuse when [Kyle's parents] said they wanted to take Kyle off the drug. As a result, [Kyle's parents] are now on a statewide list of alleged child abusers, and they have been thrust into an Orwellian family court battle to clear their name and to ensure their child isn't removed from their home. "It's beyond the point of whether he should be on it. Now it's the point of them telling us what we're going to do," said Michael [Kyle's parent]. "They're telling me how to raise my child."

The [Kyle's parent's] dilemma is not unique. While there are no reliable statistics on the phenomenon, observers say public schools are increasingly accusing parents of child abuse and neglect if they balk at giving their children medication such as Ritalin, a stimulant being prescribed to more and more children.

The schools are now using child protective services to enforce their own desires and their own policies," said David [last name withheld for privacy], a New York City lawyer who has seen cases similar to [Kyle's parents]. "The parent's authority is being undermined when people have to do what some public official wants."[37]

In August, 2002, in response to an article by Douglas Montero entitled, "Parents Tell of School Pill Pushers' 'Extortion,'" the *New York Post* created an online commentary line for parents and others to write in their horror stories on this issue. Below is one of many parent's stories:

Joyce [last name withheld for privacy], 40, of Queens [New York], charges her son Bryan, 11, was held back in the fourth grade even though he passed his statewide reading and math test because she resisted pressure from school officials to medicate. "It was extortion," said [Joyce], who felt the pressure to medicate from . . . school officials for an entire school year.

Another commentary on this same online posting site read:

Outgoing School Chancellor, Harold Levy, [in New York City] ordered an investigation. "Parents across the city say school officials are threatening to hold their children back a grade and even file a child-abuse complaint if they don't medicate. [Parent] Advocates support their claims."[38]

Here are more examples of public schools across America coercing parents into giving their children Ritalin or similar drugs, from www.Ablechild.org, a web site devoted to this issue:

• Daniel [last name withheld for privacy] at three, suffered from a severe exposure to carbon monoxide from a leaky furnace that left him brain injured. By kindergarten, the schools were determined to pin a label of ADHD on him after he showed difficulties in learning, and demanded that his mother, Cindy [last name withheld for privacy], put the child on Ritalin, taking her to court to enforce it. Five more medications were tried in the next two years that turned Daniel psychotic and suicidal. Moving to another state to escape, Cindy was again forced to drug her child by court order. Daniel was hospitalized due to psychosis three times and tried on four more medications not even approved for children. Moving yet again to escape forced drugging, a third state demanded Daniel be drugged after the original state, NY, insisted Daniel was ADHD/ODD/bipolar, despite Cindy's pleas that he was brain injured.

• Robert [last name withheld for privacy], a Hispanic TV writer from Los Angeles, was separated from his wife Georgina, who had primary custody of their son Briant. In 1996, when Briant was in first grade, Georgina was pressured by her son's teacher to "medicate" him because he was "hyperactive." After repeated meetings and school pressure, Georgina agreed to medicate her son. According to Robert, "I felt that the school and mental health officials took advantage of Georgina, in part, because she was Hispanic and spoke very little English. Georgina couldn't really communicate nor ask questions easily. The Latin culture does not question authority; we simply trust what is told to us by those in charge." A prescription was filled for Ritalin, and the boy began experiencing side effects, including nervousness, insomnia, loss of appetite and he would become angry very easily. Additionally, Briant was making no academic progress. Fed up with their son's lack of academic progress and adverse reactions to the drug, [Robert] transferred Briant to a private school where he has become a normal student making excellent progress.

• Michelle L. [last name withheld for privacy], an African-American housing counselor for a non-profit agency, said . . . school officials repeatedly pressured her to drug her 6-year-old son, Dominick, claiming the first-grader had ADHD because he was "disorganized, forgetful, and had a problem sitting in his seat." School officials were unrelenting, despite her continued objections. Then when she complained to the district superintendent's office, she felt even more intimidated. Pressured to take Dominick to the . . . Psychiatric Hospital, here a doctor reviewed a school report and prescribed Ritalin after a 45-minute talk with the boy. Still battling to keep her son off the drug, officials later threatened to file child-abuse complaints against Mrs. L. with the city's Administration for Child Services. According to Mrs. L., these officials "basically said they were going to take my rights as a parent away." At this point she decided her only recourse was to take her son out of the public school system and enroll him in private school.[39]

• A mother says her son's behavioral problems got worse after school officials gave her an ultimatum: Put the first-grader on Ritalin or he'll be placed in special-education classes.

• Patricia W. [last name withheld for privacy] has filed notice that she will sue the . . . . Central School District on behalf of her son, Michael, for the mental and physical pain she says he suffered for two years starting in

1997. Michael, she said, had trouble focusing and was easily distracted. Officials in the . . . . County school referred her son to a pediatrician who prescribed Ritalin, [Patricia] W. said.

By the third grade, Michael was suffering from insomnia, he lost his appetite and was so anxious he chewed his shirt sleeves, collars and pencils, she said.

School officials suggested more medication, she said. Michael began taking another version of Ritalin plus Paxil, an anti-anxiety drug. He was having side effects that were making him literally psychotic at one point, she said. Michael's behavior improved on weekends and over breaks, when she would not give him the drugs, she said. She finally stopped medicating her son in December 1999 after he told her voices in his head were telling him to do bad things, she said. Michael, now 12, was prohibited from entering the school, [Patricia] W. said. She now homeschools him and another son.[40]

A public-school system that coerces parents into giving their children mind-altering drugs that are potentially addictive, dangerous, or even lethal, is a moral abomination. A public-school system in which millions of children have to take Ritalin to make them pay attention in class, is a frightening and embarrassing failure.

Who Profits by ADHD and Giving Mind-Altering Drugs To Children?

As I noted earlier, the *No Child Left Behind Act* has put increasing pressure on schools and teachers to make sure their students pass standardized math and reading tests. Under the new federal guidelines, if a school gets on the "failure" blacklist and fails to improve its performance over time, the school can lose tax funding or even be shut down. So teachers' and principals' *jobs* are at stake here. This intense pressure pushes school authorities to resort to extreme measures to make sure teachers can maintain discipline in class. Hence, public schools now use a bogus disease called ADHD to justify pressuring parents to give normal, active children mind-altering drugs to keep them quiet in class.

Also, by promoting the myth of ADHD, public schools can pretend that their failure to educate our children, year after year, is partly the children's fault. We can't blame school authorities or teachers for a child's academic failure if the child has ADHD, can we? If slow-learning or "hyperactive" kids who have alleged ADHD disrupt classes, teachers can't teach the rest of the class. So how can we blame teachers and the schools for the third-rate education our kids get? By blaming the children, by blaming the victim, public schools benefit from this convenient disease called ADHD.

Schools also profit because ADHD is now officially classified as a "disability." The Individuals with Disabilities Education Act (IDEA) passed in 1990 gives public schools federal special-education funds for children labeled as having a disability. As noted earlier, public schools can get in excess of $16,000 a year in tax money for a student in a special-education class, compared to the average $7500 per student in a "normal" class.[41] Even worse, special-education funding costing from $20,000 to $100,000 per year, per student, has become common.[42]

As a result, for every student a school classifies as ADHD and puts in a special-education class, the school can get from $10,000 to $90,000 per year in additional tax funds. That is because the Individuals with Disabilities Education Act *specifically forbids schools from considering cost* [italics added] when designing their special-education instruction programs. [43]

By joining the ADHD bandwagon, public schools have literally hit the jackpot for federal funds. The moral obscenity of pressuring parents to give their children Ritalin is compounded when the schools get more tax dollars by putting alleged ADHD children into special-education classes. Morally, this is akin to a prison warden putting inmates who demand better conditions into solitary confinement, and then getting an extra

$10,000 to $90,000 per inmate in tax funds for doing so.

Who else profits from ADHD? Of course, pharmaceutical companies make millions of dollars selling drugs used to treat this alleged disease. Mind-altering drugs are profitable winners because school children are literally a captive audience. School authorities can use the law to threaten and pressure parents to give their children these drugs for years while the kids are in school. Private organizations that promote ADHD and get funding from drug companies also profit.

Then we have the medical and psychiatric professions. Pediatricians, general physicians, and child psychiatrists all get more business when the ADHD diagnosis is promoted in the public schools. Five million children with alleged ADHD translates into a lot of office visits. Also, drug companies sometimes give free dinners in fancy restaurants, and other perks to doctors and psychiatrists as part of the drug company's marketing efforts.

Am I saying there is a conspiracy here? No, I'm not. I believe most medical professionals truly believe in ADHD and think they are doing their best for their young patients. However, human nature is such that medical or psychiatric professionals' self-interest can influence them to believe in a bogus disease that brings them more business.

Some characters in this story, however, may not be so innocent. Breggin, in his books *Toxic Psychiatry* and *Talking Back To Ritalin*, explains the American Psychiatric Association's (APA) pivotal role in the rise of ADHD as a "disease." You can read the whole shocking story in Breggin's books, but here is one excerpt from *Talking Back To Ritalin* that should raise the hairs on the back of your neck:

In the 1970s, the APA was going broke. Many psychiatrists were having difficulty filling their practices. Always near the bottom of the medical-income scale, psychiatrists were floundering economically. Competition from non-medical professionals was cutting heavily into private practices. Psychologists, social workers, counselors, family therapists, and other non-psychiatrists were taking over the mental health field. They charged smaller fees and yet often provided better service as "talking therapists." With a larger proportion of women among the new breed of therapists, they drew increasing numbers of women patients to them for therapy.

Psychiatry discussed its economic crisis in its newspapers and journals, as well as within its conferences and board meetings. Psychiatry had to convince the American public that psychological suffering should remain under the ultimate control of physicians, including psychiatrists. To do this, psychiatry had to convince the public that emotional or spiritual suffering is rooted in genetics and biology, requiring drugs, electroshock and other "medical" interventions [only psychiatrists and other medical doctors can prescribe drugs].

A major step was to revise the *Diagnostic and Statistical Manual of Mental Disorders*, the ultimate source of "official" diagnoses, in order to make the diagnoses sound more medical. This resulted in the evolution of the concept of ADHD into its present form. By elaborating on ADHD as a "disorder," psychiatric interventions with drugs became more justified.

However, rewriting and publicizing the diagnostic manual requires money. Deep in financial trouble, the APA did not have the resources to mount a national PR campaign on behalf of psychiatry.

In the early 1980s, APA made a decision that changed its history and that of our society. It decided to create an economic and political partnership with the drug companies. The partnership would enable psychiatry to use drug company funds to promote the medical model, psychopharmacology, and the authority and influence of psychiatry. Backed by the multi-billion dollar drug industry, psychiatry hoped to defeat the threat from non-medical professionals, such as psychologists and social workers. Within a scant few years, APA transformed itself from a failing institution into one of the most powerful political forces in the nation.

This is not the story of a covert "conspiracy." Psychiatry's decision to save itself by going into partnership with the drug companies was an openly discussed survival plan whose historical details I have documented in *Toxic Psychiatry* (1991) . . . . *Psychiatric News* (1997b), the official newspaper of the American Psychiatric Association now brags about revenues from drug company ads in APA's newspaper and journals . . .[44]

How do these actions by the psychiatric profession relate to the current massive use of Ritalin in our schools today? Breggin writes:

It is no exaggeration to say that teachers are being heavily propagandized to believe in ADHD. In a sample of 147 elementary and middle-school teachers from a suburban district, "over 85% of the teachers indicated that they had attended at least one workshop regarding ADHD." Almost without exception, such workshops will be presented by *professional advocates of ADHD/ Ritalin* [italics added]. They will convince the teachers that medication is far more effective and appropriate than improved teaching strategies in dealing with children who seem inattentive, restless, bored, distractible, or fidgety in class.

School guidance counselors are also instructed on how to identify possible ADHD children. Their goal is to "direct and advise the parents" toward further evaluation, and to resources such as CHADD and its biologically oriented network of professionals. Despite their psychological and social traditions, counselors are now being instructed to inform parents that "ADHD is a physiological problem."[45]

The *Diagnostic and Statistical Manual of Mental Disorders,* the standard reference source published by the APA that describes various mental diseases, lists possible behavior patterns of ADHD. These include: if a child is easily distracted, makes careless mistakes, doesn't pay attention to the teacher, doesn't like to follow instructions carefully, frequently loses or forgets things, is restless, fidgets his hands or feet, squirms, runs around, climbs things, leaves a seat when not supposed to, blurts out answers to questions before the teacher asks the whole question, and doesn't like waiting in line or taking his turn because he is impatient.[46]

With behavior patterns like these, what child does *not* have ADHD? Having to sit in boring classes for six to eight hours a day, what child or teenager would *not* want to squirm, fidget, run around, not pay attention, or escape any way they can? These are the kinds of things that *normal, energetic* children want to do when they are bored or frustrated, as any mother will tell you. To call these behavior patterns a disease, however "carefully examined" by a child psychologist or psychiatrist, is absurd (in most cases) and immoral. To then use these normal behavior patterns as an excuse to feed mind-altering drugs to children, borders on the criminal or worse.

It seems that drug companies, child psychiatrists, and other medical professionals are all having a field day with ADHD and mind-altering drugs, at the expense of *millions* of innocent children who may be irreparably damaged by these drugs. It seems, also, that we cannot blame teachers or principals too much, since the ADHD propagandists are, in effect, attempting to "brainwash" school employees about this bogus disease and mind-altering drugs. If teachers and principals only hear one side of the story, what else are they to believe? However, school authorities also benefit from this bogus disease. ADHD gives them the rationalization they need to coerce parents into giving Ritalin to their children to solve the boredom and discipline problem in public schools across America.

I implore teachers, principals and school health workers to consider what you are doing. Consider the irreparable damage you could be doing to innocent children who are forced to take mind-altering drugs. Do you want this on your conscience?

Why Do They Get Away With It?

Nothing condemns our public-school system more than the fact that over five million school children take Ritalin to keep them from fidgeting in their seats and make them pay attention in class and focus on their studies.

Too often, school authorities refuse to accept the blame for our public schools' failure to teach our children or hold their interest in class. Under intense pressure to solve the "discipline" problem, school authorities resort to the quick fix—they pressure parents to give their children Ritalin.

Is there any hope on this issue? Yes and no. The good news is that, as of April, 2003, at least nineteen states have introduced or passed bills and/or resolutions that forbid school personnel from forcing parents to place their children on drugs as a requirement for their kids to stay in school.[47]

Also, under pressure from distraught parent groups, in May, 2003, the U.S. House of Representatives overwhelmingly passed the Child Medication Safety Act of 2003. This Act prohibits school personnel from requiring that a child take any psychotropic drug under the Controlled Substances Act as a condition of attending school or receiving school services.[48]

However, the bad news is that this bill was stopped cold in the Senate. In an article on EtherZone.com, Samuel Blumenfeld, author of eight books on education and public schools, wrote why he thought the Senate hasn't passed this desperately needed bill yet:

> But something happened to this bill on the way to the Senate. The Pharmaceutical and Mental Health lobby got to the Senators on the Health, Education, Labor and Pension (H.E.L.P.) Committee before the bill arrived. Democrat members of that committee include such liberal heavyweights as Ted Kennedy (MA), Christopher

Dodd (CT), Tom Harkin (IA), Barbara Mikulski (MD), Jim Jeffords (VT), John Edwards (NC), and Hillary Clinton (NY). Concerned parents contacted Ted Kennedy and Chris Dodd to get their support. So far, the reply has been negative. Yet, all of these Senators are the most vociferous supporters of public education.[49]

So, while there has been some progress, the majority of states have still not passed laws that forbid schools from pressuring parents to give their children Ritalin, and the Senate has blocked the Child Medication Safety Act of 2003 in Congress. As of this writing, therefore, millions of innocent children are still taking mind-altering drugs in classrooms across America. Public schools have indeed become a menace to our children.

Let me quote Mr. Blumenfeld again on this issue:

There must be something wrong with an education system that requires so many children to be drugged just to attend school.

Last year I spent a week in Beijing, China. During that week I visited a school where I was able to observe about 500 children doing their morning physical exercises in the school yard. I asked my host how many of these children were on Ritalin. He asked what was Ritalin. He had never heard of it. In short, in China they don't have ADD and they don't drug schoolchildren.

Are American children more mentally handicapped than Chinese children? Are they afflicted with a mental disease that is more prevalent in the United States than anywhere else on the globe?[50]

We've had a drug war in this country now for over fifty years. We spend billions of dollars on law enforcement to keep cocaine off the streets. Police in every city and state in this country spend millions of man-hours running down drug dealers. First-time offenders for mere possession of crack cocaine now get a five-year mandatory prison sentence. First-offence, low-level crack dealers go to prison for at least ten years. Our prisons are filled with millions of drug users and pushers.[51]

Police in some cities have raided public schools, searching for drugs in kids' lockers. Many public schools now test students for drugs, sometimes without parents' permission. Yet while police are searching children's lockers, and the school nurse is testing kids for cocaine or marijuana, other school employees are dispensing Ritalin to children like it was aspirin.

Is there something wrong with this picture? School children taking drugs like Ritalin is moral and acceptable if it is government approved? Why are school employees allowed to dispense potentially-addictive mind-altering drugs to children, while police search kids' lockers for cocaine or marijuana? Why do school authorities get away with this, just as they get away with turning our children into illiterates? In the next chapter we will explore this issue.

6

Why Do They
Get Away With It?

If a store sells inferior products or a business gives bad service, most customers will not come back and that store or business will eventually go bankrupt. If public schools sell bad education, year after year, why don't they go bankrupt? Why aren't they shut down? Why are these schools allowed to coerce parents into giving mind-altering drugs to their children?

The answer is that public schools are protected by *government compulsion*. Unlike private schools, public schools are a government-controlled education system that stays in business through naked compulsion. Local governments pass laws that give school authorities near-monopoly powers over our children's education. Compulsory-attendance laws force children to go to these schools. School taxes force parents to pay for these schools. Unlike private schools, public schools rarely go out of business, no matter how bad they are, because they get their "customers" and their money by force.

Compulsion rears its ugly head in our public schools in many other ways. School authorities threaten to expel students unless parents allow the schools to give mind-altering drugs to their children. Laws or school authorities in many states force teachers to join teacher unions, and force local school boards

161

to negotiate with these unions. Licensing laws dictate who can work in public schools, and prevent unlicensed educators or outside experts from teaching in the schools. Many public schools now require high-school students to do involuntary community service in order to graduate. School authorities force children to sit in their classrooms for six to eight hours a day, and to study only the subjects they set up in their curriculums. Like prison wardens, school authorities also dictate how long children must stay in school before they will be "allowed" to graduate.

Public schools also stay in "business" by deceiving their customers. They deliberately dumb down tests, textbooks, and curriculums, and mislead parents about their children's progress to keep them pacified. *Public schools don't shut down because the whole system rests on a foundation of force and deception.*

Socialist Schools in America?

Many parents might think it a bit farfetched to compare our public schools to schools in socialist or communist countries. However, if we look closer, we will see striking similarities between the two systems.

In the former socialist-communist Soviet Union, for example, the government owned all property and all the schools. In America, public schools are also government property, controlled by local government officials. In Soviet Russia, the government forced all parents to send their children to government-controlled schools. In America, compulsory-attendance laws in all fifty states force parents to send their children to public schools.

The Soviet rulers taxed all their subjects to pay for their schools. Here, Americans pay compulsory taxes to support public schools, whether or not the taxpayer has children or thinks the schools are incompetent. In the Soviet Union, all teachers were government employees, and government authorities controlled and managed the schools. In America, public-school employees are also government employees and state school authorities control the schools.

In the Soviet Union, most government employees could not be fired—they had a "right" to their jobs. Public-school employees in America also believe they have a right to their jobs, enforced through tenure laws. As we will see later, in America, it's almost impossible to fire tenured teachers. In communist Russia, competence and working hard didn't matter very much—the government paid most workers regardless of their performance on the job. In America, public-school teachers' salaries depend on length of service—competence is irrelevant. In communist Russia, the elite ruling class had estates in the countryside while peasants starved. Here, public-school authorities get fat salaries, pensions, and benefits while our children starve for a real education.

In communist Russia, government control of food supplies created eighty years of chronic famine. In America, one hundred and fifty years of public schools has created an educational famine. Millions of public-school children can barely read while the system wastes twelve years of their lives.

Still think the comparison to communist schools is too farfetched? Albert Shanker, former president of the American Federation of Teachers, the second largest teacher's union, once said: "It's time to admit that public education operates like a planned economy, a bureaucratic system in which everyone's role is spelled out in advance and there are few incentives for innovation and productivity. It's no surprise that our school system doesn't improve. It more resembles the communist economy than our own market economy."[1]

Finally, schools in some communist countries like China seem to give a better, more disciplined education in the basics of reading, writing, and math than our public schools. International math and reading test-score comparisons often find American kids lagging far behind children from China.

But what *values* do Chinese communist schools teach their children? Here is another apt comparison between communist schools and our public schools. In both cases, either a central or local government controls the curriculum and the values it teaches its students. The Chinese government can and does indoctrinate all school children with its communist ideology and loyalty to the communist leaders.

Similarly, in our public schools, school authorities control the curriculum and values they teach our children. As we saw in Chapter 2, values-clarification programs and distorted American history courses in many public schools now indoctrinate our children with anti-parent, anti-religion, and anti-American values. In both communist schools and our government-controlled public schools, parents can rarely stop school authorities from teaching harmful or immoral values to their children.

Why Public Schools Are
Un-American in the Deepest Sense

Compulsory-attendance laws force parents to send their children to public schools. These laws presume that the politicians we vote into office, our agents, have the right to take away parents' liberty and inalienable rights. Compulsory education means that in America, in contrast to the common view, we no longer live in the land of the free. Local and state governments that claim the right to control our children's education also claim, in effect, that they own our children's minds and lives for twelve years. That is an appallingly arrogant claim, especially in America.

One reason public schools get away with educational murder, year after year, is because local governments violate parents' liberty and parental rights with impunity. Local governments don't own or run food stores, auto showrooms, office-supply stores, or pre-schools and private colleges in America. Yet they own the public schools and control 1st through 12th grade education in America.

Should government officials have any right to dictate how we educate our children? To answer this question, we have to examine what our Founding Fathers understood to be the real function of government. In the Declaration of Independence, Thomas Jefferson clearly stated the moral nature and purpose of government:

> We hold these truths to be self-evident, that all men are created equal, that they are endowed by their creator with certain inalienable rights, that among these rights are life, liberty, and the pursuit of happiness—*that to secure these rights, governments are instituted among men, deriving their just powers from the consent of the governed . . .* [italics added].

The Declaration of Independence affirms that we have natural rights as human beings to "life, liberty, and the pursuit of happiness." It establishes the principle that we, the people, acting individually and by free consent, created our government *only* to protect and secure our natural rights as human beings. That is government's sole legitimate function.

Look again at the phrase from the Declaration that says, "governments are instituted among men, deriving their just powers from the consent of the governed." The "governed" means *all* the people, not just some, not a minority, and not a majority. It means that *all* citizens, including parents, have the same inalienable rights.

That phrase also means that government is our *agent*, not our master. It means that we, as free human beings, voluntarily grant limited powers to government for a specific purpose—to protect our natural rights. It means that government should only have those powers we specifically grant to it for that purpose. Yet, nowhere in the Constitution is the word "education" mentioned. The Constitution did not give the federal government any right or power to control how parents educate their children. By implication, state governments do not have any such right or power either, because such a power would violate our fundamental liberties.

Nature and justice confirm that parents have the right to

decide who educates their children. Like parents of all species, most human parents protect and nurture their children and teach them the skills and knowledge they need to survive. Parents in all cultures make teaching their children a first priority. Since reading, writing, and arithmetic are skills needed to prosper in a modern society, it stands to reason that most parents will find a way to teach these skills to their children if the means are available.

If parents have the natural right to nurture and educate their children, then any law that interferes with or violates that natural right is illegitimate. Any such law violates the basic liberties we all have as parents, human beings, and Americans. A public-school system that depends on these illigitimate laws to stay in existence is therefore deeply un-American. Let us examine how compulsory education laws violate our natural rights as parents and citizens, and thereby let public schools stay in business, no matter how bad they are.

Compulsory-Attendance Laws

All fifty states have compulsory-attendance laws. These laws force parents to send their children to public schools if they can't afford a private school. This legislative gun at parents' heads is how public schools get their "customers," our children. Compulsory-attendance laws are the main reason public schools get away with educational murder, year after year, because the schools get their students by force.

Why do we need compulsory-attendance laws? Why *compel* parents to send their children to public schools? Wouldn't parents naturally educate their children *without* compulsion? Human nature and history prove this to be the case. All over the world, parents push to educate their children, with or without public schools.

In Japan, school is compulsory only up to the equivalent of middle-school level in America (ninth-grade). High schools in Japan, like colleges in America, are voluntary and charge tuition. Middle-school Japanese students compete fiercely for a place in high schools even though their parents must pay to get them in. Most Japanese parents push their kids to apply for high school and scrape up the money for tuition without the Japanese government's pressuring them to do so.[2] In America, millions of parents voluntarily pay thousands of dollars a year in tuition to send their young children to private pre-schools and kindergartens, and their older children to private colleges. Obviously, most parents think that educating their children is very important. So why do we need compulsory-attendance laws for first through twelfth grades?

Common sense and history also prove that government does not have to force parents to educate their children. As I noted earlier, by the 1850s, *before* we had public schools in America, the literacy rate was over 90 percent. Yet most parents taught their children to read at home. They did not need town officials to force them to educate their children. All over the world, most parents' want to give their children a good education so they can have a secure future.

Compulsory-attendance laws imply that government authorities believe *some parents are too ignorant or indifferent to their children's welfare to educate their kids*. If this was not the case, then why compel parents at all? Local governments therefore believe they have to force these "bad" parents to deposit their kids in public schools, for the alleged good of the children.

Most teachers, principals, and administrators who have children naturally believe that *they* are good parents, but don't seem willing to extend this belief to the rest of us. As good parents, many public-school teachers wisely value high-quality education for their kids, and send their children to private schools. A June, 2002 article in *Reason* magazine pointed out that about 40 percent of Cleveland public-school teachers, 45 percent of Boston teachers, and 36 percent of public-school teachers in Chicago and Philadelphia send their kids to private schools.[3] It is safe to assume that the vast majority of loving parents, like public-school teachers, also value giving their children the best education they can afford.

Of course, most parents are neither perfect nor angels, and some bad or indifferent parents will neglect their kids' education, just as they might neglect giving them the right food. There are no statistics or studies on how many parents are "bad" in this sense. However, for argument's sake, let us assume that 15 percent of parents don't educate their kids because the parents are poor or indifferent to their children's welfare.

I believe this percentage of potentially neglectful parents is a reasonable assumption, given the literacy statistics we examined in Chapter 1. As I noted earlier, the literacy rate in this country was over 90 percent by the 1850s. This high a literacy rate among the general population could only be possible if the vast majority of parents valued education for their children, and made sure their children learned how to read well.

So if we assumed that 15 percent of parents might be indifferent to their children's' education, why should school authorities have the right to punish the *other 85 percent* of caring, dedicated parents? Why should school authorities have the right to commit over forty million children to inferior public schools because a relatively small number of parents *might* be bad apples? In effect, local governments and school authorities punish 85 percent of the parents in this country because the other 15 percent *might* not "do the right thing" by their children.

By "punish" I mean that school authorities force almost forty-five million children to suffer through eight to twelve years (depending on the state) of mind-numbing education in schools that barely teach children to read. School authorities also indoctrinate children with anti-parent, anti-religion, and anti-American values, and coerce parents into giving kids mind-altering drugs if the kids get bored or fidgety in class.

This punishment of millions of innocent children and their parents is not only a moral crime, but violates the following fundamental principles of civilized law (again showing why the public-school system is deeply un-American):

• *Under criminal law, a person cannot be punished for doing something where there was no criminal act or intent involved.* The vast majority of parents and children have committed no crime whatsoever. Yet, compulsory-attendance laws punish these parents and children by forcing the kids to attend public schools.

• *There is no crime without a victim.* Many school authorities believe that if a parent fails to send their children to public school (if they cannot afford a private school), then these children are victims of child abuse. Compulsion is needed, the argument goes, to prevent such alleged child abuse and ensure that these children get an education. Yet, considering the dismal record and real dangers of public schools, we might say that it is *public schools* that commit child abuse, and on a massive scale. If and when parents find alternatives to public schools, they are *protecting* their children, not abusing them. In such cases, there are no victims, so there is no crime. Also, even if some parents did nothing to educate their kids, this could be preferable to the real dangers of public schools.

Remember, before we had public schools, millions of children stayed at home and worked on family farms. Many of these children eventually learned to read, even if their parents never taught them. Just because an older child doesn't know how to read, doesn't mean he is dumb. His common sense will tell him that he should learn how to read if he wants to get a decent job. With all the low-cost learn-to-read books and computer software we have today, an older child who stays illiterate would be rare, even if his parents totally neglected his education. Most such children would remain illiterate only because they chose to.

• *A person cannot be punished for the crimes or actions of another.* School authorities force the vast majority of caring parents to send their children to public schools because a relatively small number of irresponsible parents *might* not educate their children without compulsory-attendance laws. Local governments and school authorities therefore punish our estimated 85 percent of all parents for the actions or inactions of the remaining 15 percent.

• *A person is presumed innocent until proven guilty.* Public-school authorities cannot know in advance which parents would fail to educate their children without government compulsion. To solve this problem, they have to lump all parents together. They have to assume that any parent might not educate their children "properly" if school authorities didn't put a legislative gun to their heads. They must assume that *all* parents are potentially guilty. Compulsory-attendance laws therefore presume all parents guilty of child abuse or neglect until proven innocent, rather than innocent until proven guilty. If school authorities had to *prove* this assumption in court, the judge would throw out their case.

I believe that most public-school authorities and employees have good intentions. Most teachers, principals, and administrators do not want to deliberately hurt children or punish parents. School officials always talk about protecting the children, leaving no child behind, and other such high-sounding phrases.

However, school authorities might want the best for children but they use *compulsion* to ensure this goal. They impose *their* opinions of what is best for our kids, rather than letting parents decide. School authorities force *their* views of the best way to educate our children on millions of parents who might not agree with them if given the choice.

In effect, school authorities say, "we know best, and if you don't agree with us, we will compel you to give us your children." Such an attitude is incredible gall since most public schools certainly don't "know best." They can't even teach millions of children to read well in twelve years. Their attitude is also arrogant and tyrannical presumption, especially because they are our *employees* whose salaries we pay with our taxes.

Also, many school authorities might care about our children, but *good intentions mean nothing*. Only *results* matter. Public schools are a disaster and a menace to millions of children. Lord Acton, an English philosopher, once said, "Power corrupts, and absolute power tends to corrupt absolutely." Despite their good intentions, school authorities have near-absolute power over our children's education. They have become education tyrants. Compulsory-attendance laws are the proof.

Compulsory School Taxes

Another reason public schools get away with failure, year after year, is because our taxes keep them alive. A business prospers only so long as customers are satisfied with, and willingly pay for, its products or services. Businesses have to *earn* their customers' patronage. In contrast, public schools are financed by taxes. They do not have to earn their customers' loyalty because parents don't pay them directly, as they would a private school. As a result, in public schools, the crucial link between performance and financial survival is broken. School authorities can give our kids a third-rate education, year after year, because they *suffer no financial consequences* from selling an inferior product.

In fact, in contrast to a business, public schools often *profit* by selling an inferior product. As we will see in the next chapter, school authorities constantly blame lack of money and resources for the continued failure of public schools. Too often, parents and local governments fall for this excuse and vote to give the schools more money and teachers and principals higher salaries. So the more public schools fail, the louder they cry for money and the more the schools and its employees profit. Public schools operate under these perverse incentives only because they get their money from compulsory taxes, rather than from voluntary payments by parents.

Many people believe that local governments have the right to tax everyone to pay for public schools because our elected representatives pass tax laws by majority rule. Many parents don't want to send their children to failed or dangerous public schools. Yet compulsory-attendance laws force these parents to submit to the majority, and school taxes force them to help pay for the schools.

Compulsory school taxes are an example of how majority rule can lead to tyranny. If a majority is allowed to pass any law it wants, it can hurt or even destroy people who are in the minority group. To give an example, suppose most voters in America did not own homes. Under unlimited majority rule, they could simply vote to confiscate the minority group's homes.

Unlimited majority rule, or pure democracy, is not what our Founding Fathers had in mind for America. Madison and Jefferson were brilliant men who knew their history, and consequently feared pure democracy. They knew what happened to ancient Athens and other failed democracies. They also had a healthy distrust of human nature and knew how men lust after power. So, in America, they created a republic, not a democracy. They designed the Constitution and Bill of Rights to *protect* us from unlimited majority rule. These documents limit the power of government and confirm the fact that all of us have natural, inalienable rights that no majority or government has the right to violate.

In a republic like the United States, majority rule is only a method legislators use to pass laws. In theory, local and state governments have no right to violate our basic liberties such as freedom of speech, or to arbitrarily confiscate a person's property simply because a majority of legislators votes for such an action. Our republic was founded to protect our individual, inalienable rights, not to let a majority violate these rights.

That is the way our republic is supposed to work. Unfortunately, over the past 100 years both State courts and the Supreme Court have made decisions that undermined our natural and Constitutional rights. Too often today, unlimited majority rule *does* rule, no matter whose rights get violated. These court decisions gave state and local governments the right to set up compulsory public schools and impose taxes to pay for them.

These school taxes are unfair because they tax all citizens for services they may not use or benefit from. Parents with one child often pay the same heavy school taxes as their neighbors who may have four children. Many young married couples don't have school-age children. Millions of parents have children over 18 years old who already graduated high school. Millions of Americans are single and never had children. Parents who send their kids to private school pay twice for their children's education because they pay both tuition and school taxes. Parents with no school-age children still have to pay school taxes for as long as they own their homes. So parent-homeowners without school-age children, and parents who send their children to private schools pay school taxes for nothing.

A typical homeowner currently pays about $1,500 per year in school taxes.[4] Married couples with homes pay school taxes before their children reach school age and after their children graduate from high school. A typical homeowner can pay constantly rising school taxes for forty years while they own their home. If school taxes remain at only $1,500 a year, a homeowner can pay over $60,000 total in school taxes over forty years. But children attend public schools for just eight to twelve years, depending on the state. For the remaining twenty-eight years, the homeowner pays school taxes when they have *no* children in school.

State and local school taxes therefore violate the Constitutional founding principle of equality before the law. Local governments have no right to tax parents with no school-age children, or parents who don't want public schools to educate their children. It is unjust to force parents or single adults with no school-age children to pay for the education of other parents' children. Public schools therefore turn out to be a kind of educational welfare system, supported by legalized looting through taxes.

No one has the right to steal your money, especially your elected representatives who are your agents. This moral law is even written in the Ten Commandments—"thou shalt not steal." What we earn by our own effort is *ours* by natural and legal right. If we go to a supermarket and do not buy bread or apples, we should not have to pay for bread or apples. Similarly, if we don't have school-age children or don't like the public schools, we should *not* have to pay taxes to support them. Neither those we do business with nor legislators whose salaries we pay with our taxes have the right to steal from us.

Some people argue that school taxes are justified because we all allegedly benefit when all children get a public-school education. Children who are illiterate and uneducated can turn to crime, drugs, or welfare, which can hurt innocent people.

Yet the notion that *all* people benefit is hardly true, and also depends on how you define "benefit." Millions of Americans without school-age children who pay heavy school taxes don't benefit. Millions of Americans who live in relatively stable neighborhoods with little crime don't benefit. Certainly millions of inner-city minority parents don't benefit by drug-infested, failed public schools in their neighborhood.

Also, failed public schools often leave many children little choice but to turn to drugs, crime, or welfare. Some teenagers who drop out of public school commit crimes or sell drugs to support themselves. Millions of other kids who graduate high school can barely read their own diplomas. They are poorly-educated and find it hard to get a decent job or succeed in college. Dismal public-school education can also embitter children and make them lose ambition and self-confidence. Is *this* the kind of education that benefits all of us?

School taxes are compulsory for a good reason. Parents would not voluntarily pay a grocery store for rotten food. Similarly, parents would not voluntarily pay taxes for public schools that do a bad job educating their children. That is why local governments threaten homeowners with foreclosure if they don't pay their school taxes. Rather than paying these taxes, parents should get a tax *refund* if the schools give their kids an inferior education.

A society's tax system is a barometer of its citizens' liberty. Education often involves teaching children values as well as how to read and write. Religion also teaches children values. Imagine for a moment that Congress passed compulsory *religious* laws that created a government-controlled, monopoly religion like the Church of England in the eighteenth century. Under these laws, suppose that Congress proclaimed Buddhism to be the official state religion, forcing all citizens to attend only government-approved Buddhist churches. Suppose also that a Federal Religion Board forced all children to attend state-controlled Buddhist schools.

Imagine that Congress then passed a new religion tax,

charging taxpayers $2000 a year to pay for these Buddhist schools and the salaries of Buddhist monks who taught in these schools. Suppose also that if you refused to send your child to an approved Buddhist school, you could be charged with child abuse, arrested, and have your child taken from you.

Would you accept this religious tyranny? You would probably refuse to obey the new laws or pay the religion tax because they violated your religious freedom and your right to decide the religious beliefs you teach your children.

Public schools have become today's religious monopoly, and indoctrinate children with values that millions of parents despise. As we saw in Chapter 2, many parents and parent groups throughout the country bitterly complain to local school boards about classes in sex education, homosexuality, pagan religions, and anti-American and anti-family values. Also, as we've seen, outcome-based education programs teach children warped values—that honesty, hard work, perseverance, and personal responsibility are unimportant or meaningless. In many public schools, children learn that they can get away with doing little work, not paying attention, and cheating on tests.

Public schools' education tyranny is no different than the religious tyranny system I imagined. In both cases, government authorities dictate the values taught to your children. These schools are able to enforce their education tyranny only because of compulsory-attendence laws and school taxes.

As we've seen, school taxes and compulsory-attendance laws keep public schools afloat, despite the third-rate, drawn-out education they give our kids. Teachers, principals, administrators, and other school employees are therefore the prime beneficiaries of our public-school system. These laws and taxes artificially keep public schools in business through compulsion, thereby *guaranteeing* jobs and benefits to school employees. So, in effect, public schools are a form of involuntary servitude where our children are sacrificed to benefit public-school employees, the real "owners" of the system. Yet, involuntary servitude was outlawed by the 13th Amendment to the Constitution.

As parents, we love our kids, cherish them, feed them, clothe them, worry about every little sniffle, and would fight to the death against a stranger who wanted to harm them. Yet, school authorities, strangers who are supposed to be our *agents*, not our masters, put millions of children in grave danger. School authorities believe *they* own our children's minds for eight to twelve years and have the right to decide how, when, where, by whom, and for how long our children get educated. Compulsory-attendance laws and school taxes therefore show utter contempt for our natural rights as parents, and for our inalienable political rights under the Constitution and Bill of Rights.

One example of this contempt was the literacy fiasco in California when the state switched from phonics-based reading to the whole-language method in 1987. As you might recall, after six years of this disastrous experiment, California children's reading scores plummeted. California public schools got away with this education crime for six years, only because they are a state-run monopoly that depends on compulsory-attendance laws and school taxes to stay in business. As a result, these schools were not accountable to parents.

Such a fiasco would *never* take place in a private school. No private-school owner would be suicidal enough to turn his customers' children into semi-illiterates. Parents would not wait six years or even six months for a private school to improve its teaching methods. Parents would exercise their freedom to choose and move their children to a better school.

Throughout history, totalitarian governments like the Soviet Union always set up state-run public schools. Their goal was to indoctrinate the children—to teach them the supremacy of the government and obedience to the government's leaders. A government-controlled public-school system is the hallmark of a totalitarian state or a country whose school authorities have a totalitarian mind-set.

I am certainly not saying our public-school authorities are Nazis or communists. Most are dedicated, well-intentioned, but misguided educators who have our children's welfare at heart. However, the means they use to achieve their ends, such as compulsory-attendance laws, are the same means totalitarian-state school systems use, and bring the same results. Good intentions mean *nothing* if the means used are immoral and create terrible consequences for our children.

A Government-Owned Monopoly

Another reason public schools get away with educational failure year after year is that they are, in effect, a government-owned and operated monopoly. Former U.S. Secretary of Education, Rod Paige, confirmed the true nature of public schools when he said:

> I believe that one of our most grievous sins has been to tie a child to a school that is failing him—and insist that he stay at that school and continue to be crippled. Under the current *monopolistic system* [italics added], public schools have no incentive to embark on substantial reforms or make major improvements because, no matter how badly they perform, their budgets will not be cut; their enrollment will not decline; and the school will not close down."[5]

Yet how can I claim that public schools are a monopoly when parents have other options such as home-schooling or sending their children to a private school? To answer this question, let's examine what I mean by a monopoly.

We usually think of a monopoly as a big corporation that can charge customers high prices because it has little competition from other companies. We think of the Standard Oil corporation in the early 1900s as the classic monopoly because for a short time, this corporation had almost a 90 percent share of the oil refinery market.

However, a private corporation, no matter how big, can keep its monopoly only through competence. It can't use force to stop other companies from competing with it, and it can't force customers to buy its product. It can only be so efficient that it manufactures products that millions of customers want at a price that undercuts all competitors.

Standard Oil accomplished this feat by the early 1900s. Before this time, Americans used kerosene lamps at night to light their homes, but the kerosene was expensive. Standard Oil's highly efficient refining operations eventually reduced the price of kerosene from more than two dollars per gallon in the early 1860s to approximately six cents per gallon by 1907.[6] As a result, few oil companies could compete with it.

Standard Oil's efficiency gave Americans a valuable product they wanted at an unheard-of low price. Standard Oil's short-term monopoly on kerosene did not gouge customers. Instead, low-cost kerosene brought light into millions of Americans' homes after nightfall because even poor people could now afford kerosene.

Eventually, the invention of electric lights and competing oil companies broke Standard Oil's monopoly. In the same way, every company's short-term monopoly in a free market sows the seeds of its own demise. The monopoly's huge profits become an irresistible magnet for competing companies in the same field, or companies that offer less-expensive substitute products. In the end, this unrestrained competition eventually breaks the monopoly.

In contrast, a government-created monopoly doesn't have to worry about competitors because government makes such competitors *illegal*. The U.S. Postal Service is a classic example. It loses millions of dollars a year, yet it stays in business and doesn't go bankrupt. That's because general taxes keep it afloat, and federal laws *forbid* private companies from competing with it for first-class mail delivery. In the past, some private companies tried to deliver first-class mail in direct competition with the Postal Service. The government shut them down.

A government-created monopoly forbids competition because it knows free-market competition would destroy its monopoly and put it out of business. A government monopoly like the Postal Service also gets intense pressure from its employee unions to keep competition out. Postal Service workers know that if private companies could compete with the Postal Service for efficient mail delivery, they might soon be on the unemployment line. Postal Service employees therefore have an intense financial interest in keeping their monopoly alive.[7]

In the same way, public-school employees and their unions benefit by defending the public-school system and blocking school choice for parents. Teacher unions have spent huge amounts of money fighting against voucher referendums in California, Florida, and other states. Public-school employees and their unions know that vouchers give parents more choice. They also know that ending compulsory-attendance laws and school taxes would break their monopoly. If public schools were privatized, they would have to compete with private schools, and many school employees might lose their jobs.

That is why public-school employees want to keep their government-controlled monopoly. School choice, competition, and eliminating compulsory-attendance laws and school taxes could be a deadly threat to their jobs.

I can understand school employees' fears on this matter. If I was a public-school teacher or principal and saw the kind of education public schools give our kids, I would fear competition from the private sector also. I would fear for my job if my public school was privatized.

However, do our schools exist to serve our children, or do our children exist to serve the self-interest of public-school employees? *Should we betray our children to protect the jobs of teachers, principals, and school bureaucrats?*

Having discussed monopolies, how can I say that public schools are a monopoly if we have private schools and home-schooling? Supreme Court decisions have upheld parents' rights to direct their children's education, so local governments can't outlaw private schools or home-schooling.

However, even though school authorities can't outlaw their competition, they have an *effective* monopoly created by other government taxes and regulations. Parents can send their children to a private school only *if they can afford it*, and homeschool their children *only if they have the time* to do so. The problem is that city, state, and federal taxes and regulations often rob parents of the money to pay private-school tuition. Heavy taxes can also rob parents of the time to homeschool their kids because in many families, after taxes take their bite, both parents now have to work to make ends meet.

Public schools are supported by taxes. As a result, local governments can stifle real competition from private schools by keeping school taxes relatively low compared to private-school tuition. Businesses have to make a profit to stay solvent, but public schools don't. They can be grossly inefficient, waste money, and give parents a bad product and still stay in business. All they do, like the Post Office, is ask for more tax money to cover their expenses.

Even though about 12 percent of children go to private schools and 2 percent are homeschooled, this unfair competition helps public schools keep their near-total monopoly. School taxes average about $1,500 a year. However, about 80 percent of private-school students go to religiously-affiliated schools whose average tuition rates in 2002 were about $3500 to $4000 a year. Average tuition at non-religiously-affiliated private-schools ranged from about $7000 to $14,000 a year.

As a result, parents are often willing to put up with inferior public schools that charge a lot less than private schools.[8] The demand for private schools then shrinks, which in turn reduces the number of private schools parents can choose from, which further reduces the competition from private schools.

Also, as I noted earlier, parents who send their children to a private school must still pay school taxes that support the public schools. They therefore pay twice for their children's education. Relatively few parents can afford this heavy burden, which further decreases the demand for private schools and reinforces public schools' near-total monopoly.

According to the U.S. Census Bureau, median household income for 2002 was $42,409.[9] However, federal, state, local, sales, real estate, social security, and other taxes slash the average family's income down to about $26,000 a year.[10] That is what's left to pay for rent or the mortgage, food, utilities, clothing, car payments and insurance, dental bills, and expensive health-insurance premiums. After paying all these expenses, relatively few families can afford to send their children to a private school, which again reinforces public schools' near-total monopoly.

Government regulations also add heavy financial burdens to the average family by inflating the cost of everything we buy. For example, thousands of local, state, and federal regulations have sharply increased the cost of all materials and labor that go into building a house.

Home builders and contractors have to obey and pay the cost of zoning, building department, highway department, and other agency regulations. They have to file complicated and time-consuming environmental impact statements. Lumber now costs more because environmental laws restrict lumber production. Steel, cement, roofing, plumbing, and sheet rock manufacturers and contractors also have to obey and pay for regulations in their own industries, which increases the cost of these materials. Builders and contractors also have to pay sharply higher labor costs because of state and federal labor laws. Environmental regulations hinder oil exploration and development, inflating oil prices. Higher oil prices in turn inflate the cost of steel, lumber, and most other products that use oil heat to manufacture these products. Higher oil prices also inflate homeowners' fuel and electric bills after the house is built.

That is why in the year 2003, new house prices averaged about $244,000, yet in 1979 the same house cost around $71,800.[11] Government regulations over the past twenty-five years have been partly responsible for this shocking increase in the price of homes, which sharply increases homeowners' mortgage payments. Similar regulations have inflated the cost of cars, food, clothing, health insurance, and most other products or services parents must pay for. Heavy taxes and sharply higher living expenses now drain a family's income, leaving it little extra money for private-school tuition.

Regulations also increase the cost of every product or service that goes into building and operating schools, including desks, paint, books, paper, computers, and teachers' salaries and benefits. Increased school costs lead to higher school taxes, which further drains families' net incomes.

Strangling government regulations also contribute to rising tuition costs at private schools. These private schools then find it increasingly more difficult to compete with post-office-like public schools that are propped up by school taxes. Once again, this government-created assault on families' incomes shrinks the demand for and number of private schools, and further strengthens the public schools' effective monopoly.

Heavy taxes and strangling regulations put parents in an economic pincer. After paying taxes and all the inflated bills, the average family has little money left over. Most Americans go from paycheck to paycheck. The average family in America now saves less than 1 percent of its annual income, far below the savings rate in Japan, England, and many other countries.[12] Because money is so tight, almost 75 percent of mothers with school-age children now have to work part- or full-time to meet expenses.[13]

As a result, millions of mothers can't homeschool their children, even if they want to. Because they have to work, they usually can't find the time (I'll discuss how parents can solve this problem in Chapter 8). Local, state, and federal taxes and regulations have helped create a public-school monopoly not by outlawing private schools or home-schooling, but by robbing parents of the money to pay tuition for a private school or the time to homeschool their kids. Simple economics now leaves millions of parents with no choice but to send their children to the local public school.

The Absurdity of a
Public-School Monopoly

The notion that local governments should have almost total control over our children's education is not only unjust and tyrannical, it is also absurd. Children need education, to be sure, but they also need food, clothing, and shelter. The same poor or irresponsible parents who public-school apologists claim will not educate their children without compulsion, might not feed, clothe, or shelter them either. Yet, we do not see local governments owning and operating supermarkets, department stores, or apartment houses. Instead, government food-stamp or rent-subsidy programs give temporary financial help to those parents who are too poor to provide for their children.

When it comes to education, however, instead of giving vouchers or other temporary loans or subsidies to poor families so they can pay for their children's education, we've created a government-owned-and-operated monstrosity called public schools. As I noted earlier, millions of parents now pay for private pre-schools, kindergartens, and colleges for their children in a vibrant, competitive, education free-market. Most parents who can't afford college tuition for their kids usually apply for student loans either from a bank or a government agency. Yet for 1st through 12th-grade education, suddenly government must step in, treat all parents like idiots or potential child abusers, and own and operate all the schools.

To more fully understand the absurdity of this system, imagine for a moment that well-intentioned government authorities want to make sure that every child has enough to eat, that no child gets "left behind" when it comes to food. To insure this goal, local governments across the country take control of all supermarkets and grocery stores in your town. Under this new system, bureaucrats now own and operate all food stores, and store workers become tenured civil-service employees who can't be fired. Your local government then passes a new "food tax" to pay for these stores and employees' salaries. This tax is added to your current real-estate tax bill. If you don't pay this new tax, local government officials can and will foreclose on your home.

Under this new system, suppose the local Food Board forces you and your family to buy from a particular store. The store clerks know you have to shop in their store, and that they can't be fired. As a result, they soon become indifferent to their customer's needs. The store managers can't be fired, so they manage the stores badly. The stores can't go out of business because they are supported by taxes, so they give you poor service and rotten food. If you want to change stores, you have to ask *permission* from your local Food Board bureaucrat, who will usually refuse your request. Also, changing food stores doesn't accomplish much because they are all the same—all owned and operated by the same government food monopoly.

If this system sounds absurd to you, if you would scream bloody murder at having to put up with such a system simply to buy food, why do you put up with such a system when it comes to your children's education?

Those we elect to office are our *agents*, not our masters. They derive their powers from our consent. They are supposed to represent our interests and follow our instructions. Politicians, bureaucrats, and school authorities therefore have as much right to dictate how we educate our children as a real-estate agent has to dictate who we sell our house to and at what price.

The following passage from Isabel Paterson's book, *The God of the Machine,* sums up the proper response to local governments and school authorities who think they have the right to dictate how you educate your child:

> The most vindictive resentment may be expected from the pedagogic profession for any suggestion that they should be dislodged from their dictatorial position; it will be expressed mainly in epithets, such as reactionary, at the mildest.
>
> Nevertheless, the question to put to any teacher moved to such indignation, is: Do you think nobody would willingly entrust his children to you or pay you for teaching them? Why do you have to extort your fees and collect your pupils by compulsion?[14]

Tenure — Lifetime Guaranteed
Jobs For Public-School Employees

Another reason public schools get away with education failure year after year is because tenure laws make it almost impossible to fire incompetent public-school employees. After a probationary period of two to four years (depending on the state), most teachers get tenure. Each state's tenure laws allow school boards or principals to fire a teacher for different reasons, such as incompetence, a criminal act, insubordination, unprofessional conduct, neglect of duty, drug abuse or alcoholism, a felony conviction, or physical or mental disability.[15]

On paper, this sounds like tenure laws let school boards fire teachers or principals for many of the same reasons a private company might fire an employee. However, the catch is that in most cases, a school board has to go through a legal nightmare to fire a teacher or principal. Under tenure laws, teachers and principals can only be fired for "just cause" and have the right to "due process" before they can be fired. Unlike owners or managers of private schools or businesses, school boards can't simply fire a public-school teacher or principal after making a fair review of their conduct or competence. Instead, teachers have the right to take their case before various review boards, and then appeal a decision to lower and superior courts set up for these cases.

To dismiss teachers or principals, school boards usually have to file lengthy, aggravating, and very expensive lawsuits. Since most school boards have the sense to avoid such lawsuits like the plague, tenure laws, in effect, give public-school employees a *guaranteed job for life*.

Sykes provides an example of the sometimes outrageous consequences of tenure laws:

> In some districts, the combination of aggressive unionism and arcane tenure rules has made it virtually impossible to fire teachers short of their commission of a felony. In some cities, even felony conviction isn't enough

for a school district to get rid of a teacher. In New York City, a special education teacher who was arrested, convicted and sent to prison for trying to sell $7000 worth of cocaine to undercover police officers in 1989 was not only able to keep his job, but continued to receive his full salary while he was in prison.

Even after five years—and $185,000 spent on disciplinary hearings—New York's schools were unable to fire the convicted drug dealer Jay [last name withheld for privacy], who was protected by tenure and the teachers union. The board's failed attempt to fire [Jay] dramatically illustrated the Byzantine disciplinary process required to remove teachers—even those who were accused of the most extreme misconduct. In eight hearings spread out over ten months, [Jay's] lawyer argued that his client had been unfairly dismissed and explained that [Jay] was forced to sell drugs to support his own $300-a-day habit. In mid-1994, now out of prison, [Jay] still had a job.

Despite the cost, complexity, and futility of the effort to fire [Jay], his case was not really all that unusual. In New York State, school districts spend an average of $194,520 to fully prosecute each case of teacher misconduct, a process that takes 476 days. Not surprisingly, many districts simply choose to look the other way rather than descend into the Kafka-esque maze of tenure protections, litigation, and union agitation.[16]

In June 1997, a Jacksonville teacher threw books at her students and in rambling letters wrote that she saw evil spirits in her students' eyes. Some time later this teacher changed her name to "God." Because of Florida tenure laws, it took the local school board *three years* to fire her, during which time this teacher repeatedly hurt other students she threw books at.[17]

Gerald A. Pound, a former Michigan public-school district superintendent, confirmed the extraordinary cost to discharge a teacher. In an article about tenure on the Mackinac Center For

Public Policy website, he noted that a legal case to discharge a tenured teacher may cost a school district between $250,000 and $500,000.[18]

Because school boards have to go through a legal nightmare to fire a teacher or principal, very few are discharged. A Pacific Research Institute press release noted the following:

In the entire state of Florida in 1997, only 0.05 percent of teachers were removed involuntarily from their jobs. Across the state's economy as a whole, 7.9 percent of all employees were fired. In two large Georgia counties, not a single tenured teacher was fired from 1995 to 2000. In New York City, where the public schools employ 72,000 teachers, the school board sought to fire three teachers for incompetence in a two-year period. In California, which employs some 350,000 teachers at any given time, only 227 cases reached the final phase of the dismissal process from 1990 to 1999—only one of these from Los Angeles, the second largest school district in the country.[19]

How do tenure laws contribute to public schools' educational failure, year after year? If most school boards won't go through the time and enormous expense of firing an incompetent teacher or principal, students suffer because these teachers and principals remain on the job.

Even worse, tenure entrenches mediocrity in public-school education. It's not just the incompetent teacher who's the problem. Far more devastating for our children's education is the much larger number of teachers and principals who are simply mediocre at their jobs. Private schools or companies usually won't allow their teachers or employees to produce mediocre work, year after year. Most private businesses demand more from their employees because their profits and competitiveness depend on having quality employees who continually improve their skills and knowledge.

In contrast, most public schools don't require or enforce

high teaching standards. That's because lazy or mediocre teachers or principals know they can't be fired for using the same lesson plans or boring teaching methods year after year. A private-school owner can and will dismiss mediocre teachers whose teaching skills never improve. To have high standards in public schools, school boards need the same right to dismiss mediocre teachers or principals. Tenure laws prevent this. As a result, millions of school children must suffer with a third-rate education.

In every other business or industry, employers have the right to judge their employees' performance, and dismiss those employees who are not doing a good job. A business's very existence depends on its employees' competence and quality of work. Teachers in private kindergartens, grammar schools, trade schools, and many colleges don't have tenure. Why should public-school employees have a lifetime job, irrespective of their talent, effort, or ability?

Tenure laws are not the only employment policies that create mediocrity in our public schools. Public-school teachers and principals are civil-service employees. Like most other civil-service employees, their salaries depend on length of service, not competence. The National Education Association (NEA) is the biggest teachers union in the country, with branches in every state. The NEA publishes an annual *Handbook* that outlines the union's goals for public schools for the coming year. In their 2001 *Handbook*, Resolution F-8 repeats the NEA's consistent opposition to merit pay for teachers.[20] Merit pay means paying teachers based on their competence and performance, rather than on training and seniority.

The NEA and AFT (American Federation of Teachers), the two biggest teachers unions, powerfully influence wage structure and employment practices in many public schools. That's because collective bargaining laws in many states *force* school boards to negotiate with teachers unions rather than individual teachers. As a result, most teacher-employment contracts base teacher-salary schedules on the unions' criteria—training or preparation, professional growth, and length of service, *not* on merit.

Preparation usually means if a teacher has a Bachelor or Master's degree in education. Professional growth usually means if teachers take further education courses after they get their license and are teaching. Length of service simply means how long a teacher has been on the job. Notice that the most important criteria to children and parents is missing here—can these teachers teach, and are they competent?

School-employee salary levels are all about *inputs*, not outputs. Because a teacher has a bachelor's degree and a license doesn't mean she knows how to teach kids to read. Even if she took so-called professional-growth courses after she got her license, she may know nothing about the subject she teaches. As we will see later, so-called teacher preparation and professional growth in no way guarantees that teachers are competent or even have training in the subjects they teach.

Suppose a man took all the required training to be an airline pilot. He gets his bachelor's degree, passes the pilot training tests, and gets his pilot's license. However, every time he takes a plane up, he forgets what he learned in pilot school and almost crashes the plane. Should this pilot get a guaranteed tenured job because he graduated pilot school and got his license? Should he keep getting higher pay the longer he is a pilot? Or, should he be fired? I'm sure we can guess the answer his passengers would give.

The same absurdity applies to public-school teachers or principals, where salary is based on seniority rather than merit. Because of civil-service salary schedules, both a mediocre and great teacher both get the same pay if they've been on the job the same number of years. Also, a mediocre or incompetent teacher who's been teaching for twenty years, gets a higher salary than a great teacher who's only taught for five years.

For example, here are some salary-schedule statistics for North Carolina licensed teachers for the 2003-2004 school year. Those with a Bachelor's degree in Education who have been teaching for three years get an annual salary (10 months work) of $27,640. Teachers on the job for twelve years make $35,110 a year. Teachers with a Masters degree in Education who have worked for three years get $30,400 a year, while those who have worked for twelve years make $36,620 a year. Salaries vary depending on the state, but such schedules are typical for most public-school teachers. Nowhere on these salary schedules is there a column marked "competence," or "parent satisfaction with teacher."[21]

The way employees are paid affects their behavior. When schools pay teachers based on how long they've been teaching, rather than competence, three bad things happen. First, if a great teacher sees that she is not rewarded for all her extra effort and dedication, that she gets the same pay as an incompetent teacher with the same number of years on the job, why should she keep trying? Why should she make that extra effort anymore? Second, the mediocre teacher can just coast along, boring her students for the next twenty years, but still get a higher salary every year. So why should she try harder or be more creative teaching her kids? Third, the incompetent teacher does not have to care that her students can't read or do arithmetic. Why bother learning her job if most school boards won't risk a protracted and expensive lawsuit to fire her? So, too often, incompetent teachers remain incompetent and stay on the job.

In short, if school boards or principals can't judge or dismiss teachers based on their competence or real-world results with their students, *mediocrity becomes entrenched* throughout the public schools. Naturally, our children suffer from this mediocrity.

Public-School True Believers with a Mission

Another reason public schools get away with education failure year after year is because they are run by school officials who passionately believe in what they are doing. As the great English writer C. S. Lewis wrote, "Of all tyrannies, a tyranny sincerely exercised for the good of its victims may be the most oppressive. Those who torment us for our own good will torment us without end, for they do so with the approval of their own conscience."[22] Public-school true believers often fall into this category—for over a hundred years, education "experts" have been tormenting our children with public schools, allegedly for the children's good. These people believe that *they* know what is best for our children and society.

From the 1850s to the 1920s, public-school activists such as Horace Mann and John Dewey worked to create a public-school system like the one they admired in Prussia. Mann and Dewey considered public education a religion, with a holy mission to mold children and society. Simply teaching children to read, write, and do math was too commonplace a goal for them. Mann and Dewey wanted the schools to have total control over children's lives. This meant removing parents' influence over their children. Mann put it this way: "We who are engaged in the sacred cause of education are entitled to look upon all parents as having given hostages to our cause."[23]

Dewey also had a utopian vision for America and he wanted the common schools to achieve his vision. To create a socialist America, public schools had to mold generations of children into the habit of obedience. In his *Pedagogic Creed* of 1897, Dewey wrote, "Every teacher should realize he is a social servant set apart for the maintenance of the proper social order and the securing of the right social growth . . ."[24]

By the early twentieth century, public schools had expanded their functions into areas undreamed of in the 1850s. Schools took on the role of social agencies, with nurses, social centers, playgrounds, school showers, kindergartens, and "Americanization" programs for immigrants. Public schools became a major agency for social control.[25]

Unfortunately, today's public schools are fulfilling Mann's and Dewey's socialist vision with a vengeance. There is hardly any area of children's lives that school authorities don't push to control or manipulate. Politicians and public-school apologists in many states are now pushing programs that would make kindergarten compulsory. Public schools also now spend billions of dollars for programs like socialization classes, psychological counseling, school-lunch programs, parent welfare-outreach programs, special-education classes, bilingual classes, early-childhood programs, drug and sex-education classes, as well as programs for millions of "at-risk" or "special-needs" children.

The NEA's *2001 Handbook* claimed that public schools should focus on the whole child. It claimed that the NEA has an obligation to deal with all the issues that shape a child's life, such as health and safety, the economy, and the distribution of wealth in this country.[26]

This government-knows-best philosophy is the deepest reason why public schools get away with educational murder and can never be fixed. True-believer school authorities think that your children's minds and lives belong to them, to the government, for twelve years. By implication, they believe that parents are an annoyance at best, and at worst a danger to their children's education. Public-school true believers will never voluntarily give up their power and monopoly control. They see themselves as noble idealists who know what is best for our children.

Licensing

Teacher licensing in public schools does not insure better teachers for our kids. A license does not insure teacher quality. It does not even insure that a teacher knows anything about the subject she teaches. In fact, like salary schedules based on years on the job, licensing leads to ill-trained and mediocre teachers instructing our children.

The notion that only state-approved, licensed teachers can guarantee children a good education is proven wrong by history and common sense. In ancient Athens, the birthplace of logic, science, philosophy, and Western civilization, city authorities did not require teachers to be licensed. Plato and Aristotle did not have to get a teaching license from Athenian bureaucrats to open up their Academies. A teacher's success came only from his competence, reputation, and popularity. Students and their parents paid a teacher only if they thought he was worth the money. Competition and an education free market created great teachers in ancient Greece.

As noted in Chapter 1, parents in America gave their children a superior education at home or in small grammar or religious schools for over two hundred years *before* we had public schools or licensed teachers. School authorities' claim that teachers have to be licensed for our children to get a quality education, is therefore false.

Today, in millions of companies across America, owners or their managers teach new employees job skills, from the simplest to the most complex. Private schools and trade schools teach millions of students valuable, practical skills. Thousands of college professors with masters or doctorate degrees in the subject they teach, instruct hundreds of thousands of college students in subjects ranging from philosophy to electrical engineering. Over a million home-schooling parents teach their children reading, writing, and math with learn-to-read or learn-math books, computer-learning software and other teaching materials. These teachers are not licensed, yet they usually give children a far better education than licensed public-school teachers.

To get their license, most public-school teachers have to take their state's prescribed number of education courses in a university education department or state-approved teacher college. The problem is that education departments and teacher colleges are notoriously mediocre.

Many university education programs and so-called teacher colleges only require their students to take courses in education theory, the history of education, and how to "socialize" children. They don't train students in the subject they will teach, or how to teach in the real world. They give their students little practical training in how to teach children to read and other basic skills. Thousands of education-department or teacher-college students only have to pass dumbed-down teacher-education courses to graduate and get their license.

Many education students are bright, truly want to teach, and love children. However, education departments and teacher colleges are also filled with many other high-school graduates who may lack ambition, have low self-confidence as students, don't know what they want to do with their lives, or have never found a subject they want to pursue as a career. Students like these would have a hard time finding a job with employers who demand real knowledge and job skills. So many of these students go into teaching as a last resort because they want a government job that gives them lifetime security.

Shockingly, many student-teachers today not only lack college training in their subject areas, but they are also barely literate. Fred Bayles, in a column titled, "Those Who Can't Spell or Write, Teach," gave an example:

On April 1, 1998, the Massachusetts Board of Education gave applicants who wanted to teach a basic reading and writing test. The results of the test were that 59 percent of the applicants failed. If you think these test results made the Board of Education do something constructive, think again. It promptly lowered the test's passing grade from 77 to 66 percent. Under the "new" standard, *only* 44 percent failed. Note that all the applicants were college graduates."[27]

Also, these same education students often score lowest in academic achievement among other high-school graduates. Thomas Sowell, senior fellow at the Hoover Institution, wrote about this issue in his book, *Inside American Education.*

Despite some attempts to depict such attitudes as mere snobbery, hard data on education student qualifications have consistently shown their mental test scores to be at or near the bottom among all categories of students. This was as true of studies done in the 1920s and 1930s as of studies in the 1980s. Whether measured by Scholastic Aptitude Tests, ACT tests, vocabulary tests, reading comprehension tests or Graduate Record Examinations, students majoring in education have consistently scored below the national average.

At the graduate level, it is very much the same story, with students in numerous other fields outscoring education students on the Graduate Record Examination—by from 91 points composite to 259 points, depending on the field. The pool of graduate students in education supplies not only teachers, counselors, and other administrators, but also professors of education and other leaders and spokesmen for the education establishment.[28]

Sowell also notes that these same professors of education are not held in high esteem by other university faculty members:

Professors of education rank as low among college and university faculty members as education students do among other students. After listing a number of professors of great personal and intellectual distinction teaching in the field of education, Martin Mayer nevertheless concluded: "On the average, however, it is true to say that the academic professors, with many exceptions in the applied sciences and some in the social sciences, are educated men, and the professors of education are not. . . Education schools and education departments have been called the intellectual slums of the university."[29]

Sowell sums up his study of teacher colleges, university departments of education, and teacher training this way: "In short, some of the least qualified students, taught by the least qualified professors in the lowest quality courses supply most American public school teachers."[30]

The low-level quality of teacher college or university education-department training can be seen in graduate education majors' doctoral theses. Below are some of the "subjects" these students spend years researching to get their doctoral degrees in education.

> Selected clothing characteristics and educator cred-
> ibility" . . . "The effect of the three-point rule-change
> in college basketball" . . . "Teacher humor in middle
> school and educational criticism" . . . "An ethnographic
> study of the use of puppetry with a children's group" .
> . . "Weather conditions and productivity of junior high
> school students" . . . "Effects of lunchtime instruction
> on student attitudes towards science" . . . "The contex-
> tual realities of being a lesbian physical educator: Liv-
> ing in two worlds" . . . [and my personal favorite] "An
> investigation into the personal meaning of golf."[31]

These are the actual titles of dissertations by graduate students who earned doctorate degrees in education. Some of these
same graduate students become education professors in teacher
colleges and university departments of education, and train the
student-teachers who become our children's teachers in public-
school classrooms—in effect, the blind leading the blind.

Paul Craig Roberts lists the following courses as a sample
of those offered by the Education Department at the University of Massachusetts: "Embracing Diversity, Diversity and
Change, Oppression and Education, Introduction to Multicultural Education, Black Identity, Classism, Racism, Sexism,
Lesbian/Gay/Bisexual Oppression, Jewish Oppression, Oppression of the Disabled, Erroneous Beliefs."[32] Education departments throughout the country have curricula filled with such
politcally-correct courses, none of which have anything to do
with teaching children how to read, or traditional elementary-
school subjects.

Many bright, dedicated education students who truly love
teaching and children, find teacher colleges and university
education departments insufferable. Listen to one student-
teacher's experience in a teachers college, as quoted in Sykes's
Dumbing Down Our Kids:

I didn't decide to teach because I couldn't think of anything else to do with my life. I didn't decide to teach because it was a "cushy" job. I wanted to be a teacher because I thought I could make a difference. Idealistic? Naive? Certainly. But I truly believed that I could be the kind of teacher that students remembered long after they had left my classroom. I believed that teaching was my destiny. Then I went to college.

I remember looking at my schedule that fall and having a shadow of doubt cross my mind. To my untrained eye, the education classes appeared to be theoretical in nature, not practical: Reading, Visual Arts, Educational Psychology, Fundamentals of Education. Where were the "roll-up-your-sleeves, dive-right-in" classes that would teach me how to be a teacher? I was looking for "real life" preparation for the classroom. But instead I learned about Piaget and the history of public education. I spent three hours a week for several months learning how to thread a projector and make laminated copies of phony lesson plans.

The instructors wanted journals and projects and early morning meetings where we were all supposed to sit around and talk about how it "felt" to be a teacher. We were sent to observe classrooms at the local high school, as if by watching these teachers at work, somehow we would know what to do when we stood up in front of thirty bored ninth-graders. I had been watching and listening to teachers for almost sixteen years. I knew what they did. What most of them did was boring—especially to a twenty-one-year-old college senior. I didn't want to be that kind of teacher. I had my own ideas about how I would teach—how I would spark interest and creativity in the mind of reluctant middle-school grammar students. I was dying to get out there and try it for myself.

One afternoon, in a fit of frustration, I confided in an instructor who had appeared to me to be one of the few college instructors who really cared about teaching.

I told him I was bored. Frustrated. That I was having trouble sitting through all these senseless classes, filled with their self-important gobbledy-gook. I told him I thought the education department at the college was not preparing me to teach—that I wanted to be shown the practicalities of teaching and be given the freedom to experiment with some of my own ideas.

The instructor was furious. How could I understand something that I didn't have a degree in? Didn't I realize that the people I was criticizing had spent their lives studying these theories and knew more about education than 99.9 percent of the population? Creativity? Was I crazy or something? I had to be extremely naive to believe that a "cocky, arrogant college senior" like me would be afforded the privilege of creativity. Who in the hell did I think I was, anyhow?"

And then it occurred to me—these so-called educators were not teachers. They had never taught a single day in any secondary classroom. They were not interested in showing me or any other student-teacher how to be a "good" teacher. For these instructors, with their doctorates in education, the primary goal was to indoctrinate all of us teacher wanna-bes into the subjective, mediocre ideologies of the professional educator. We were told to leave our creativity, uniqueness, and youthful enthusiasm outside of the college classroom and cheerfully conform to the bloated rhetoric of educators who designed their courses to be intimidating, complicated, and filled with senseless jargon that only sounded impressive.

As a student teacher, I spent eight weeks watching and listening to a junior-high English teacher who had become jaded and mean-spirited after too many years of clocking in and clocking out of a job she hated. She told me and anyone else in earshot how she despised the children she taught. She was not interested in her students or in her student teacher. She couldn't wait to dash out of the classroom at the end of the day. I did my best to ignore her zealous advice that I should be more intimidating—more threatening—and I found that the only reason the whole experience was tolerable was because of the wonderful support and encouragement I received from my students.

Some of my innocence was lost that year. For my entire life, working hard and being myself were two things that had always led to success. But that semester of student teaching turned my world upside down. The things I valued most about myself—my creativity, my tenacity, my enthusiasm, my individualism, my intellect—were tossed aside and deemed inappropriate. In her evaluation, my supervising teacher concluded I wasn't cut out for the job.

I often think that if I had been the kind of teacher she had wanted me to be, it all would have turned out differently. But I loved teaching. I loved the students and the moments where I knew that I was getting through to them. I had spent four years preparing to make teaching my life. I wanted to make a difference. I never taught again."[33]

Here is the real truth about these so-called teacher colleges from a woman who loved children and wanted to teach—that in many of these colleges, ivory-tower education professors with little public-school teaching experience, teach pedantic, meaningless, psycho-babble, so-called education courses. Here we also see the sad story of a woman who loved teaching, but ended-up feeling contempt for teacher colleges and public-schools. How many other potentially fine teachers give up in disgust because their student-teaching experience destroys their enthusiasm, creativity, and initiative?

This would-be teacher's story is not unique. Steve Wulf, writing in *Time* magazine, confirmed that many other student-teachers had the same opinion about their teacher training:

Six hundred experienced teachers surveyed in 1995 were brutal about the education they had received, describing it as "mind-numbing," the "shabbiest psycho-babble," and "an abject waste of time." They complained that fragmented, superficial course work had little relevance to classroom realities. And judging by the weak skills of student teachers entering their schools, they observed, the preparation was still woefully inadequate.[34]

Not all student-teachers drop out, of course. Once student-teachers get their official government stamp of approval (a license or teaching certificate), they can, after their probationary period, stay in the system until they retire. Some states require licensed teachers to take further education courses, but these again are only *inputs*—ivory-tower "education" courses that have little relevance to teachers' classroom competence or knowledge of the subject they teach.

The poor quality of teacher-college or university-education-department training obviously means that teacher licensing does not guarantee competent teachers. In fact, this training almost guarantees that our children's teachers will be ill-trained or totally unprepared to teach in real classrooms. This so-called teacher training almost guarantees that many public-school teachers will be mediocre or worse (of course there are exceptions, because there are some excellent teachers in our public schools). The fault is mostly the teacher-training system, not the teachers. If teacher colleges taught proven teaching skills like the phonics reading method, and required student-teachers to prove they are knowledgeable in the subject they will teach, our children would have better teachers.

Why don't more talented writers, scientists, engineers, businessmen, or historians in the private sector teach in our public schools? First, most won't put up with school authorities telling them what and how they must teach. Second, anyone with real knowledge in their field won't spend years of drudgery and boredom in a college education department or teacher college to get a license to teach. They value their time too much. That is one reason the best teachers work in private schools or universities, not in public schools. Sowell summarizes this issue well:

> With teachers as with their students, merely throwing more money at the educational establishment means having more expensive incompetents. Ordinarily, more money attracts better people, but the protective barriers of the teaching profession keep out better-qualified people, who are the least likely to have wasted their time in college on education courses, and the least likely to undergo a long ordeal of such Mickey Mouse courses later on.[35]

Licensing laws imply that only so-called education experts can judge a teacher's competence. This makes little sense because these "experts" are usually graduates of our illustrious teacher colleges and university education departments, and are the same "experts" responsible for the depressing failure of our public schools.

Licensing also implies that parents can't and shouldn't judge a teacher's competence. Yet millions of parents in all fifty states send their children to private pre-schools, kindergartens, grammar schools, and colleges. These allegedly ignorant parents have no problem judging the competence of teachers in private schools, and withdrawing their children if the schools don't live up to their expectations.

We all judge the competence of our doctors, accountants, and car mechanics every day of the year, and we do so reasonably well. Is there some mysterious reason we can't judge whether our children are learning to read, write, or do math and other subjects? Public-school officials' claims that parents are too ignorant to judge their children's education are often self-serving. If we allegedly can't trust parents with this job, obviously we then have to turn to so-called education experts, which guarantees their jobs.

School authorities also claim that we need licensing to

guarantee competence, so no charlatans become teachers. Yet, as noted above, many licensed public-schools teachers are barely literate themselves or are ill-trained or have little knowledge of the subject they teach. Of course there are also incompetent teachers in private schools. In any profession, there are always some "bad apples."

However, as we've seen, public-school authorities hire ill-trained or mediocre teachers on a massive scale, which causes untold damage to millions of children. Parents have no recourse to oust these teachers, for all the reasons we discussed above. In contrast, in a private school, a truly incompetent teacher will not last long. Parents will complain, and the school owner will have to fire this teacher to keep parents happy. Also, for the same reasons, a private-school owner will make every effort to find out if a teacher is competent before he hires that teacher. The school owner's livelihood and the success of his school depend on having competent teachers and happy customers. *Public schools have no such constraints.*

Most parents naively assume that if a teacher is licensed, he or she is a trained professional. Parents will therefore lower their guard with licensed teachers because they assume that a licensed teacher must be competent. Unfortunately, as we've seen, this is often not the case.

One solution offered for this problem is "merit" pay for teachers. Merit-pay programs would judge all school employees on competence. Better teachers would get paid more. Bad teachers, principals, or administrators could be fired or demoted. How one judges merit, of course, is a whole separate issue, but just as private-school owners devise methods to judge the merit of their teachers, so too could public schools.

If teacher licensing produced competent teachers, why would school authorities and teachers unions fight so hard against merit pay? The answer seems obvious—the system produces many teachers, principals, and administrators who may not "merit" their pay, and might lose their jobs under merit-pay rules.

In effect, public-school employees say to parents: "You have to pay our salary and benefits, but how dare you demand proof that we know how to teach your children? How dare you judge our merit? How dare you demand that you get your money's worth?" Only frauds or charlatans are afraid to be judged by the people who pay them. So licensing does not keep charlatans out of our public schools. Instead, it practically guarantees that we employ charlatans or ill-trained teachers.

Public-school apologists say that merit pay, like teaching without tenure, could lead to teachers being fired on a whim for personal, subjective, or political reasons by principals or school boards. Such things can and do happen of course, even in private schools and private industry. Employees have no guarantee that their boss is not an idiot. However, most employers are ruled by self-interest. An employer only hurts himself if he fires a great employee, since that would hurt his business and his profits.

Public schools have no such constraints. School administrators' or principals' jobs are not usually threatened by incompetent teachers, nor does a public school go out of business if most of its teachers are mediocre. Yes, merit pay could lead to subjective or politically-motivated firings for a few teachers. However, most principals or school boards would not want to fire good teachers today, especially because the *No Child Left Behind Act* now punishes failing schools. In contrast, merit pay could finally lead to some accountability in our public schools (assuming we should keep our public schools in the first place).

If licensing doesn't work, what is the alternative? The answer is, *no* licensing. If anyone could teach without a license like home-schooling parents or private-school teachers, then millions of new, competent, creative teachers would flood the market. These new, unlicensed teachers would compete with one another and drive the price of education down, much as competition drives down the price of computers. They would, thankfully, also put public schools out of business, since millions of parents and free-market schools would now hire these new competent, low-cost teachers.

Without licensing laws, anyone with a special skill or knowledge could simply put an ad in the Yellow Pages or their local newspaper and advertise themselves as a tutor in English, math, biology, history, or computer skills. Retired cooks, engineers, authors, plumbers, musicians, biologists, or businessmen who love teaching could easily open a small school in their homes. If there were no licensing laws, these talented new teachers would not have to worry about school authorities stopping them from teaching because they didn't have a license.

How would parents be sure they were not hiring a charlatan if there were no licensing laws? The same way they judge their doctor, accountant, or car-mechanic—by results, reputation, and by being careful consumers. Naturally, parents would make occasional mistakes in judgment because they are human. However, they would quickly become careful consumers because they would now be spending their hard-earned money for teachers. It is amazing how fast we learn to judge the work of others when we have to pay for their services. Also, if a parent does make mistakes in judging an unlicensed teacher, by watching her child's progress she will soon catch her error. At that point, she can quickly fire the teacher and find a better one. Can a parent do that with her children's public-school teachers?

The worst nightmare for public-school authorities is a true free market of teachers with no licensing requirements. Fierce competition by millions of new, unlicensed, competent, highly-skilled teachers might destroy the public schools, the teacher unions, and teachers' lifetime security in tenured jobs. That is one unspoken reason why school authorities fiercely defend licensing laws—real competition terrifies them. That is also one of the best reasons to eliminate licensing.

The only way to insure good teachers is to let *parents* decide who will teach their children, not bureaucrats. Millions of parents making individual decisions about who should teach their children, will bring forth the best teachers. Fierce competition and an education free market would raise all boats in the teaching profession. Teachers who want to succeed in their profession would have to prove to parent-customers or private-school owners that they have what it takes. They would have to prove by *results* that they know how to teach and motivate children to read, write, and learn.

Public School Deception

Another reason public schools fail year after year and get away with it, is because they deceive many parents into thinking the schools do a good job educating their children, when they don't. If parents knew how bad the schools really were, they might demand that public schools be shut down or teachers or principals fired. Consequently, school authorities and employees benefit when parents don't know the facts.

Public schools across the country have succeeded in deceiving parents. Despite study after study showing the appalling illiteracy rates and dropping SAT test scores, many Americans don't think there is anything seriously wrong with *their* children's schools or the education their kids are getting. Many parents are convinced that the dumbing-down of American education does not include their own children and that their kids are doing well in math, science, and reading.

In 1994, the American Association of School Administrators did a survey on parent's attitudes towards their local public school's performance. The study found that nearly 90 percent of parents rated their schools an A, B, or C, and more than half rated their schools an A or B. An *Associated Press* poll the same year found 62 percent of parents rated their local schools as good or excellent. Only 10 percent of parents surveyed said their local schools were doing a poor job.

However, when *employers* were asked how they rated the academic skills of high-school graduates they had recently hired, a very different opinion emerged in the survey. Only 22 percent of employers thought the newly-hired graduates had sufficient math skills. Only 12 percent thought they had good writing skills and only 30 percent were satisfied with their new employees' reading abilities.

Colleges and universities were equally disappointed with these high-school graduates' poor academic abilities. Only 27 percent of the colleges and universities thought the recent high-school graduates had adequate math skills, only 18 percent rated their writing abilities highly, and only 33 percent said that the high-school graduates had good reading skills.

In contrast, parents of college-bound high-school graduates expressed satisfaction with their public schools. If anything, these parents were either totally deceived or deeply into denial. Seventy-one percent of the parents gave the public schools favorable ratings in teaching math, 77 percent gave favorable ratings for teaching writing well, and 82 percent gave the schools positive ratings for teaching reading well.

Besides grossly overrating their children's academic skills, surveys have found that parents often overrate their *own* skills. In a 1993 survey, the U.S. Education Department found that 90 million American adults—about 47 percent of the population—had a low level of literacy. Yet the survey found that most Americans describe themselves as being able to read and write English "well" or "very well."[36]

Herein lies an important reason why many parents don't demand that we shut down the public schools—because *they don't see a problem*. Many parents are complacent because their local public school has deceived them into thinking it is doing a good job educating their children.

Also, intelligent parents can be deceived by public schools because the system limits competition among schools. When shopping for a car, or clothing for their children, these same parents are careful consumers who use comparison shopping to find the best price and quality for the products they buy. Competition among many car dealers or clothing stores gives parents the opportunity to do this comparison shopping.

However, parents do *not* have this same opportunity with their children's education. Public schools are government-controlled and have a near-total education monopoly. If every school in a district is run by the same school authorities and gives the same third-rate education, how are parents to know that their children's school is doing a bad job? Parents don't have dozens of other elementary, middle, or high schools run by private companies from which they can compare and choose. The compulsory, near-monopoly structure of public schools denies parents the ability to do comparison shopping for their children's education.

In the next chapter, we will examine some of the endless excuses that school authorities use to rationalize why, despite their constant failure to educate our children, we still need public schools.

7

Excuses, Excuses

School authorities find themselves on the horns of a dilemma—they preach an educational morality they don't practice. They repeat over and over, like a mantra, that they support excellence in education, and that no child should be left behind. Yet year after year, public schools cripple children's ability to read, damage their self-esteem, and graduate millions of semi-illiterate teenagers who are badly prepared for college or a career.

The huge gap between school authorities' good intentions and their dismal results in educating our children, forces them to invent a laundry list of excuses and rationalizations to defend the system. This chapter will examine many of their most common excuses.

Excuse #1 — Give Us More Money!

Suppose that a contractor was building a house for you, and for some strange reason he convinced you to build your house on a garbage dump. The house was supposed to cost $150,000, but the contractor is having problems. Every time he tries to lay his foundations, the foundations sink into the garbage-filled earth. So the contractor keeps trying new ways to reinforce the earth to hold the foundations. He tries steel rods. He uses a different concrete mixture. But everything he tries fails because the garbage dump won't support any foundation he pours. Every time the contractor tries something new, the price of the house goes up. His experiments push the price to $350,000.

Of course you become disgusted and start to think that the problem may be a structural one that can't be fixed—that you'll never be able to sink a solid foundation on a garbage dump. The contractor, who doesn't seem to have a waiting list of other customers, keeps saying that if you give him another $100,000, then another $100,000, he's sure he can find a way to lay your foundation and build your house. But you're bankrupt by now, so you have to walk away from the house.

The same scenario has been running for the past fifty years in our public schools. To cover their embarrassment at their constant failure to educate our kids, school authorities endlessly demand more tax dollars. They point to all the alleged deficiencies of our public schools. They claim that the schools are overcrowded and run-down, and that good teachers expect high salaries. They demand more tax dollars to modernize the schools, reduce class sizes, expand programs for struggling students, and always, increase teacher pay to recruit and retain better teachers.

The problem with public schools, however, is not lack of money. The real problem is that the public-school system is, in effect, an educational garbage dump. No matter how much money we pump into these schools, they will not improve because the system's foundation is rotten. It is a compulsory government-controlled near-monopoly—*that* is the rot under its foundation. Just as the government-controlled food system in the communist Soviet Union produced failure and famine, so our government-controlled public schools produce educational failure for our children. In both cases, that failure is built into the system because compulsory government control strangles free choice and competition.

Government control guarantees mediocrity in our schools. We have falling SAT scores, high dropout rates, and depressing math and reading scores across all grades. As we saw in Chapter 1, the grim statistics are endless. Yet school authorities have the gall to continually ask for more money.

Giving more money to public schools is usually a waste of time. Paul Craig Roberts describes a 1984 Kansas City public-school experiment that eloquently illustrates this point. Because of a desegregation lawsuit, Roberts writes,

> Kansas City spent $2 billion building the most expensive school system in the world. Beginning teacher salaries rose from a low of $17,000 to a high of $47,851. Fifteen new schools were constructed and 70 had additions or renovations. The luxurious facilities include a planetarium, a vivarium [a little zoo for frogs], greenhouses, a model United Nations wired for language translation, radio and television studios, movie editing and screening rooms, swimming pools, a zoo, a farm, a wild land area, a temperature-controlled art gallery, and 15 computers per classroom. Students can study Suzuki violin, animal science, and robotics. Language instruction spans French to Swahili.
>
> Despite the extraordinary facilities and massive sums of money, student performance is so low that recently the state had to strip the Kansas City School District of its accreditation. The school district has fewer students and is less integrated than in 1984 when Judge Clark took control of the school district in order to achieve "mathematical racial balance."[1]

If more money meant better education, our public schools should have vastly improved over the last 75 years. Yet the reverse is true. In dollars adjusted for inflation, public schools spent about $876 per year for elementary and secondary school students in 1930, when student literacy rates were close to 90 percent.[2] In 2003, as I noted earlier, public schools spent an average of $7300 per student, while literacy rates for millions of students fell to the 50 percent level (see Chapter 1 statistics).

In the year 2000, the five states whose students got the highest SAT scores were North Dakota, Iowa, Wisconsin, Minnesota, and South Dakota. Yet, per-pupil spending in North Dakota ranked forty-first among the states, in Iowa twenty-fifth, Wisconsin tenth, Minnesota sixteenth, and South Dakota a lowly forty-eighth. In contrast, the District of Columbia had the fourth highest per-student spending of all the states but ranked almost at the bottom of the list (50th out of 50 states and the District of Columbia) in student achievement.[3] Clearly, there is little correlation between money spent per student and student achievement.

Many studies have shown that most private Catholic and Protestant-affiliated schools do a better job educating children than public schools. A 1990 Rand Corporation study examined big-city high schools to find out how education for low-income minority children could be improved. The study compared thirteen New York City public, private, and Catholic high schools that had many minority students. In the Catholic schools, 75 to 90 percent of the students were black or hispanic. The study found that:

The Catholic high schools graduated 95 percent of their students each year, while public schools graduated slightly more 50 percent of their senior class; over 66 percent of the Catholic school graduates received the New York State Regents diploma to signify completion of an academically demanding college preparatory curriculum, while only about 5 percent of the public school students received this distinction; 85 percent of the Catholic high school students took the Scholastic Aptitude Test (SAT), compared with just 33 percent of the public school students; the Catholic school students achieved an average combined SAT score of 803, while the public school students' average combined SAT score was 642; and 60 percent of the Catholic school black students scored above the national average for black students on the SAT, and over 70 percent of public school black students scored below the same national average.[4]

Recent studies confirm many of the Rand report's findings. A 1997 study by Derek Neal, then associate professor of economics at the University of Chicago, analyzed the effect of Catholic high-school education on high-school and college graduation rates. Neal found that when inner-city students transferred to Catholic schools, their probability of graduating from high school increased from 62 percent to at least 88 percent. He also found that hispanic and black Catholic-school students were more than twice as likely to graduate college than minority students who attended public schools.

Protestant-affiliated-school students also consistently show superior academic results compared to public-school students. The National Center for Education Statistics (NAEP) administers the National Assessment of Educational Progress (NAEP) to test the knowledge and skills of the nation's students in grades 4, 8, and 12.

The NAEP's 2003 test results showed that students in the Protestant-affiliated schools (as well as Catholic-school students) consistently scored well above public-school students in math, reading, writing, history, and geography. At all three grade levels, a significantly higher percentage of Protestant-affiliated-school students scored at or above the *Basic, Proficient,* and *Advanced* levels compared to public-school students. Protestant-affiliated-school students also consistently scored higher on both verbal and math SAT scores compared to public-school students. Similarly, hispanic and black students in Protestant-affiliated schools were more than twice as likely to graduate college than low-income minority students who attended public schools.

Yet, the average annual tuition costs for Catholic and Protestant-affiliated schools for the 2002-2003 school year were about $3500-$4000 per elementary-school pupil and $5500-

$6000 per Secondary school pupil. The average public-school cost per pupil was approximately $7300.[5]

These studies show that Catholic and Protestant-affiliated schools give a superior education to public schools, especially for inner-city minority students. They give a better education at half the cost for elementary-grade students and about 30 percent lower cost for secondary or high-school students compared to public schools. Something is clearly wrong with public schools if they do an inferior job educating children for almost twice the cost of religiously-affiliated schools. Obviously, more money does not mean better education.

When we compare the academic record of home-schooled vs. public-school students, the cost vs. achievement differences are even more startling. In 1998, the Home School Legal Defense Association commissioned Larry Rudner, statistician and measurement expert at the University of Maryland, to do a study on the academic achievement levels of home-schooled students. The study tested 20,000 home-schooled students on the Iowa Test of Basic Skills (ITBS). The study found that home-schooled students did extremely well on the test compared to public-school students. Home-schooled kids scored in the 75th to 85th percentile range, compared with the 50th percentile national average for public-school students across the country.

The study also found that in every subject and grade level of the ITBS battery of tests, home-schooled students scored significantly higher than public and even private-school students. On average, home-schooled students in the first to fourth grades performed one grade level higher than comparable public and private-school students. By the fifth grade, the gap began to widen, and by the eighth grade, the average home-schooled student performed *four grade levels* [italics added] above the national average.[6]

Home-schooling parents not only give their kids a superior education, but spend on average far less than even Catholic or Protestant-affiliated schools to achieve these superior results. For example, Samuel Blumenfeld's excellent basic *Alpha-Pho-*

nics program (see Resources section) can help teach a child to read through several grade levels and currently costs about $30. Another good phonics program called *Turbo Reader*, written by Phyllis Schlafly, only costs about $50. Even if we assumed that an average home-schooling parent spent about $1500 a year on learning materials, that is less than one-quarter of what the average public school spends per student, and less than half the tuition cost at the average Catholic or Protestant-affiliated school. Clearly, once again, it is obvious that more money does not guarantee a better education for children.

Teacher Salaries

Another money-related excuse school authorities constantly use is that teachers allegedly aren't paid enough. To get good teachers and therefore better education for our kids, the argument goes, we need to pay teachers more. But salary statistics don't bear out this claim.

In 1998, Michael Antonucci of the Educational Intelligence Agency did research on teacher wages and found that teachers made more than the average worker in every state.

Mr. Antonucci's research found that:

• In Pennsylvania, teachers' wages exceeded other worker's wages by 65.2 percent—the biggest gap in the nation. In Washington D.C., which had the smallest gap, teachers still made 2.9 percent more than average workers.
• In Vermont, Rhode Island, Wisconsin, Oregon, and Alaska, teacher salaries exceeded the state's wage average by more than 50 percent. In Texas, teachers exceeded the average by 19 percent, and by 12.2 percent in Louisiana.
• With the exception of Texas and Louisiana, teachers' salaries exceeded state average wages by 25 percent or more.[7]

Teachers are not the only school employees who earn above-average wages. School janitors in New York City public schools got paid an average $57,000 a year in 1996, but had to mop the schools' floors only three times a year.[8]

More recent statistics tell the same story. An AFT (American Federation of Teachers) website press release noted that the average national salary for teachers was $44,367 for the 2001-2002 school year. Yet, according to the U.S. Bureau of Labor Statistic's National Compensation Survey (USBLS), the average annual salary in 2002 for all workers in this country, including blue-collar workers, was about $32,000.

The same 2002 USBLS survey also showed that public-school teachers' average hourly wage was about $31 an hour. Yet the average hourly wage was $26.64 for architects, $29.41 for metallurgical engineers, and $32.86 for computer systems analysts.[9] Engineers and computer systems analysts go through years of rigorous, difficult training, and need an extraordinary amount of specialized knowledge to do their job well. In contrast, public-school teachers get their psycho-babble alleged "training" in teacher colleges and often lack even rudimentary knowledge of the subjects they teach.

Not only that, public-school teachers get the entire summer off, so they only work about 185 days a year. In contrast, the average worker in private industry works about 230 days a year, yet gets a *lower* annual salary than teachers. Based on these facts, the claim that public-school teachers are underpaid is false. If the average worker in other occupations can do a good job for less money than teachers make, giving teachers even higher salaries than they now make would be an *insult* to every worker in private industry in this country.

We've previously noted that most Catholic and Protestant-affiliated schools give children a better education than most public schools. Yet the average annual Catholic-school teacher salary for the 2001-2002 school year was about $35,000,[10] compared to the average $44,367 a year public-school teachers made in 2002.[11] Obviously, if Catholic and Protestant-affiliated-school teachers do a better job educating children for less pay, public-school teachers have little justification in asking for higher salaries.

Also, why should mediocre or incompetent public-school employees get higher salaries if public schools keep failing our children? When parents pay school taxes, they expect to get their money's worth, as they should. They expect the schools to teach their children to read and not waste their time. They expect teachers to be competent and know the subject they teach. Yet too often that is not the case. Not only that, public schools do real damage to children's reading ability and self-confidence—they hurt the innocent customers they are supposed to teach.

If public schools do not perform the tasks parents pay them for, why should we pay teachers and principals even higher salaries than they get now? If you hired a roofer who couldn't fix the leak on your roof, should you pay him simply because he's a decent person with good intentions?

Again, it's not teachers' fault if they are ill-trained or don't know the subject they teach very well. As I noted earlier, the teacher-training system is the real culprit. Teachers can't teach what they never learned, and can't be competent if teacher colleges never taught them how to teach. However, parents should not have to sacrifice their children and pay school taxes to prop up an incompetent teacher-training system.

Giving more money to public schools doesn't make sense. If a drug addict came up to you on the street and asked for a hand-out, an addict who had approached you many times before, would you give him money? What if you knew that he spent every dollar you gave him on more drugs? Would you believe him when he insists that *this* time he will straighten out his life? Wouldn't you make his condition worse by feeding his habit? That is exactly the moral status of giving more money to public schools. Doing so gives them more money and power to cripple your children's education and waste their time.

Excuse #2 — Classes Are Too Large

School authorities often complain that classes are too large. They claim that teachers can't be expected to give their students the individual attention they need if there are too many students in the class. On the surface, this excuse seems to have some merit. Common sense tells us that in smaller classes, teachers can give more time and attention to each student.

However, many studies show that smaller class size does not guarantee that children get a better education. The pupil-to-teacher ratio in public schools in the mid-1960s was about 24 to 1. This ratio dropped to about 17 to 1 by the early 1990s, which means the average class size fell by 28 percent. Yet, during the same time period, SAT test scores fell from 954 to 896, a decline of 58 points or 6 percent.[12] In other words, student academic achievement (as measured by SAT scores) *dropped* at the same time that class sizes got smaller.

Eric Hanushek, a University of Rochester economist, examined 277 published studies on the effects of teacher-pupil ratios and class-size averages on student achievement. He found that only 15 percent of these studies showed a positive improvement in achievement with smaller class size, 72 percent found no statistically significant effect, and 13 percent found a negative effect on achievement.[13]

It seems to go against common sense that student academic achievement could drop with smaller class sizes. One reason this happens in public schools is that when class sizes drop, schools have to create more classes to cover all the students in the school. Schools then have to hire more teachers for the increased number of classes. However, public schools across the country are already having trouble finding qualified teachers to fill their classrooms. As a result, when reduced class sizes increase the need for more teachers, schools then often have to hire less-qualified teachers.

As we might expect, teacher quality is far more important than class size in determining how children do in school. William Sanders at the University of Tennessee studied this issue.

He found that teacher quality is almost twenty times more important than class size in determining students' academic achievement in class. As a result, reducing class sizes can lead to the contrary effect of hurting students' education, rather than helping.[14]

According to the U.S. Department of Education, class sizes in America range from seventeen to twenty-seven children, depending on the location and economic status of the school district. These class sizes are smaller than those in many other countries.[15] Another study from the U.S. Department of Education comparing class size in American schools to that in other countries showed that China and Taiwan have larger class sizes than our schools, yet their students do better than American kids in verbal and math test scores. According to Casey J. Lartigue, Jr., policy analyst with the Cato Institute's Center for Educational Freedom:

> Although American students lag behind other students in international testing, American classrooms have an average class size of 23 students [at the time of this study], incredibly few compared with the averages of 49 in South Korea, 44 in Taiwan, and 36 in Japan. Washington, D.C. has an average class size below the national average, yet ranks near the bottom in academic achievement.[16]

Similarly, a study on class size by policy analyst Jennifer Buckingham of the Sydney-based Center for Independent Studies found no reliable evidence that students in smaller classes do better academically or that teachers spend significantly more time with them in these classes. Buckingham concluded that a 20 percent class-size reduction cost the Australian government an extra $1,150 per student, yet added only an additional two minutes of instruction per day for each child.[17]

Reducing class sizes can't solve the underlying problems with public schools. No matter how small classes become, nothing will help if the teachers are ill-trained or their teaching methods are useless or destructive. For example, if teachers use whole-language reading instruction, they can cripple students' ability to read no matter how small the classes are. Even if classrooms had *one* teacher for every student, that child's ability to read could still be crippled if the teacher used whole-language instruction. In fact, smaller class sizes would give this teacher more time to do damage to each student.

Here's an analogy on this issue of class size vs. teaching methods: Suppose a horseback-riding instructor was teaching one little girl to ride. This instructor's teaching method was to tell the bewildered girl to sit backwards on the horse, facing the horse's rump, and control the horse by holding its tail. Does it matter that the student-teacher ratio in this horseback-riding class is one-to-one if the instructor is an idiot or uses bad teaching methods?

Excuse #3 — Working Moms, and Kids Watch Too Much TV

School authorities often claim that American children do poorly in school because they watch too much television or because they have working mothers. But these excuses don't hold water, either. Studies have shown that Japanese fifth-graders watch as much as or more television each day as American kids do.

Also, while an average of 35 percent of American mothers work full-time, so do 30 percent of mothers in Japan, 33 percent of mothers in Taipei, and 97 percent of mothers in Beijing.[18] Since Japanese, Taiwanese, and Chinese children consistently outperform American children on standardized tests, these excuses don't explain why American kids do so poorly in school.

Excuse #4 — Poverty

School authorities argue that public schools can't give inner-city kids a good education because poor parents have less time and resources to help their children in school. While it is certainly true that struggling poor parents often have to work longer hours to support their children, the facts do not support the poverty excuse. As I noted earlier, a 1990 Rand Corporation study of Catholic versus public schools in New York City confirmed the fact that poverty has little to do with academic achievement.[19]

A few inner-city public schools manage to give their students a better-than-normal education. These schools prove that poverty can't be used as an excuse for bad education. Samuel Casey Carter, researcher and Bradley Fellow of the Heritage Foundation, investigated twenty-one of these schools where low-income children received a better education than kids in other inner-city schools:

> Under principal Irwin Kurz, the 6th grade at P.S. 161 in Brooklyn, New York, has the second highest reading scores in all of New York State.
>
> KIPP Academy in Houston, Texas, under Michael Feinberg, is 95 percent low-income and 90 percent hispanic. Within one year, students who enter the middle school with passing rates of 35-50 percent on the state assessment test are passing by more than 90 percent in both math and reading.
>
> Seventy-eight percent of the students in Bennett-Kew Elementary in Inglewood, California are low-income. For 20 years, Nancy Ichinaga's school has been one of the highest performers in all of Los Angeles County.[20]

Carter found that these principals succeeded where most other public-school principals failed because they followed seven important rules in running their schools:

> 1) Effective principals are free to decide how to spend their money, whom to hire, and what to teach; 2) Effec-

tive principals use measurable goals to establish a culture of achievement; 3) Master teachers bring out the best in a faculty; 4) Rigorous and regular testing leads to continuous student achievement; 5) Discipline is anchored in achievement; 6) Effective principals work actively with parents to make the home a center of learning; 7) Effective principals require hard work.[21]

Many charter and private schools use these same education rules, which is why low-income minority kids succeed in these schools. In contrast, millions of low-income children fail in public schools because the schools don't apply these rules.

One more example will suffice to show that poverty is no excuse for most public schools' dismal performance. Harvard University did a two-year study of tuition-scholarship programs for minority children in New York, the District of Columbia, and Dayton, Ohio. Students were picked by lottery to receive the tuition scholarships. Low-income minority students who transferred to a private school from a public school soon did better in their studies.

Critics of previous tuition-scholarship studies where public-school students did better in a private school had claimed that students' performance could have improved because of other factors, such as motivation or family background. In the Harvard study, however, children were randomly assigned by lottery to private or public schools. As a result, neither poverty nor parents' motivation explained the difference in achievement.[22]

Excuse #5 — Parents Are AWOL From Their Children's Education

School authorities often complain that many parents are indifferent to their children's education. School officials often aim this charge at low-income minority parents. Teachers complain that many low-income minority parents don't come to parent-teacher conferences. They also claim that many parents don't show up for meetings the teachers arrange and don't respond to the messages teachers send home with the children.

However, low-income minority parents often complain just as passionately that teachers don't treat them with respect, that they give up on their children, and are only interested in collecting their paychecks.[23]

Teachers' complaints on this issue implies that black or hispanic parents don't value their children's education as much as white or asian-american parents do. Inner-city minority parents allegedly don't monitor their children's progress in reading and other subjects, push their children to do their homework, or meet with teachers to go over problems their kids are having in school. Without parents' cooperation, school authorities ask, how can we educate their children?

Who is right here? Are minority parents AWOL, and if so, why? If some low-income minority parents are AWOL, it is not because they don't love their children or want the best for them. It is because these parents believe that teachers and principals don't listen to them, don't respect them, and don't care about their kids.

The following scenario at a typical parent-teacher conference illustrates why some parents might go AWOL. Low-income minority and other parents who attend a conference might bitterly complain to the teachers and principal that their children can't read, and that the school is doing a lousy job teaching their kids.

In turn, to defend themselves, the teachers will give these parents their list of excuses. They might explain to the allegedly uninformed parents that teachers are the experts, and that their teaching methods are based on the latest scientific research. If parents press them, they might claim that it is the parent's or child's fault for the child's continuing failure. Or they might tell parents that their kids have been getting passing grades, so why complain. But the parents might then respond, "but my kids can't read!"

If parents tell teachers and the principal that they want the school to change its teaching methods, do you think it will? If parents insist they want their children to learn to read with the phonics method instead of whole-language instruction, many principals will probably say it is out of the question. They will say that school authorities set the curriculum and tell him to use whole-language instruction. *Parents have no choice or power in the matter.* That is the message many teachers and principals will convey to them.

Many teachers don't know *how* to teach phonics anymore —their so-called teacher colleges never taught them. Principals have to obey the orders of their superiors in the local or state Board of Education who insist they use the whole-language method. If schools had to teach phonics reading, that would require complete retraining of teachers. Most school authorities with tight budgets are just not interested.

So the teachers and principal at this "friendly" parent-teacher conference often politely look down their noses at parents and tell them, in effect, to buzz off. They say or imply that they know what is best for their children's education, and they will make no changes in how they teach their kids.

In a parent-teacher's conference, the school's final argument with parents is, in effect, a gun. That is, compulsory-attendance laws force low-income minority parents to send their children to these schools, and school authorities can dictate what and how children learn. Remember that teachers and principals are tenured civil servants who are almost impossible to fire, and they know this. In response to every frustrated demand and complaint by parents, teachers and principals can simply say, "Too bad, we're doing it our way, and you can't do anything about it." They may not use those exact words, but that is the underlying message.

Parents quickly learn that their complaints fall on deaf ears. If a school refuses to act on parents' complaints or give parents some control over their children's education, naturally parents feel helpless. No matter how many parent-teacher conferences they go to, parents can't change the system in any meaningful way, and it is the *system* that betrays their children. Teachers and principals are just little cogs in the system's machinery. They can't change the system, even if they wanted to. So low-income minority and other parents see that no matter how much they complain, nothing changes. Isn't it understandable why they might go AWOL, why they might give up? Wouldn't you?

Here is one parent's experience with parent-teacher meetings as described in *Education Week* magazine:

> Parents are welcome in the building for the traditional cookie-bake fund-raiser. But when PIE [Partners in Education], our Nyack group [Nyack, NY], organized 30 volunteers to read aloud to children, they were not welcome. The program was arranged with the principal and teachers through the shared decision-making team. But once district employees realized this meant parents would be inside—with a chance to see how the school worked—the program was nixed. I don't believe ours is the only district with a tendency to see parents as spies. . . . Parents are welcome in the building—but not for too long.[24]

Another reason many parents may go AWOL is because they think public schools are free. There's a simple law of human psychology that says, *when you pay, you pay attention.* When we pay for something out of our own pockets, we become careful consumers. This applies even more to low-income families or single, working mothers. A single, working mom might work longer hours or take on a second job to pay the bills. Her hard-earned money is precious to her, so she can't afford to waste a penny. If she pays tuition to a Catholic or Protestant-affiliated school for her child, she is far more likely to watch like a hawk how the school is teaching her children. She will constantly check how her children progress in reading and other subjects. She doesn't have a second chance with her children's education because she doesn't have much money to spare.

As a result, she will push her children to study, do their homework, and listen to the teacher. She will encourage her children and consult with their teachers. She knows her hard-earned money and her children's only chance at a future will go down the drain if she does not pay attention to her children's education.

In contrast, low-income parents who think public schools are free because they don't pay school taxes, are less likely to pay attention to their children's progress in school. That's because of another law of human psychology—*if you don't pay for it, you don't value it as much.* Low-income parents who don't own a home and don't pay property taxes aren't losing their tax money if their children's public school does a lousy job. Of course, most parents will be angry with the schools because they love their children and want the best for them, but for low-income minority parents, the financial sting is gone. Low-income parents who don't pay school taxes for public-school education might value it less, so might pay less attention to their children's progress.

Yet another law of human psychology applies in this matter —*if you don't pay for it, you don't think you have the right to complain.* If a stranger gives you something for free, you probably won't complain if there's something wrong with it. If parents think public schools are free, many might think they have no right to complain. They may think that because the education is free, whatever their children learn is better than nothing. If those same parents pay school tuition for a private school with their hard-earned money, they complain loud and clear if the school doesn't teach their children to read.

Another question is why public schools need all these parent-teacher conferences in the first place. Sure, parents getting involved in their kids' education is a good thing and can only help their children learn better. Home-schooling parents know this first hand. However, if you paid a tutor to teach your child to read, you expect him to know his job and earn his pay. If school authorities were the education experts they claim to be, why do they need so much help from parents?

Children are learning machines. They *love* learning—that's their nature. Learning is wired into their brains. You only have to watch young children at play to confirm this truth. If children are passionate learners, why do public schools constantly need parents' cooperation to push their kids to learn?

When children find something that interests them, no one has to push them to learn. In fact, kids constantly ask their parents hundreds of questions, and love when their mothers or fathers teach them a new skill such as cooking or riding a bike. Millions of kids today are more computer literate than the average public-school teacher. I've seen articles about young children who were teaching their teachers how to use the computer. When most children learn a new skill they enjoy, they don't need much parent involvement. Children often become so absorbed in their new toys or skills that they forget all about their parents, until mom calls them to dinner.

When children go to summer camp, they learn boating, archery, baseball, drawing, dancing, and camping skills. Do the camp counselors constantly call parents and ask for their help to get the kids to learn these skills? No. If anything, there is only one parent-visiting day the whole summer when kids show their parents all the exciting new things they've learned, *without* the parent's involvement.

When self-motivated high-school graduates go to the college of their choice to study something they love, do college professors constantly whine that they need parent involvement? Do the professors tell parents to nag their children to study and do their homework? No. If anything, parents complain that their college kids don't call them enough and only see them on holidays.

When children constantly need parental involvement to learn, *something is terribly wrong.* As John Holt, author of *How Children Fail,* pointed out, what is wrong is that public schools strangle children's innate love of learning. In public school, passing the next test is the goal, not learning anything useful or interesting. Each child's unique interests, strengths, and weaknesses are ignored for the sake of covering the material and making sure kids pass the standardized tests. Children must sit in a class for six to eight hours a day and learn boring facts that don't interest them from often ill-trained or mediocre teachers.

Is it any wonder that public schools can't keep children interested, and cripple their natural passion to learn? That is why teachers and principals constantly complain that they need more parent cooperation and involvement. The schools wreck children's love of learning, so they try to enlist parents to help undo the damage.

Low-income minority parents do not want to be AWOL. In fact, they fight for school choice because public schools hurt their children the most, and because they have the least options. George A. Clowes wrote in *School Reform News*, "African-Americans are no longer willing to accept that poverty and dysfunctional families are the reasons black children cannot learn. Black parents are demanding that their children be taught to read, write, compute, analyze, think."[25]

When the free market gives parents real school choice, these formerly AWOL parents become involved parents. Theodore J. Forstmann and his business partner John Walton are successful entrepreneurs with a passion for helping children get an education. They created a multimillion-dollar, private scholarship program called the Children's Scholarship Fund. Forstmann and Walton pledged $100 million of their own money to fund 40,000 scholarships for kids trapped in the worst public schools. With the help of other prominent business leaders and celebrities such as Oprah Winfrey, they raised another $70 million in matching funds. They made these scholarships open to low-income families across America.[26]

The demand for these scholarships was explosive, especially from low-income minority parents. These are the same parents that principals and teachers claim are AWOL from their kids' education. Forstmann's program received over 1,250,000 applications. In many areas, huge blocks of the eligible population applied: 26 percent in Chicago; 29 percent in New York, 33 percent in Washington, D.C., and 44 percent in Baltimore.

In his September, 1999 testimony before the U.S. House of Representative's House Committee on the Budget, Forstmann pointed out that the incredible demand for his scholarships revealed a huge dissatisfaction with our public schools, and the need for alternatives.[27]

In short, many parents go AWOL from public schools because they have little control over their kid's education, the schools keep failing their children, and no matter how much they complain, nothing changes. When these same parents get school choice, all of a sudden they spend lots of time and energy on their children's education.

Excuse #6 — It's Society's Fault

School authorities often blame "society," meaning the American economic and political system, for the public schools' continuing failure. They say that society makes it hard for parents, especially low-income parents, to do the right thing for their kids. Bob Chase, former National Education Association (NEA) president, noted this point in his November 16, 2001 speech before the National Press Club. He spoke about the time-crunch problem many parents faced. He referred to surveys and interviews in which parents consistently say they want to be more involved in their children's education, but that employers don't give them the time to do so.

The reason for this time crunch, according to Mr. Chase, was that many unskilled or low-income minority parents work long hours for low wages, especially single mothers. Because they often have to work two jobs just to pay the bills, many single mothers don't have time to attend parent-teacher conferences or to keep up with their children's educational progress.

Mr. Chase talked about employers who don't give single mothers paid leave, flextime, or day-care benefits so they can have more time for their children. So society, in the form of uncooperative employers (or allegedly needed laws that would force employers to be more cooperative), creates this time crunch for parents. Without employers' cooperation in this matter, the argument goes, parents don't have the time to give schools the backing and cooperation that teachers need.[28]

This argument doesn't hold up under scrutiny. As we will see in Chapter 8, the average parent needs to spend only two to three hours a day home-schooling their children to give their kids a great education. Most working parents or even single moms could manage this if they schedule their time right. So employers don't necessarily have to give parents flextime or paid leaves for parents to give their kids an excellent education at home.

For over two hundred years in this country, before public schools became entrenched by the 1890s, families of hard-working farmers, craftsmen, and even laborers managed to teach their children to read at home. Colonial farmers and laborers often worked from sun-up to sun-down, but still managed to find the time to teach their children to read, write, and do arithmetic. These parents didn't blame "society." They just made sure they found the time to educate their kids.

Paul Barton, working for the Educational Testing Service, conducted a 1993 study called "America's Smallest School: The Family." Barton found that one of the important factors determining a child's educational performance was the presence or absence of two parents in the home. As evidence, he pointed out that North Dakota ranked first in math scores and second in the percentage of children in two-parent families, while the District of Columbia ranked next to last in math scores and last in two-parent families (meaning that it had the most single-parent homes).[29]

Barton's study reflects a disturbing trend—American family stability has indeed declined badly over the last fifty years. George Will, one of our most thoughtful syndicated columnists, pointed out in one of his columns that the percentage of children born to unmarried women in 1958 was 5 percent. In 1980, it was 18 percent. By 1999, it was 33 percent. In 1999, 48.4 percent of all children born to women of all races and ethnic background, ages twenty to twenty-four were born out of wedlock.[30]

However, this explosion of single-mother families does not

explain or justify public school's never-ending failure. Neither do the long hours that low-income parents, single or married, must work. As noted earlier, if public schools knew their job, they would not need constant parental involvement. Also, children of these same hard-working mothers suddenly become much better students if they are lucky enough to transfer to a private school. In spite of poverty, society, or their uncooperative bosses, these parents push their kids to succeed in a Catholic or Protestant-affiliated private school. The fact that single mothers often work long hours has little to do with public-school failure.

Excuse #7 — If We Allow School Choice, Public Schools Will Be Destroyed

Public-school defenders often argue that school choice would destroy the public schools. Almost 90 percent of children in this country attend public schools. If we had vouchers, no compulsory-attendance laws, and an unregulated education free market, millions of parents might transfer their children to private schools. This would drain hundreds of millions of tax dollars from public schools. Those children left behind in the shriveled public schools would then get an even worse education than they do now. Therefore, the argument goes, we have to fight school choice to protect the public schools.

School authorities use the same argument against charter schools. They claim that charter schools, like vouchers, divert millions of taxpayer dollars from regular public schools and can therefore undermine these schools.[31]

In effect, public-school apologists argue that despite their schools' never-ending failure and betrayal of our children, we should just keep using the same old failed solutions—spend more money, hire more teachers, and reduce class sizes—and hope we get better results (which of course we never will).

In the meantime, what happens to forty-five million children forced to suffer through eight to twelve years of public school? School authorities don't seem to care about what happens to children who are forced to stay. Instead, they care far more about what happens to the public-school *system* if children are free to leave. By this reasoning, no matter how bad the schools get, we must not help children escape these failed schools because that might threaten the system. The question therefore is, *do our children exist to serve the system, or should our education system exist to serve our children?*

Asking a parent to keep her child in public school when she has a chance to give her child a better education in a private or charter school, is absurd and immoral. It is like asking a parent to tell her child not to escape from a prison or concentration camp because it would upset the warden. Parents' first priority is to protect their children and give them the best possible chance in life, not to worry about a rotten public-school system. Parents and their children are not sacrificial animals. Why should a parent care more about protecting the jobs of public-school employees than the welfare of her child?

Moreover, if millions of parents took their children out of public school, they would be doing a great service to the children remaining behind, *not* a disservice. If all parents kept their kids in public school to "protect" the system, they would simply be helping to perpetuate the system. By taking their children out of public school, parents voice their protest *against* the system. If enough parents vote with their feet, the public schools might shut down from lack of students. This would greatly benefit all parents and their children. Parents would then find alternative education options in the free market that could give their kids a quality, low-cost education.

The argument that vouchers and charter schools might destroy the public schools is therefore one of the *best* arguments *for* school choice. Government-controlled public schools, not school choice, cripples our children's education and future, and banishes millions of inner-city kids to a lifetime of poverty and ignorance. We need to scrap the public school system once and for all, and the sooner the better.

Excuse #8 — The "Diversity" Problem

American classrooms, especially those in big cities like New York and Los Angeles, are filled with children from many diverse ethnic groups speaking different languages. School authorities claim that this diversity makes teaching these children an almost superhuman task.

It is certainly true that America has a diverse population, especially in big cities, but public schools are not the solution to educating these children. Any immigrant child who does not speak English will have a difficult time in school, just as an American child whose parents moved to Japan or Turkey would have a hard time in Japanese or Turkish public schools because he or she couldn't speak the language.

So the first order of business for these children is to learn the language of their new country. Immigrant parents naturally expect their children to learn English. Yet look who we give this crucial job to—public schools, the same schools that can barely teach *American* kids to read. Public schools are the *worst* place to teach English to non-English-speaking children, for many reasons:

First, these children get stuck with maybe twenty other kids in the class, including children from other cultures who speak different languages. It is almost impossible for even the most competent English as a Second Language (ESL) teacher to handle this diversity. These children need intense one-on-one instruction designed for their specific language to get them quickly up to speed.

Second, public-school classes lump together children of different learning abilities. Out of alleged fairness, teachers often gear instruction to slower-learning students. Students who want to learn faster get bored and may take out their frustration on non-English speaking or slower children. The non-English speaking students can be shamed and humiliated by the other kids (children can be cruel). This treatment can cripple these children's self-confidence and make them hate school and learning.

Third, as we saw in previous chapters, public-school children often get stuck with poorly-trained teachers. This is especially true in low-income minority neighborhoods that are more likely to have many non-English-speaking immigrant children.

Fourth, many public schools teach reading with whole-language instruction, not phonics. As we saw in Chapter 3, this reading method is an unmitigated disaster. Whole-language instruction used alone turns non-immigrant *American* children into functional illiterates with dismal reading-test scores. To use this same method to try to teach non-English-speaking immigrant children to read English is absurd. For all the reasons indicated above, public schools are the *last* place we should be sending immigrant children to learn English.

Many public schools try to solve this diversity problem with bilingual education classes. The schools teach non-English-speaking kids reading, writing, math, and other subjects in their native language for sometimes up to four years while the children learn English through assimilation. There is a lot of controversy surrounding bilingual education. Advocates say it lets kids keep up with their studies while gradually learning English. Opponents say these classes retard immigrant children's academic growth by not forcing them to learn English sooner.

In 1998, California's successful Proposition 227 initiative eliminated bilingual classes and instead mandated "English Immersion" programs for hispanic and other non-English-speaking students. In these programs, all instruction is in English and geared specifically to teaching students English as fast as possible. Some studies have shown this method to be successful in helping immigrant children develop fluent conversational English in one to two years.

Even without these programs, young immigrant children often become fluent in conversational English in this same time period. They do this by assimilating into the culture and learning from other immigrant members of their community who have been in America longer and learned the language.[32]

If young immigrant children can learn basic conversational English in this relatively short time period, then the diversity excuse does not hold water. Once these kids learn to speak English, they are in a similar position to American students who are learning to read from scratch. At this point, the serious disadvantages of public-school instruction kick in, and the immigrant kids are stuck with the same public schools American children have to suffer with.

The only system that can effectively handle diversity is the *free market*. The problem can be solved if private companies or former immigrants who now speak English set up local schools in their neighborhoods. If Chinese, Indian, Spanish, Italian, or Vietnamese entrepreneurs, churches, or social organizations opened local schools to teach new immigrants English, the problem would be quickly solved.

Why don't we see more of these local schools in immigrant neighborhoods? One reason is that many immigrants struggle financially when they first come here, so allegedly "free" public schools seem like a better deal than paying tuition to a local private school. However, if we scrapped the public schools, the explosive demand for English-instruction schools would push local entrepreneurs to open such schools. As long as "free" public schools are around, local entrepreneurs have little incentive to risk their money opening private schools in low-income neighborhoods.

Excuse #9 — Education Is Too Important to Be Left to the Free Market

The notion that we need public schools because education is too important to be left to the free market is one of the strangest excuses public-school apologists invent. On the contrary, I would argue that the exact opposite is true. Education of precious children is too important to be left in the hands of failing schools that never shut down no matter how bad they are, and public-school employees who are almost impossible to fire no matter how ill-trained they are. Only the free market can give kids the superb education they deserve.

Many public-school authorities either distrust the free market or don't have the faintest idea how it works. Yet, they live in a free-market economy that gives them the highest standard of living in human history. These people live in big, clean houses on paved streets. They have cars, computers, televisions, refrigerators, electric lights, indoor plumbing, supermarkets full of fresh food, airlines to whisk them away to vacations in the Bahamas, and modern antibiotics that can save their lives. All these marvels are products of the free market.

However, public-school employees' jobs depend on keeping the public-school system intact. To justify their tenure-guaranteed jobs and power, they must loudly defend the public schools and attack school choice and free-market education.

In October 1995, Pepsi company officials announced in front of Jersey City Hall that Pepsi would donate thousands of dollars into a scholarship fund that helped low-income kids attend a private school of their choice. What was the immediate response of the local teachers' union? They threatened the possibility of a statewide boycott of all Pepsi products. Three weeks after their announcement, Pepsi company officials withdrew their scholarship offer.[33]

Why would a teachers' union do this? As we noted earlier, teacher unions and many school employees view private or government vouchers as a threat to their jobs and the public-school system. Vouchers allow children to leave failed public schools and take tax money with them. Teacher unions don't want to deliberately hurt children, but to protect their system at all costs, they try to chain students to the wretched public schools by fighting vouchers.

School authorities claim that children's minds and futures should not be left in the hands of potentially dishonest, commercial, for-profit schools. To school authorities, making a profit seems to be incompatible with giving kids a good education.

Yet, most of the wonderful, time-saving, often life-saving

products and services we buy in the free market are produced by for-profit companies. Take food, for example. As a basic necessity of life, food is more important than education. Without food, we die. Without education, we only lack knowledge. Would school authorities say that food production is too important to be left in the hands of the free market? Should we close down all our for-profit supermarkets and local grocery stores? Should local governments own and operate all farms and supermarkets, as the Soviet government did in communist Russia?

The Soviet Union tried government-controlled collectivized farms for seventy years. The end result was seventy years of perpetual famine. Meanwhile, for-profit American farmers produced so much food that they exported millions of tons of wheat to the Soviets every year. In fact, American farmers produce so much food that federal bureaucrats now pay them subsidies to *not* grow food in order to prop up farm prices.

Do public-school authorities claim that for-profit farms, supermarkets, and local grocers do a bad job giving us fresh food every day? I think not, because we do not hear teachers, principals, or school administrators clamoring for socialization of food production in this country. They don't do so because for-profit farms and supermarkets make their lives better by giving them a huge variety of fresh food at reasonable prices. If we ever socialized food production in this country, I believe public-school employees would scream bloody murder because they would hate the rotten food and lousy service in the new government-run food stores.

Yet, when it comes to our government-controlled *education* system, public-school authorities and employees defend the system to the death. One reason they may do so is because they *personally benefit* by the system, so are willing to turn a blind eye to its failures and overlook the damage it does to millions of school children.

As I noted in Chapter 1, public schools only became fully entrenched and compulsory in this country by the 1890s. Before then, for over 200 years, our education system was voluntary and mostly free-market. Parents were free to educate their kids at home or at relatively inexpensive local grammar schools, religious schools, or colleges. Education was widespread, literacy rates were over 90 percent in the major cities, and parents had complete control over their children's education. The free-market education system worked great before public schools came along.

We also have a thriving education free-market in our preschools and colleges right now. Millions of parents pay for and enroll their kids in thousands of these schools and colleges across the country. Parents are free to choose which pre-school, kindergarten, or college is best for their kids, and can easily change schools if they are not satisfied with its performance. Most parents appreciate the choice and quality these schools offer. If the free market can give kids a great pre-school, kindergarten, or college education, there is no reason it cannot also give us a superb 1st through 12th grade education system if public schools were privatized.

Japan has proved how effective an education free-market can be. It has a thriving, multi-billion-dollar education industry called *juku* schools. These are private, for-profit "after-school" schools that Japanese children start as early as the first grade. The schools are so popular that by the fifth grade, 30 percent of students attend a *juku* school. In 1991, it was found that over half of eighth-graders and an estimated 70 percent of ninth-graders attended these schools. A Tokyo survey found that 90 percent of students had studied at a *juku* by the time they advanced to the ninth grade.[34]

Why do millions of Japanese parents send their children to private *juku* schools? In Japan, competition is intense to get into the most prestigious universities because students who attend these universities get the best jobs after graduating. Entry into these universities strictly depends on admission-test scores.

In general, Japanese public schools give children a better and more disciplined education than our schools. However, Japanese parents who want their children to get into the best

universities are often not satisfied with their children's public-school education. Parents send their kids to *juku* schools
for three primary reasons. They want to improve their child's
chances on high-stakes entrance exams, get remedial help for a
child who is falling behind in public school, or give their child
more advanced instruction if the child is a fast-learner and is
not challenged by public-school instruction.

The *juku* system is huge, vibrant, and fiercely competitive
because there is such a big demand for these schools. Instead
of forcing a one-size-fits-all curriculum on all students, these
schools cater to the needs of individual students and parents
who are their *customers*. They ask what parents and students
want and need, and design their curriculums and teaching
methods accordingly. In *juku* schools the parent-customer is
king, not the public-school employees.

The *juku* schools test students before admission to discover
their current academic skill levels. Then, unlike public schools
in America, they group students by *ability*, not age, so class
instruction can be specifically geared to students' individual
needs and abilities. Also, the schools don't allow slower students to be "warehoused," as that would be bad for business.
Instead, school administrators give frequent tests to determine
each student's progress and then revise their curriculum or
teaching methods to ensure that each student gets the exact
kind and level of instruction he or she needs.

Slower students are therefore not embarrassed or humiliated in class as they are in America's public schools that group
children by age, not ability. Also, faster-learning students can
study more challenging material and progress more quickly in
their studies.

Teachers have a special and highly honored place in the
juku system. There are no hiring or licensing restrictions for
teachers as there are in Japanese public schools. The teachers
come from many backgrounds. Some of them are professional
educators, but many others are scientists, economists, college
professors, other professionals, and even college students who
like to teach. The fierce free-market competition between *juku*

schools forces school owners to hire the best teachers they can find and dismiss those who are ill-trained or incompetent. The juku system is also good for Japanese teachers. They enjoy giving individualized instruction to motivated students. Good teachers are appreciated both by their employers and parents. Their salaries are based on *performance*, not how long they have been teaching. Also, some top *juku* teachers who are in high demand earn as much as professional Japanese baseball players. Public-school teachers in America should take special note of this fact. It shows that a competitive free-market education system could give them high status and huge financial rewards if they do a great job educating children. [35]

Excuse #10 — For-Profit Schools Are Unaccountable to Taxpayers

School authorities often defend public schools because they claim the schools are accountable to the public. In contrast, they attack private schools for being allegedly unaccountable to taxpayers. They claim that private-school owners, unlike public schools, don't have to open their records or their decision-making process to the general public. For-profit schools, they point out, are not subject to the Freedom of Information acts and don't have to hold open public meetings about their policies. Private schools also don't have to publicize student test scores, dropout rates, or their financial status.[36]

These facts are true, but that does not make private schools unaccountable to the public. The absence of government oversight does not affect the general quality of education in for-profit schools, or the quality of most other products we buy in the free market. Would school authorities claim that most private airlines, homebuilders, or supermarkets sell bad products because they don't have to open their books to the public?

Of course there are always some mediocre companies who sell inferior products or services. However, the free-market system eventually rids itself of such businesses. An airline that has many crashes, a homebuilder whose houses fall apart in a few years, or a supermarket that sells rotten, high-priced food, will soon go out of business because of fierce competition. Only businesses that give customers consistent value and accountability over the long term—quality products at reasonable prices—will last in a competitive free market.

Private schools may not have to open their records or decision-making process to the public, but neither do car manufacturers, homebuilders, or supermarkets. All customers care about is if the car or house is well constructed, and the supermarket sells fresh food at a reasonable price. Customers care about *results*, not about the dubious privilege of looking into a company's records. Likewise, private schools have to satisfy their parent-customers. Private-school owners are accountable to parents because they know if they do a bad job and parents withdraw their children from their schools, *they will go bankrupt.*

Moreover, open school records do not in themselves guarantee accountability. In many public schools, records have been distorted because tests and coursework are often dumbed-down and grades manipulated to make a good impression on parents. What good are "open" records, if you can't trust the people who created those records?

Even if parents had access to true student achievement records in public schools, that record is often dismal, as we saw in Chapter 1. What does it matter if schools' records are open to the public, if the schools can barely teach children to read? What is more important to parents, good record keeping or good teaching and academic results?

Despite appearances to the contrary, public schools are wholly *unaccountable* to taxpayers—the customers who pay teachers' salaries and school upkeep. These schools could not have stayed in business after committing education negligence on millions of children for the past fifty years, if they were accountable to parents.

Public schools are unaccountable to parents because they work by compulsion. Parents can't tell school authorities what or how to teach their kids. They have little control over the moral values the schools teach their children. They can't sue these schools for educational fraud and negligence. They can't refuse to pay school taxes to support these schools. It is public schools, not private schools, that are unaccountable to parents.

If public schools had to depend on voluntary contributions from parents, most of them would soon be out of business. That is why school authorities fight tooth and nail to deny school choice to parents—they want to *stay* unaccountable to the public they allegedly serve.

Excuse #11 — For-Profit Schools and Vouchers Would Lead to Segregated Schools

Public-school apologists claim that we need these schools to prevent education from becoming segregated again. They claim that school choice would create a separate-and-unequal system of segregated schools. Yet current enrollments in Catholic schools don't support this assertion. Since 1970, the percentage of minorities in Catholic schools has more than doubled to 26 percent. For the 2003 school year, 11.2 percent of students were hispanic, 7.8 percent black, 3.7 percent asian-american, and 2.0 percent multiracial.[37]

Just as for-profit supermarkets serve black, hispanic, asian-american, and other minorities, for-profit schools, both secular and religious, accept students of every race and color. Like most other businesses, the color most private schools are interested in is green, the color of money. If these schools reject eligible applicants because of their race, they only reduce their profits and hurt themselves.

In contrast, many public schools are as segregated today as Southern schools were before the civil-rights movement in the 1960s, particularly in poor, inner-city urban areas like Chicago and New York City. The wholesale failure of our public-school system has helped create thousands of segregated schools throughout the country. The Civil Rights Project at Harvard's

Graduate School of Education found that:

> 70 percent of the nation's black students now attend predominantly minority public schools, with 36 percent of the nation's black students attending schools with a minority enrollment of 90 to 100 percent. Researcher Jay Greene found in a national study that 55 percent of children in public schools attended classes where 90 percent of students came from a single ethnic group. In comparison, 41 percent of private school students attended schools with similar conditions. The alleged resegregation caused by school choice is occurring in places where vouchers are still just a rumor.[38]

Public schools resegregate because they continually fail low-income minority students. Inner-city, low-income parents who work hard to move up the economic ladder, quickly relocate and move to middle-class suburban neighborhoods to find better schools for their kids. This process leaves behind poor minority families, and low-income neighborhoods then become even more segregated. This resegregation is reflected in the local public schools, where neighborhoods with 90 to 100 percent black or hispanic residents then have public schools with 90 to100 percent black or hispanic students. Also, the lack of real school choice for low-income minority parents means that students have no alternative but to attend these segregated and often violent public schools.

Excuse #12 — The Right to an Education

One of the most common arguments school authorities use to justify public schools is that all children have a right to an education. Public-school apologists claim that all children have a right to the best education possible regardless of their parents' ability to pay.

As I will explain below, the claim that all children have a

right to an education actually *hurts* the children it was intended to help. I must therefore ask a seemingly shocking question—*do all children have a right to an education?* If they do, public-school apologists are correct in assuming that we need government to guarantee that right.

An economic "right" means that a person has an alleged claim on the rest of society (other Americans) to give him some product or service he wants, regardless of whether he can pay for it or not. For example, if we claimed that everyone has a right to a car, that would mean if someone couldn't afford a car, government would give that person the money to buy it (the payment might be called a car voucher).

Similarly, if we say that all children have a right to an education, regardless of their parent's ability to pay tuition, then only government can guarantee this alleged right. Government has to guarantee this right because no private, for-profit school will admit a student if the parents don't pay tuition (unless the student gets a scholarship). This is not because of "greed" or "selfishness," but because of simple economic reality—if a private school doesn't get paid for its services, it soon goes out of business.

Local or state governments can guarantee this alleged right in two basic ways. They can own and operate all the public schools and force all children to attend these schools, or they can give subsidies (vouchers) to parents to pay for tuition in the private school of their choice. Most school authorities strongly oppose vouchers. That means they support only a government-controlled system of compulsory public schools and school taxes to guarantee children this alleged right to an education.

But government produces nothing by itself, including education. Government gets its money by taxing us. To guarantee this alleged right to a product or service, government tax collectors must therefore take money from one person to give it to another. They must take from Peter to pay Paul, as the saying goes. So, in effect, a person who demands food, housing, or medical care as an alleged right, is really demanding that government tax agents take money from his neighbor to give him an unearned benefit he didn't work for.

Education, like housing or medical care, does not grow free in nature. Just as someone must pay doctors, nurses, and hospitals for all the services they provide, someone must also pay for teachers' salaries, textbooks, janitorial services, and school upkeep. Other than air, nothing that we need is free.

The average public school now gets about $7,300 a year per student, paid from taxes. To guarantee education as a right, local, state, and federal governments must tax all Americans to pay for these schools. All of us are taxed, whether or not we have school-age children or think these schools are worth paying for. So when some parents claim that their children have a right to an education, they are really demanding that their local or state government steal money from their neighbors to pay for their children's education.

Here's an analogy that might help clarify this issue. Imagine that your unemployed neighbor comes to you and asks you to lend him money to pay for his children's education. You reply that you sympathize with his problem, but your answer is no. He responds by saying that he is poor, points out that you have a big house and a job, and insists that his children have a "right" to an education. You say, "Sorry, my answer is still no because I need my money for my own children's education." Suppose that your neighbor then gets real mad, pulls out a gun, puts it to your head, and says, "I asked you nicely. I told you my children need an education. You have a job, and I'm unemployed, so you have a *moral duty* to give me your money." Then he clicks back the hammer on the gun.

Obviously your neighbor has no right to put a gun to your head and steal your money because his children need an education. Nor does he, or any number of your neighbors, have the right to rob you by getting government to be their enforcer— by pressuring local governments to take your money through school taxes. Any school system that uses compulsory taxes is a system based on the notion that theft is moral if it's for a "good" cause. No goal, not even educating children justifies, in effect, legalized theft.

It is only natural that all parents want the best education for their children, but do good intentions justify stealing from your neighbor? A mugger on the street who puts a knife to your throat and demands your money also has good intentions— he wants to make his life better with your money. One of the Ten Commandments says, "Thou shalt not steal." It does not say, "Thou shalt not steal, except if you need tuition money to educate your child." Since no one has a right to steal from his neighbor, no one, including children, has a "right" to an education.

Some might argue that I may be correct on this issue when it comes to adults, but surely we can't punish innocent children for their parent's failures? Just because parents are poor or un-employed, why should innocent children suffer and be denied an education? The answer to that question is one that many people find hard to accept, yet it is true—*there are no guarantees in life*, not for adults or for children. Good intentions to allevi-ate a problem do not justify hurting other people by stealing from them. Two wrongs do not make a right.

Moreover, if we agree that children have a right to an edu-cation because their parents are poor, then shouldn't they also have a right to food, a bicycle, a nice house in the suburbs, and a *college* education? If poor kids (and all children) have an alleged right to an education, don't they also have an alleged right to everything else that other kids have whose parents are well-off? Why not then say that anyone, poor, middle-class, or rich who has less money than his neighbor, has the "right" to steal from his neighbor? *Where do we stop* if some people can legally steal from others because they claim their kids need this or that?

The answer is, we don't stop, and we haven't stopped. That is why our country has turned into a welfare state that is drown-ing in debt. When I use the word "welfare," I don't mean only for the poor. Rich, poor, and middle-class alike in America now claim the right to everything from corporate tax breaks and subsidies, to price supports for farmers, to Medicare, to rent subsidies for unwed mothers. When we let government steal money from taxpayers to give unearned benefits or subsidies to special-interest groups, we open up a Pandora's box. We become a nation of thieves stealing from each other. Is this what we want America to become?

It is true that a free market does not and can not guarantee that all children have enough to eat or live in a comfortable house. Likewise, a free-market education system in which all parents have to pay for their children's education obviously can't guarantee a quality education for every child.

However, government-controlled public schools *also* can't guarantee that every child gets a quality education. These failed schools can barely teach our children to read. Also, neither system can make guarantees because there are no guarantees in life, and because each child's abilities, personality, and family background are so different that such guarantees are impossible. The real question, then, is not which system is *perfect*, but which system is more likely to give the vast majority of children a quality education that most parents could afford?

We have seen how public schools fail and betray millions of children, year after year. The only "right" most public schools give to school children is the right to suffer through a mind-numbing, third-rate education for twelve years.

In contrast, the free-market, while not perfect, gives us all the wondrous goods and services we buy every day, such as cars, fresh food, computers, refrigerators, and televisions. If we want to discover which system would give the vast majority of children a quality education at reasonable prices, I think we have the answer—the free market, hands down.

We therefore don't need a failed public-school system to enforce an alleged right to an education, when there is no such right in the first place. Each parent should be responsible for paying for their own children's education, just as they pay for their children's food or clothing.

Finally, public-school apologists use this alleged right to an education to justify keeping our public schools alive, in spite of these schools' never-ending failure. Many of those who claim that children have a right to an education do so out of good intentions. They want to give all children a chance to get a decent education. But, once again, good intentions mean *worse than nothing* if they lead to evil consequences. This alleged right to an education is used to prop up our public-school system, a system that, as we've seen, has caused and continues to cause irreparable harm to millions of children.

Low-income families today can buy quality, low-cost food in a competitive, free-market food industry full of grocery stores and supermarkets. In the same way, once compulsory public schools are out of the way, most children would be able to get a quality, low-cost education in a competitive free-market education system (I will discuss how the free-market can help parents in detail in Chapters 8, 9, and the Resources section).

Excuse #13 — What About Children From Poor Families?

Many Americans and most public-school apologists argue that if we had no public schools and an unregulated education free-market, many poor families could not afford to educate their kids. We need public schools, they claim, to make sure poor kids get an education, however bad.

School authorities point out that at least in a public-school system, local governments force parents to send their children to school and pay for this schooling through taxes. This compulsory system insures that even children from the poorest families get an education, even if this education is mediocre to miserable. In contrast, they argue, a free-market system in which children do not have a right to an education, can't guarantee even a minimum education to children from poor families.

As I noted above, it is true that the free market can't guarantee a quality education for all children. However, let's look at some poverty statistics that clarify this issue further. According to U.S. Census Bureau data, the number of families living under the poverty line in the year 2002 was 7.2 million, or 9.6

percent of all American families.[39] Census Bureau data for 2002 also indicate that 11,704,000 children under 18 years old, lived in families below the official poverty line.[40]

Let's assume for the moment that a free-market education system could not find ways to give poor children a decent education (I will discuss ways that it can, very shortly). Under this assumption, about 11.7 million children living in poverty might not get educated (however we define educated). Now contrast this number with the fact that our public-school system *guarantees* a third-rate education to the vast majority of public-school students (almost 45 million a year). Our public schools also waste twelve years of children's lives, warp their values, give millions of children mind-altering drugs, make kids hate learning, and cripple their ability to read.

In effect, those who use the poverty argument are saying that we must sacrifice the minds and futures of forty-five million children to insure that about 12 million poor kids get a "minimum" education in public schools. This system punishes the vast majority of parents who could afford tuition in a competitive free-market education system, for the sake of poor parents who *might not* be able to do so. That is like saying that all children should be put in prison to insure that children from poor families get enough food to eat. So public-school apologists' solution is *not* to give poor families the means to pay for tuition in a free-market school, but to *chain all children to the wretched public schools*.

Also, public schools already fail to give most low-income minority children a decent education, even though the schools are allegedly "free" to these children's parents. So how can school authorities claim we need public schools to ensure that poor children get a decent education? Would poor children be any *worse off* with a free-market education system than they already are in our public schools?

The answer is no, because a free-market system has a far greater chance of giving poor kids a quality education than public schools do. That's because an education free-market is extremely flexible, and has many powerful ways to give poor parents real school choice that fits their budget. Before I discuss how an education free-market would do this, let me first clarify what I mean by this term.

An education free market would have no compulsory public schools—government would be *out of the education business*. As a result, there would be no compulsory-attendance laws and no school taxes. All licensing laws would be scrapped. Anyone who wanted to teach any subject could do so without having to get a license. Also, anyone or any company who wanted to open a school could do so without having to get a license to operate. Parents would judge teachers or schools based on their reputation, competence, and real-world results. Parents would pay for their children's education out of their own pockets, just as they now pay for their children's food and clothing (just as Japanese parents now do in their free-market *juku* schools). However, parents would only pay for *their* children's education, not their neighbor's, because school taxes would be gone.

The free market, together with the elimination of school taxes and regulations, can help the poorest parents educate their children in many ways:

First, state governments can use their lottery profits to pay for education scholarships for poor children. I consider state lotteries part of the free market because they are voluntary, as opposed to taxes, which are compulsory. If millions of people choose to gamble a few dollars on their state lottery every week, that is similar to their losing a few dollars a week playing the slot machines in a private casino.

In fiscal year 2003, 39 states grossed about $45 billion from their lotteries, and after payouts and expenses had about $12 billion in net profits for education and other programs in their states.[41] If we divided this $12 billion a year by the approximately 12 million children living under the poverty level that I discussed earlier, that comes out to about $1000 per child, per year. This $1000 a year scholarship could help poor parents pay part of the tuition for a Catholic or Protestant-affiliated private school. It could also pay for most of the yearly tuition for an accredited Internet school or pay for a computer that would help parents homeschool their kids (I'll talk about Internet schools and homeschooling in detail in Chapters 8 and 9).

But the potential benefits of lotteries can go way beyond this. There is no reason why state governments should have a legal monopoly on lotteries. If state gaming regulations that forbid private lotteries were scrapped, and private companies could then run lotteries of their own (far more efficiently), more billions of dollars could be raised for educating poor children. Local governments could induce private companies to contribute part of their lottery profits to education scholarships by giving them tax credits for such contributions.

Today, state lottery money is dumped into failing public schools. This is a waste of precious money and resources, since the public-school system is beyond repair no matter how much money it gets. Instead, if public schools were scrapped, every cent of state lottery profits could fund tuition scholarships for children from poor families.

Second, state and local governments can also offer tax credits to individuals or businesses that contribute to an education fund used for scholarships for poor kids. In 1997, Arizona passed a law that let taxpayers deduct up to $500 from their taxes for contributing the same amount to a "tuition organization" that gives education scholarships to kids from poor families. As of this writing, Arizona has thirty-one such scholarship organizations. In 1999, over 30,000 Arizona residents contributed almost $14 million to these scholarship clearinghouses, which helped almost 7,000 low-income students attend private schools. Many other states have created similar tax-credit programs, including Iowa, Illinois, and Minnesota, raising tens of millions of dollars in scholarship funds for poor children. [42]

Third, private donors are another source of funding to help low-income children get a decent education. Americans are enormously compassionate. In 2001, they gave over $187 million to various charities in New York State alone.[43] Many philanthropist-entrepreneurs have also created multimillion-dollar private scholarship programs for poor kids. One example I noted earlier is Theodore J. Forstmann's $170 million Children's Scholarship Fund that provides about 40,000 scholarships to poor kids.

Fourth, if we scrapped the public schools and eliminated all school taxes, homeowners would get back thousands of dollars a year in tax refunds for school taxes they no longer had to pay. School-tax refunds will help families who own homes. However, everyone pays state, local, and federal income and sales taxes that are used to support the public schools. If states and the federal government lowered their income and sales tax rates after we dismantled the public schools, *everyone's* taxes would be less. Less state, local, and federal taxes would give low-income families extra money they could put aside for tutors or private-school tuition for their kids.

The greatest help for poor parents, however, would come from the free-market itself. If we no longer had public schools, the parents of 45 million school children would be shopping for education alternatives. This would create a huge, multi-billion-dollar market demand for private teachers and schools. As a result, we would then see an explosion of new, low-cost, competitive schools created to meet this demand.

Every former public-school teacher could tutor children or open a small school in her home or a local, storefront space. Any adult with a special talent or knowledge could tutor neighborhood kids for a reasonable fee. Major corporations like Disney or Microsoft might enter the education business and create thousands of local schools throughout the country. Children could learn valuable skills and earn money in work-study programs with local businesses. Local entrepreneurs in low-income minority areas could open low-cost neighborhood schools without having to worry about getting a license to operate or competing with "free" public schools. In Chapters 8 and 9, I will examine in depth other free-market education options such as the new Internet schools, computer learning software, and home-schooling.

Cristo Rey Catholic School is one example of the many ways free-market schools can give poor kids a quality education. This school has created a study-work program in partnership with businesses to help cover tuition costs.

Cristo Rey Jesuit High School is a Catholic School in Chicago, where 93 percent of the students come from low-income families. To give these poor kids a chance in life, the school developed a creative new way to finance their private education that other cities are now adopting. Student tuition at Cristo Rey is about $8500 a year, but the poor kids pay only about $2200. The students pay off the rest of the tuition by working five days each month, eight-hours a day, at participating banks, law firms, and other companies in Chicago. Each company pays about $25,000 a year in exchange for the clerical work done by four rotating students. This work-study-tuition program has paid off big for these kids; currently, about 85 percent of the children in this program graduate and go to college.[44]

For many years, the free market has been satisfying millions of parents' need for quality private pre-schools, kindergartens, and colleges. When children are ready for college, parents have thousands of local or out-of-state colleges to chose from with a wide range of tuition costs. Many parents or high-school graduates take out college student loans and pay back the loans after they graduate. Parents could take out similar low-interest loans to pay for 1st through 12th grade education for their kids.

Fortunately, in an education free-market, parents would *not* have to pay tuition for twelve years of private school. Public schools have been around so long that most parents think that education requires going to a school for twelve years. *Nothing can be farther from the truth.*

In Chapter 1, I talked about John Taylor Gatto, New York City Teacher-of-the-Year in 1990. Mr. Gatto taught English and reading for twenty-six years in some of the worst public schools in New York City. Let me repeat here what Gatto wrote in his book, *Dumbing Us Down*, because it is worth repeating: "The truth is that reading, writing, and arithmetic only take about one hundred hours to transmit as long as the audience is eager and willing to learn."[45]

One hundred hours is less than three months of public-school time for the average child. Even if we *triple* the time to three hundred hours for slow-learning or less enthusiastic kids, that's still less than *one year* of school time to teach a child to read, write, and do basic arithmetic. This statistic is shocking if we remember that millions of public-school students take reading and English literature classes right into high school, yet still barely read at minimum levels by the time they graduate. If Gatto is right, most parents would only have to send their children to a good free-market school (or pay a tutor) for a maximum of two years for their children to become good readers and know basic arithmetic.

If most children could become proficient readers in two years, then why do they need public schools to waste *twelve years* of their lives? Most public-school education is a waste of time, anyhow. Whether kids learn history, science, or English literature, teachers make them read the next chapter in a dumbed-down textbook, and then give them boring lectures and tests on that chapter.

John Holt, teacher and author of *How Children Fail*, pointed out that most kids quickly forget the facts they memorized for the next test, because they usually have little interest in the subject they memorized. If they soon forget what they studied, what have they really "learned" in twelve years? Also, kids resent having to sit through boring classes six to eight hours a day, so public-school "education" becomes a mind-numbing drudge.

Also, why should children waste their time studying trigonometry, biology, or foreign languages if these subjects bore them? Why should kids spend years studying a subject they will probably never use later in life, unless they really like the subject and will make it their college major? Why don't we value our children's time as much as we value our own?

Once children learned to read proficiently, if there were no compulsory-attendance laws or required subjects to study, children could study whatever interests them, for as long as they like. Many parents might think I'm naïve to believe that children would read and study without being forced. However, parents should remember how their children loved to learn when they were very young, *before* they started public school. Young children love to learn about new things all the time, and constantly ask their parents questions about the world around them.

Older children can also be self-motivated learners. When they study subjects that fascinate and have meaning for them, they can be absorbed for hours on end, especially if you let them learn in their own way and at their own pace.

So parents would *not* have to send their children to school for eight to twelve years, as they do now. After learning to read well and do arithmetic, most kids could continue their education through self-study, tutors, Internet schools, computer learning software, home-schooling or other relatively inexpensive options.

Also, fierce competition would drive down tuition costs to levels that most parents, even the poorest, could afford. The free market would create so many new schools and options that we would have an education supermarket. Happily, most parents' biggest worry would not be the cost of tuition. Their biggest worry would be trying to choose among the thousands of high-quality, low-cost tutors, local schools, computer software, and Internet schools competing for their business.

Most people who buy a car today finance the purchase with a car loan, paid off over four to five years. The average car today costs around $20,000. If children attended school in an education free market for only two to three years, parents could similarly pay off the tuition costs with a bank loan. If tuition costs were $3000 to $4000 a year, parents could take out a $12,000 education loan, and pay it out over five years. Sharply reducing the time children must spend in "formal" schooling greatly expands parents' financial options to pay tuition costs.

These are only a few of the many ways a free-market education system could help poor parents give their kids a quality, low-cost education. So school authorities' excuse that we need public schools to ensure that poor children get an education, doesn't hold water.

Why Do They Need These Excuses?

Having dissected public-school apologists' most common excuses, let us now ask a seemingly simple question—why do they need all these excuses in the first place? If you hire a roofing contractor to fix the roof on your house and he does a good job, does he make excuses? No. *He lets his work do the talking for him.* You show your appreciation for a job well done by paying him, recommending him to your friends, and using him again in the future. You become a loyal customer because he proved he is competent, trustworthy, and gave you your money's worth.

On the other hand, an incompetent or dishonest roofer who leaves holes in your roof, will make excuses. He makes excuses because he wants you to pay him even though he botched the job. He makes excuses to try to fool you into paying him, even though he doesn't deserve your money.

This contractor, like most people, also has to justify himself in his own eyes. He doesn't like to think of himself as dishonest, incompetent, or a bad person—that would wound his self-image. So he rationalizes to himself and makes excuses to you why his work isn't so bad. He might tell you that he's the expert on roofing, that you don't know good roofing work when you see it, or that no roofer could do a better job.

If the roofer does a lousy job for all his customers and keeps giving excuses, what happens? In a free market, where you have dozens of other roofers to choose from, you will fire this roofer and look for a better one. So will his other customers, and soon he will be out of business.

Just like our roofer, incompetent public schools benefit by inventing a constant stream of excuses. What can these excuses accomplish?

1. Personal justification — Every public-school employee believes he is a good person, and most of them are. School employees do not want to believe or admit to themselves that they work for a school system that continually betrays millions of innocent children. These excuses let them justify themselves and the system in their own eyes.

2. Justify their privileged position — Public-school employees need excuses to justify why they have a unique, privileged position in the work world. Most employees in the real world can be fired if they are incompetent. Most companies that do shoddy work can and do go out of business. Few workers in the real world have job guarantees like tenured school employees. Few workers get the fat benefits and pensions that public-school teachers, principals, and administrators do, especially for mediocre or incompetent work. Teachers who work in private pre-schools, kindergartens, grammar or secondary schools, and many colleges do not have these same benefits or job guarantees. So public-school employees have to pretend they are somehow unique. They have to rationalize why they deserve their privileged position. Hence the excuses and self-delusion.

3. Fear of parents — If public-school employees don't make these elaborate excuses, they are afraid of open rebellion by parents. Already, over a million parents are voting with their feet by home-schooling their children. Every year, thousands more parents give up in disgust with their local public schools and join the ranks of home-schoolers. Public-school authorities see this as a frightening and dangerous trend. As a result, they need a constant stream of excuses to stem the flow and convince parents to keep their children in public school.

4. To induce guilt — School authorities invent excuses to make parents feel guilty if they take their kids out of public school. No one likes to feel they are a bad person, that they support policies that harm children. Americans are a kind, wonderful, generous people. Public-school apologists play on our good nature. They keep telling scare-stories about how school choice would hurt the children, destroy the public schools,

leave minority children behind, and bring back segregated schools. Guilt is a powerful weapon. These excuses are a guilt-trip sword aimed squarely at parents' hearts.

5. Loss of funding — Every time a parent takes her child out of public school, the school loses an average of $7300 a year in tax money. If the child was in a special-education class, the school can lose $16,000 a year or more (on average). When schools lose tax money, they lose power and control. If enough parents quit the public schools, many teachers might be fired because the schools would need fewer teachers. Hence the endless list of excuses to stop the loss of tax dollars and the threat to teachers' jobs.

6. Fear of legislators — If enough parents or parent organizations complain to local or state legislators about bad public schools, legislators may (a) reduce funding to the schools and education programs, (b) pass new laws that require merit pay, accountability, and teacher-competence testing, (c) require teachers to know their subject as a prerequisite for a license, (d) eliminate tenure rules that guarantee jobs, (e) pass new laws or repeal old ones to make home-schooling easier for parents, and (f) pass new laws that require schools to prove their competence with standardized tests, or lose funding. School authorities want to avoid such legislative punishments. Hence the frantic excuses to keep politicians at bay.

7. Greed — If school employees fool parents and legislators with their excuses, they then feel safe to demand higher teacher salaries and fatter benefits and pensions. Parents should get value for their hard-earned tax dollars. These excuses fool parents into thinking that public schools do a good job, and that school employees deserve their higher-than-average salaries, generous benefits, and guaranteed job security.

School authorities constantly repeat these excuses to make parents doubt their own judgment and common sense, justify the continued existence of failed public schools, and fool or appease parents and legislators who want real school choice. Public-school apologists seem to believe that if they repeat these excuses long enough and loud enough, parents and legislators will believe them. They thereby show their contempt for parents' and legislators' common sense and intelligence.

Parents who want quality education for their children cannot depend on a public-school system whose only real achievement is an endless list of excuses why it can't educate their children. Instead, parents should seriously consider leaving this system behind and finding education alternatives for their children. We will examine these alternatives in depth in the following chapters.

Part II

How Parents Can Give
Their Children a Great,
Low-Cost Education
Without Public Schools

8

Great Education Options
For Parents and Children

With rare exceptions, public schools cannot and will not give your children the quality and enriching education they deserve. If your children hate school, are always bored in school, are failing in their studies, or you are concerned about the poor quality of education your kids are getting, you should seriously consider removing your children from public school. If you value your children's minds, their ability to read, their self-esteem, their love of learning, their precious time, their future, even their physical safety, think about finding better education alternatives for your kids.

Twenty-two Danger Signals
From Your Children

How do you know if public school is bad for your child? What signals from your child tell you it's time to think seriously about other education options? Here is a useful list of common danger signals from Jerry Mintz of the Alternative Education Resource Organization (AERO).

1. Does your child say he or she hates school? If so, something is probably wrong with the school because children are natural learners. When they're young, you can hardly stop them from learning. If your children say they hate school, listen to them.

2. Does your child find it difficult to look an adult in the eye, or to interact with children younger or older than they are? If so, your child may have become socialized to that very narrow group which many children ordinarily interact with in most schools, and may be losing the ability to communicate with a broader group of children and adults.

3. Does your child seem fixated on designer labels and trendy clothes for school? This is a symptom of the shallowness of the traditional schools' approach, causing children to rely on external means of comparison and acceptance, rather than deeper values. [Children fixate on these superficial things for two other reasons—because peer pressure in public schools pushes kids into group conformity, and because the fixations distract normally energetic kids from the misery or boredom of public school].

4. Does your child come home from school tired and cranky? This is a sure sign that their educational experiences are not energizing but are actually debilitating.

5. Does your child come home complaining about conflicts that they've had in school and unfair situations that they have been exposed to? This is a sign that your school does not have a proper process for conflict resolution and communication.

6. Has your child lost interest in creative expression through art, music, and dance? These things are generally not encouraged in the traditional system today and are not highly valued. They're considered secondary to the "academic" areas. In some cases, courses are not even offered in these areas any more. This tends to ex-

tinguish these natural talents and abilities in children.

7. Has your child stopped reading for fun, or reading or writing for pleasure? Are your children doing just the minimum for homework and going off for some escapist activity? This is a sign that these spontaneous activities are not being valued in their school and another sign that they are losing their creativity.

8. Does your child procrastinate until the last minute to do homework? This is a sign that homework is not very interesting, is not really meeting his or her needs, and is tending to extinguish their natural curiosity.

9. Does your child come home talking about anything exciting that happened in school that day? If not, maybe nothing exciting is happening for your child in school. Would you want to keep working if your job was like that?

10. Did the school nurse or guidance counselor suggest that your child has some strange three-lettered disease, like ADD, and that they should now be given Ritalin or some other drug? I suggest that it is more probable that the *school* [italics added] has some disease, Educational Deficit Disorder, and time to get your child out of that situation![1]

Here are additional danger signals to watch out for:

11. Does your child's reading or writing ability seem far below what you would expect for his or her grade level?

12. Is your child's writing and spelling atrocious, yet the teacher gives him high grades or compliments for creative spelling?

13. Is your child constantly frustrated with school and homework?

14. Does your child have difficulty doing simple arithmetic problems that he should be able to handle at that grade level?

15. Does your child come home afraid or disturbed by what he or she learned in school that day?

16. Does your child tell you that the teacher said bad things about you in class because you spanked or yelled at him at home?

17. Does the teacher tell your child not to tell you about something he or she learned in school that day?

18. Is your child embarrassed by what she learned in sex education class and doesn't want to talk to you about it?

19. Does your child come home with bruises he got from some bully who the teacher did not control?

20. Ask your child how many hours a day he or she learns reading, math, and other academic subjects, versus other classes about pagan religions, homosexuality, and other social-psychological conditioning classes. Does the school spend most of the day on these nonacademic subjects? If so, the school is wasting your child's time.

21. Ask your child about the stories she reads in class or the exercises the teachers have her do. Is the school indoctrinating your child with values or ideas that you think are harmful or dangerous?

22. Ask to see your child's textbooks. Are they dumbed-down and do they teach values you don't approve of?

If your child exhibits any of these danger signs, it may be time to take your child's education into your own hands.

Exciting, Low-cost Education
Options Outside the Public Schools

Many parents believe that expensive private schools are the only alternative to public schools. Most private-school students today go to religiously-affiliated schools whose tuition for 2002 averaged about $4000 a year. This cost can be a hurdle for many parents, especially for low-income families.

This tuition is in addition to school taxes you still have to pay to support the public schools your child is *not* attending. Also, like public schools, most private schools assume that a child's education requires eight to twelve years, and many teach subjects that your children are not interested in or are unlikely to use later in life.

The good news is that there are exciting, *low-cost* education alternatives most parents can take advantage of that will give their children a high-quality education in much less time than conventional schooling. These alternatives include the new Internet schools, Internet tutors, computer learning software, and home-schooling.

Internet Schools

Internet schools are a form of home-schooling that makes life easier for parents. Home-schooling normally requires parents to personally teach their children at home using a wide variety of educational teaching materials, including books, the Internet, computer learning software, and much more. While every family is different, most parents usually commit at least two to four hours a day for home-schooling, depending on the child's age, interests, and progress. We will talk about time constraints and other possible problems with home-schooling, and many solutions to overcome those problems, later in this chapter.

For those parents who have little time to spare or don't feel confident in home-schooling their children right now, Internet schools can be a wonderful new alternative. These schools take most of the home-schooling burden off parents' backs, yet can give children a low-cost, quality education at home.

An Internet school for children is similar to the Internet college-degree programs that many universities around the country now offer adults. There are many good Internet schools parents can choose from. Some schools only offer high-school programs. Others offer middle-school and high-school instruction or 1st through 12th grade education.

Each school has different costs, curriculum, and teaching methods, but essentially they are like secular or religiously-affiliated private schools, only they operate through the Internet.

Many universities and private schools have 1st through 12th grade Internet-school divisions that allow students to work from home. In many schools, you can enroll your child for individual tutoring on specific subjects, or a full course of study leading to an accredited high-school diploma.

Many Internet schools give a course of study similar to traditional private schools. They take children through a progressive curriculum in math, science, reading and writing, social studies, and many other subjects. The school assigns one or more teachers to each child's class, there are progressive lesson plans, and children learn at their own pace. This structured, comprehensive program is like having a personal teacher and private school in a parent's own living room. As a result, these schools can relieve parents of most of the home-schooling burden, while giving children a high-quality education.

This setup is especially helpful for single-working moms, or families where both mother and father work. Since Internet-school teachers supervise the child's education, it's less likely that parents will have to take time from work or quit their job to homeschool their kids. If their children are still young, parents would have to find friends, neighbors, or baby sitters to look in on their kids during the day to see that everything is all right. We will discuss many ways parents can handle this problem, later in the chapter.

The good news about Internet schools gets even better when we talk about cost. Many Internet schools charge *much lower* tuition rates than brick-and-mortar private schools, and sometimes thousands of dollars a year less than Catholic or Protestant-affiliated schools. Tuition costs vary with each Internet school, from as low as $350 a year to $3000 or more a year.

Internet schools can charge lower tuition for many reasons. Unlike public schools, they don't hold classes in a brick-and-mortar building, or have to pay rent, upkeep, or taxes on that building. They don't have big overhead expenses, don't need to hire an army of high-salaried administrators, and can hire competent, qualified, non-union teachers who work at lower salary levels. Yet, in spite of lower tuition costs, these schools can offer your children a thorough, high-quality, and fun education in the safety of your home.

For example, in Clonlara CompuHigh Internet school, students take a standard course of traditional subjects to earn their accredited diploma. A student can graduate in three years or less, and the current tuition cost is about $1000 a year. If you compare this cost to the average $7,000 to $14,000 a year tuition for non-secular private schools, or the average $3500 to $4000 a year tuition that religiously-affiliated schools currently charge, you can see why Internet schools can be a great resource for parents.[2]

Your children can learn faster in Internet schools because these schools concentrate on the basics, your children get individual attention, and they can work at their own pace. As a result, they can graduate sooner and save you money in tuition fees. Here is an article about a satisfied parent who sent her child to the Babbage Net School:

At age 6, Erin [last name withheld for privacy] had already taught herself to read and write. And when testing confirmed in 1991 that the precocious child was indeed gifted, her mother, Lorraine, knew educating her would not be easy. "My first thought was to make sure she got the educational challenge she needed and still be a little girl and have fun," said [Lorraine]. "She had an absolutely incredible desire to learn."

With no adequate public school program available, years of private schools and home-schooling with private tutors followed until 1999 when, having exhausted her options in the Tampa, Florida area where they lived, [Lorraine] turned in a radically different direction. She enrolled Erin in several courses offered via the Internet by the Babbage Net School, a cyberschool based about 1,200 miles away in Port Jefferson [New York].

"I was sort of fumbling in the dark," recalled [Lorraine], who describes herself as a researcher. "I checked out the school with the offices of the attorney general and the secretary of state of New York . . . . It almost sounded too good to be true."

Erin took seven courses from fall 1999 to spring 2000, allowing her to graduate *two years early* [italics added] and go on to the University of Tampa, where she's a sophomore. Kim R. [last name withheld for privacy], who taught three of Erin's online courses—sociology, economics and criminal justice— said she was an excellent student.

"I tell everyone that I was fortunate in that Erin got a New York State education, said [Lorraine] in a soft Southern accent. It really was too good to be true. But it was real. I just got lucky."[3]

There are many types of Internet schools parents can choose from based on their method of instruction. Some schools are full virtual schools where children learn online interactively with teachers, using multi-media teaching materials. Other Internet schools are more traditional. In these schools, students read the course material, take tests online, and teachers review tests and supervise further work. Some of these schools are actually brick-and-mortar private schools with online divisions. Other Internet schools are like the older high-school correspondence-course schools, where the school mails course material to the student, who then studies the material, takes tests, and advances to the next grade after they have completed their tests successfully.

Another new education option many parents can take advantage of is virtual charter schools. Like regular Internet schools, these charter schools are online. Virtual charter schools are public schools that try to combine the advantages of home-schooling, such as individual attention, with the time-saving advantages of a structured and supervised curriculum.

These schools can offer the same quality education as non-charter Internet schools, but have special advantages. Because virtual charter schools are accredited public schools, state education departments pay the school's tuition, not parents, the same way states would pay the tuition for brick-and-mortar charter schools.

The other great advantage of these schools is that they have less restrictive geographic limits. Parents can enroll their children in virtual charter schools hundreds of miles away in the same state, and their children can learn in the comfort of their own living room.

One indication that many parents love these new virtual charter schools is that some public-school authorities are trying to shut them down. In April, 2003, the Pennsylvania School Boards Association filed a lawsuit that challenged the legality of cyber-charter schools in their state.[4] School authorities fear charter schools because these schools siphon off tax dollars from public schools. Virtual charter schools give parents far more options because parents are no longer restricted to the few, if any, brick-and-mortar charter schools in their neighborhood. Giving parents more options always terrifies public-school authorities.

The huge variety of low-cost Internet schools can meet most children's needs and most parent's pocketbooks. As I noted earlier, most of these schools teach essential skills and academic fundamentals, and cover core subjects such as math, sciences, reading and writing, literature, and American and world history. Many also offer interesting elective subjects like "life skills," which can include subjects such as how to buy a car, establish credit, rent your first apartment, and much more.

Most of these Internet schools test students throughout the school year, and track students' activities and studies so parents and teachers can see students' progress or problem areas. When students complete their course of study, most of these schools provide complete transcript, course-of-study, and other materials to colleges that students apply to. Many schools also have courses that give graduating students helpful strategies for taking SAT college entrance exams.

Many Internet schools offer a somewhat traditional education similar to what children might get in a brick-and-mortar private school. While these schools offer a quality education that stresses academic fundamentals, students usually study subjects from a set curriculum. However, many parents might prefer a more unstructured, wider-ranging education for their children that gives them greater freedom to study subjects that interest them, and to explore those subjects in greater depth.

For these parents, home-schooling is ideal because it lets parents take direct responsibility for educating their kids. It also lets parents use a much wider range of resources to educate their children, everything from cooking lessons at home, planting gardens, trips to bookstores, libraries, and museums, art and music projects, and much more (I'll explore these many options in greater detail in Chapter 9). Let's examine the many ways home-schooling can benefit children.

The Benefits of Home-schooling

Home-schooling removes children from public school. That alone makes home-schooling worthwhile. Unlike public-school children, home-schooled kids are not prisoners of a system that can wreck their self-esteem, ability to read, and love of learning. Home-schooled kids don't have to read dumb-downed textbooks, study subjects they hate, or endure meaningless classes six to eight hours a day. Home-schooled kids won't be subject to drugs, bullies, violence, or peer pressure, as they are in public schools.

Home-schooled children who are "different" in any way won't have to endure cruel jokes and taunts from other children in their classes. Slow-learning or "special-needs" children won't be humiliated by their peers if they are put in regular classes, or further humiliated if the teacher puts them in so-called special-education classes.

Faster-learning home-schooled children won't have to sit through mind-numbing classes that are geared to the slowest-learning students in a class. They won't have to "learn" in co-operative groups where other kids in the group do nothing and are not cooperative.

Home-schooled children do not have to waste their time memorizing meaningless facts about subjects that bore them, just so they can pass the next dumbed-down test. Home-schooled kids don't have to endure twelve years of a mind-numbing public-school education that leaves many students barely able to read their own diplomas.

The notion that tests tell teachers and parents what children have learned turns out to be mostly false. As I noted earlier, John Holt pointed out that most children forget what they memorized for a test soon after the test is over, so the test-taking process is mostly worthless. Facts or ideas that are not useful, relevant, or interesting to children pass through them like a sieve and are soon forgotten.

Home-schooled kids don't have to study an arbitrary curriculum of subjects imposed on them by public-school authorities. They don't have to be treated like little mindless, spiritless robots that have to learn the same subjects at the same time and in the same sequence as their classmates. They are not forced under threat of punishment by the teacher to move along a pre-determined path to an arbitrary destination imposed on them.

Home-schooled children don't have to sit quietly in a class of twenty-five other students and pretend they like being in this mini-prison called public school, just to avoid being punished by a teacher for "acting-out" or fidgeting in their seats. Any adult's mind would wander if they were forced to sit through a boring lecture for just *one* hour. Yet public schools expect children to sit still for boring lectures on subjects that are meaningless to them, for *six to eight hours* a day.

Home-schooled children do not have to be fearful of displeasing a teacher because they get the wrong answers on tests. They therefore don't have to be afraid of learning and have their natural joy in learning crippled as a result of this fear. Infants and very young children embrace life and learning with a passion, which is why they learn so fast. Yet as teacher John Holt found out, by the time these same children have progressed to the fifth grade in school, most are listless, bored, apathetic, and often fearful in class.

Home-schooled children won't be hurt by test grades or comparisons to their classmates, and associate learning with this pain. They won't associate learning with having to get the *right* answer that school authorities insist on for standardized tests. They won't be made to feel that learning means passing an arbitrary test, and that failing a test is a shame or disgrace.

Home-schooling also prevents school authorities from indoctrinating children with warped values, pagan religions, or politically-correct ideas. Unlike public-school students, home-schooled children are not forced to sit through explicit or shocking sex-education classes. Also, school authorities can't pressure home-schooling parents to give mind-altering drugs to their children.

For all these reasons, keeping a child out of public school is an enormous benefit in itself. Other positive benefits of home-schooling are:

1. *Home-schooling lets parents give children a custom-made curriculum that makes learning a joy* — Parents can expose their children to many different subjects and ultimately focus on subjects that their children enjoy and benefit from. Children can also learn about subjects that are not taught in any school, and have time for non-academic subjects like art and music. Parents can choose from a wide range of teaching materials that not only engage and delight their kids, but bring real results.

2. *Home-schooled children can learn at their own pace* — Slower-learning kids will benefit by their parent's love and attention. Bright children will progress as fast as they want to. Children will learn to read or learn any other subject when they are ready, not according to a prescribed time-table. Unlike public schools, home-schooling parents treat each child as a unique individual with his or her own special interests, talents, strengths and weaknesses. Parents can also pace the instruction to match each child's personality and learning style.

3. *Home-schooling parents can give their kids a one-to-one teacher-student ratio* — This insures that children get individualized attention from a loving, attentive parent-teacher.

4. *Home-schooled kids get instant feedback* — Children don't

have to compete with twenty other children in a class for their teacher's attention. A parent-teacher can instantly answer her child's questions, or research the answer together with her child.

5. *Home-schooled kids have fewer distractions* — At home there is no peer pressure by other students, few conflicts with other kids, no children who disrupt classes, and all the other distractions of public schools. Home-schooled kids can study something that fascinates them for large blocks of time, instead of having to go to a different class and subject every 50 minutes, as they do in public schools.

6. *Home-schooled children learn faster* — Your children could learn much faster at home because you give them individual attention, and use innovative free-market education materials such as Internet schools, computer software, and independent study resources. Also, children will learn faster because you can focus their instruction on the basics and subjects they like, and not waste their time on subjects they hate or will never use.

With home-schooling, your children could be ready to take college-entrance exams by age thirteen or fourteen, not age eighteen, as in public schools. Even today, a few bright fourteen-year-old high-school graduates go to college each year.

7. *Children can interact with older and younger siblings* — Home-schooled kids can interact with and learn to relate to brothers or sisters in different age groups. This gives kids better social skills, lets them teach younger siblings and learn from older ones.

8. *Home-schooling gives children self-esteem* — Because kids get love, individual attention, and constant encouragement from their parents, they learn better. They accomplish real goals and real progress in their studies, so their self-esteem grows stronger.

9. *Home-schooled children discover that learning can be fun and exciting* — They can study subjects for their own enjoyment, rather than for external rewards. Children will be more willing to take risks and be creative, because they only have to please themselves and don't have to worry about teachers or peers

who disapprove or make fun of their efforts. Home-schooled children discover that learning is a joyous, life-long process.

10. *Home-schooling helps children to think and learn independently* — Kids don't have to worry about coming up with the one-correct, public-school textbook answer to every question. They can experiment and improvise. They can read many books or articles on a subject and research different sides of issues so they form their own independent judgments. They learn how to use many different resources to find answers to questions, instead of relying on a single teacher for answers. Unlike harried, over-worked public-school teachers, parents can nurture this independence in their children.

11. *Home-schooling brings families together* — Parents can spend many hours teaching, interacting with, and nurturing their children. The kids also interact with their brothers and sisters, sometimes helping younger ones, or asking older siblings questions. Children also learn a sense of personal responsibility by helping with family chores.

12. *Home-schooling gives parents and kids flexible scheduling* — With home-schooling, parents can adjust their schedules so that each parent spends time teaching the children. Children can learn different subjects when they are ready and interested. For example, each child learns to read or becomes fascinated with different subjects at different ages. Also, parents and kids can constantly adjust their daily learning schedule.

13. *Home-schooling gives kids better socialization skills* — We've already noted that home-schooled kids learn to interact with brothers or sisters in different age groups. Another socialization benefit is that home-schooled kids don't spend six to eight hours a day cooped up in a classroom. They therefore have more time to socialize with other neighborhood children in outside classes, sports teams, and other activities.

14. *Home-schooled kids get to choose their peers* — They can decide who their friends are and what activities they want to do outside the home with other children, rather than having to socialize with children they don't know and may not like in a public school.

15. *Home-schooling provides a superior education* — Parents can quickly teach most kids the basics of reading, writing, and arithmetic using excellent, creative, learn-to-read, or learn-math books, programs, or computer learning software. Once children become proficient readers, they can then study subjects they love in greater depth. If a child needs help on a special subject, parents can occasionally call in a tutor.

Many studies confirm that home-schooled kids learn more, learn better, and learn faster than public-school children. Christopher J. Klicka, author of *The Right Choice: Homeschooling*, cites a nationwide study of more than 2,163 home-schooling families conducted in 1990 by the National Home Education Research Institute:

The study found the average scores of the home school students were at or above the 80th percentile in all categories. This means that the homeschoolers scored, on the average, higher than 80 percent of the students in the nation. The home schooler's national percentile mean was 84 for reading, 80 for language, 81 for math, 84 for science, and 83 for social studies.[5]

Several state departments of education also conducted their own surveys on the academic achievement of home-schooled students. In 1987, much to its embarrassment, "the Tennessee Department of Education found that home-schooled children in second grade, on the average, scored in the 93rd percentile, while their public school counterparts, on the average, scored in the 52nd percentile on the Stanford Achievement Test" (the SAT-9 is a well-respected battery of multiple-choice academic achievement tests for public-school students).[6]

These studies, and many others, confirm the fact that home-schooling parents can give their kids a superior education. This shouldn't surprise us. Home-schooling parents succeed where public schools fail because parents give loving, personalized attention to their children, use innovative free-market educational materials, and nourish a love of learning in their kids.

16. *Home-schooling lets children find the career they will love early in life* — Through home-schooling and parents' guidance, children can discover the subjects they love much earlier in life. They can then concentrate on these subjects. By doing so, they will have a surer idea of the career they want and get there much quicker. When children find themselves quicker, this can take an enormous time and financial burden off parents' backs. With their children on their way to a satisfying career, parents can then concentrate on their own lives and fulfilling *their* dreams, once the kids are out of the house.

In contrast, many children who go to public school have no idea what they want to do, even by the time they graduate college. This is exactly what happened to me. I didn't know what I wanted to study for a career when I graduated high school. So I then majored in psychology in college, which is one of those liberal-arts subjects many students choose who don't know what they want to do in life.

College then became just an extended high school for me, and I wasted another four years. Millions of children go through this same desert of wasted years because public schools waste their time, give them little guidance, and kill their love of learning. Many parents then have the burden of supporting their children well into their mid-twenties or even later, while their kids are still trying to "find themselves." Home-schooling can relieve parents of this burden because it helps children find the career they will love and pursue much sooner in life.

Questions about Home-schooling

For many parents, taking their children out of public school can seem like a scary step. Certainly, home-schooling can cause some big changes in family life. Almost 75 percent of American mothers with school-age children now work either full or part-time. [7] Many working parents have limited free time. Also, taxes take almost 40 percent of the average parents' earnings, and government-created inflation sharply increases the cost of everything they buy. This economic pincer makes it hard for average families to pay their bills. Many working parents who want to remove their children from public schools therefore worry about finding the time or money to homeschool their children.

Also, it may seem that parents alone make the choice to homeschool, but children should also take part in the decision. Home-schooling should be a cooperative partnership between you and your kids. Talk to your children about your desire to homeschool them. If you don't have their enthusiastic support, you may not get the best results from teaching them at home. Discuss the homeschool program and strategy you have in mind and get their input. Then adjust as you go along, see what works or doesn't, and what your children get excited about. You and your kids can continually adjust the home-schooling curriculum to get the best results.

Over a million parents now homeschool their children, but many others fear that home-schooling may be too hard or not worth the effort and sacrifice. Many parents have little prior teaching experience, so they worry that they won't have the ability to homeschool their kids. Let's examine some of these potential problems, and see how parents can overcome them.

How Do I Know It's Worth the Trouble?

Chapters 1 through 6 described how public schools betray our children. Parents who are still not fully convinced can read additional books about public schools that I list in the Bibliography. These eye-opening books will give parents a true, detailed, and often frightening picture of our public schools.

For those parents who believe that most public schools fail our children, but that *their* local school may be an exception, please take the time to carefully examine the education your local school gives your children. As I noted earlier, ask your children to read to you or solve simple arithmetic problems. Do they read poorly for their age or grade level, or have trouble with basic math? If you ask your children to write a simple essay, are their grammar, spelling, and writing skills shockingly bad?

Ask your kids what grades they get on English tests, essays, reports, and on math tests. If your child has poor reading, writing, or math skills but gets "A's" or "Excellent" on his test grades and report cards, it means the school's teaching, testing, and scoring methods are worthless. It means, in effect, that the school is committing educational fraud against you and your children.

You can also get an accurate and independent appraisal of your children's true math and reading skills with low-cost computer-software programs and Internet education sites that test and analyze children's reading, writing, and math skills. You can do an Internet search for "test reading (or math) skills," or "reading software" using search engines like Google or Yahoo. The search will come up with many listings for skill-testing software and Internet sites you can use to test your children's skills yourself. Also, nationwide tutoring companies like Sylvan Learning Centers can give your children an independent evaluation. After testing your children, you may be shocked to discover that your children's academic skills are far below what your local public-school led you to believe.

Re-read the potential danger signals from your children described above. If your child exhibits many of these signals, then he or she is having serious problems with public school. Don't wait for public schools to wreck your children's education and waste their years. Take these potential danger signals seriously.

Use the testing and research methods noted above to make sure in your own mind that public schools are truly a threat to your children. Confirm for yourself that these schools can cripple your child's mind, self-esteem, reading ability, and future. If you then agree that public schools are a menace to your children, including your local school, then *any alternative is better*, including tutors, home-schooling, Internet schools, or private schools. Yes, home-schooling will force you to make some adjustments to your life, but don't you want to protect your children? Don't you want the best for them? Don't your kids deserve more than a third-rate public-school education?

What If Home-schooling Doesn't Work Out?

Suppose that you rearrange your life to homeschool your child and the experiment fails. You may feel that you've disrupted your life and wasted a year of your child's time. He or she may be kept back a grade by the local public school.

The answer to this concern is, can you risk *not* trying? Isn't your child's future worth the risk? If you see a bad situation, the worst thing to do is *nothing*. Then there is *no* chance of improvement. If you leave your children in public school, chances are great that their ability to read, self-esteem, and love of learning will be damaged, and they can waste twelve years of their lives. Look at the potential consequences to your child if you don't try other education alternatives

Second, if you research and use the many free-market education resources I describe in Chapter 9, it will be hard for you to fail. You can choose from a wide variety of quality Internet schools, learn-to-read (and math) books and computer learning software, and home-schooling resources to teach your children. These resources offer you a learning supermarket from which you can choose the best programs for your child. Also, Internet education sites are always there and always ready to coach your child.

These education alternatives are relatively inexpensive, yet offer high-quality instruction. Your job as a parent is to commit some time and energy to find the right education resources for your children, then help and encourage them to learn.

Also, like most kids, your children want to learn when they study subjects that interest them. When learning becomes fun, your kids can become your best home-schooling partner and help you succeed. Your kids may enjoy home-schooling so much that you may soon have to drag them away from their

books or the computer for lunch. But isn't that great? Wouldn't
you like to see your kids totally engrossed in their studies, improving their reading skills rapidly, and finding joy in learning?

Here's the beauty of an education free market—if one math
or reading book, software program, or Internet school doesn't
excite your children or provide satisfactory results, there are
many more to choose from. You may find home-schooling difficult in the beginning only because it is so new to you. If you
use the books, Internet schools and tutors, and teaching materials I describe in the Resouces section, you should do fine.
Also, you can network with other home-schooling parents to
benefit from their experiences (parent organizations are also
listed in the Resources section). Over a million parents just like
you already teach their children at home.

While I certainly can't guarantee you success, like anything
else in life, if you keep trying you will probably succeed. If you
say to yourself, "I will make this work, for my child's sake,"
you'll be surprised at what you can accomplish. Tell yourself
what Gene Kranz, actor Ed Harris's character in the movie
Apollo 13, said to his Houston crew about rescuing the astro-
nauts in trouble: "Failure is not an option." If you say this and
mean it, you're halfway to success for yourself and your child.

How Do I Know I Can Homeschool My Child?

As I noted earlier, for over 200 years, from the time the Pil-
grims landed at Plymouth Rock to the 1850s, most children
learned to read at home from their parents, or in small, local grammar or religious schools. Many of these parents were
housewives or simple farmers and tradesmen, taught by *their*
parents. They didn't have the Internet, computer software, educational videos, or *Sesame Street*, yet they taught their children
to read so well that the literacy rate in the colonies was over 90
percent by the 1840s. John Taylor Gatto wrote that,

Looking back, abundant data exists from states like Connecticut and Massachusetts to show that by 1840 the incidence of complex literacy in the United States was between 93 and 100 percent wherever such a thing mattered. Everyone was literate, rich and poor alike. In Connecticut only one citizen out of every 579 was illiterate . . . [8]

By 1850, Massachusetts residents had reached a literacy rate of close to 92 percent. This occurred *before* the state enacted its public-school, compulsory education laws in 1852. In the 1980s, Senator Edward Kennedy's office released a paper stating that literacy in Massachusetts in the early 1850s was *only* (italics added) 91 percent.[9]

If colonial mothers, farmers, and tradesmen could teach their children to read at home with only the Bible or simple readers, that means two things—teaching kids to read (and basic arithmetic) is not that hard, and that most parents today can also teach their kids to read at home. Most children are learning sponges, eager to soak up what you teach them. Also, unlike colonial farmers, you have the benefit of computers, the Internet, videos, encyclopedias, well-stocked libraries and bookstores, and the Science channel on cable TV. With all these resources at your disposal, it would be difficult not to succeed.

Many parents may be concerned because they don't have a college education and consider themselves unqualified to teach their children. Yet, of the million parents now home-schooling their kids, about 50 percent of these parents have only a high-school diploma or less.[10] If these parents can give their kids a superior education at home, there is no reason why other parents can't do the same. Finally, parents' love and undivided attention often far outweigh their alleged lack of academic credentials in determining how well their children learn at home.

If you're still unsure of your ability to homeschool your kids, try home-schooling *before* you take your children out of public school to test it out and gain more confidence that you can do it. While your kids are still in public school, enroll them in some Internet classes or try an Internet tutor. Buy learn-to-read books to teach your child to read (see the Resources section). Once you find that you and your child really like home-schooling and you feel confident that you can do it, you can then make the final break with public schools.

Some words by writer and home-schooling mother Isabel Shaw neatly expresses your role as a home-schooling parent:

> Homeschooling, seen in this light, is not about a parent becoming a teacher, in the traditional sense, but a parent becoming a guide and a partner in the learning experience. Successful home learning involves observing your child, following his lead, and respecting his choices. This can be done within the framework of core subjects like reading, math, and history—it's just done creatively.
>
> For instance, I remember studying about the Civil War when I was in school. We opened our history books, did a few activities and spent many hours memorizing large blocks of information. It was incredibly boring, and after I passed the test on Friday, I remembered very little about the Civil War.
>
> When my daughter Jessica was seven, we read a series of books about a little slave girl named Addy who lived during the Civil War. Told from the perspective of a nine-year-old girl, Addy's story fascinated Jessica. She was filled with questions and wanted to learn more: "Why were there slaves? What was the Underground Railroad? Who was Abraham Lincoln?"
>
> We found the answers to these and other questions in the colorful books and educational videotapes in our library. We cooked with recipes from that time period, and made simple garments that were (almost) historical. We also went to a Civil War reenactment—complete with soldiers camping and food cooking on open fires. But most importantly, we had fun. I never had to

"teach" her anything, and I certainly learned a lot. Six years later, Jessica still recalls just about everything we covered—now *that's* real learning![11]

What About Socialization?

If you homeschool your kids, won't they miss socializing with other children? School authorities try to scare parents away from home-schooling by claiming that only public schools can properly socialize your child. At home, they claim, your child will be isolated from other children and turn into a social misfit.

The answer to this argument is that there is good socializing and bad socializing, and public-school kids usually get the bad kind. They must sit in classes with about twenty other children, all the same age, for six to eight hours a day. Their socialization consists mostly of brief, offhand cracks or conversations with fellow students in the hallways between classes or in the cafeteria.

Also, as previously noted, these schools can be dangerous places for children, exposing them to drugs, bullies, and violence. Boys sometimes taunt or humiliate girls in class. Larger boys, full of raging testosterone, often bully smaller boys. Most teachers don't have the time or patience to be nursemaids or prison guards. No matter how caring or observant the teacher, he or she can never adequately supervise so many children. Parents have far more control over their children's socialization at home.

The only normal socialization that a public school can provide is through clubs or athletic teams. However, home-schooling doesn't eliminate such opportunities. You can encourage your children to join a local soccer or baseball team. Younger children can socialize with other neighborhood kids at local playgrounds. Children can also take music or dancing lessons, join the YMCA, talk to friends on the phone, join the Boy Scouts or Girl Scouts, go to the mall together, and do many other activities. Also, home-schooled children have far more time to socialize with other kids, because they don't spend six to eight hours a day stuck in public-school classrooms. Your options to socialize your children are limited only by your time and imagination.

If you homeschool and have several children, your kids can also socialize with you and their brothers and sisters. Socializing within the family gives a younger child the benefit of your experience and that of their older brothers and sisters. It also brings family members closer together. Before state governments forced children to attend public schools in the 1850s, home-schooling was the *norm* in this country, and children learned to socialize just fine.

A 1992 doctoral dissertation by Larry Shyers debunked the notion that home-schooled kids aren't well socialized:

> Larry Shyers of the University of Florida ... challenged the notion that youngsters at home "lag" in social development. In his study, 8- to 10-year-old children were videotaped at play. Their behavior was observed by trained counselors who did not know which children attended conventional schools and which were homeschooled. The study found no significant difference between the two groups of children in self-concept or assertiveness, which was measured by social development tests. But the videotapes showed that youngsters taught at home by their parents had fewer behavior problems.[12]

A comment by a parent named Laura hits the bulls-eye on the socialization question:

> When we were kids, we only spent maybe six hours a day at school. There was plenty of time for learning at home and pursuing our interests. Kids are in school nine hours now, plus the before-school care and after-school care programs. There is no time for the children to absorb family values and knowledge, or pursue inter-

ests apart from school programs. They are learning their social behavior from undisciplined masses of children. Socialization? Well, it would be like us having to spend nine hours a day in county jail. It's the same people in both institutions.[13]

You can also have the best of both worlds if you homeschool your children. Many school authorities won't tell you this, but the laws in most states allow home-schooling parents to take advantage of public-school facilities such as art, music, science labs, and sports programs offered by the public schools. Since home-schooling parents pay taxes that support public schools, these parents *should* have the right to use public-school facilities.

How Much Time Will Home-schooling Take?

The time you will need to teach your children the essentials—reading, writing, and arithmetic—is much less than you think. Let me quote again from Gatto's *Dumbing Us Down*:

> Were the colonists geniuses? [i.e., why did our colonial forefathers have literacy rates close to 90 percent?]. No, the truth is that reading, writing, and arithmetic only take about *100 hours* [italics added] to transmit as long as the audience is eager and willing to learn. . . . Millions of people teach themselves these things. It really isn't very hard . . .[14]

To be conservative, let's assume that because you're not an experienced teacher it takes you three hundred hours to teach your child these skills with the help of learn-to-read workbooks or computer software. If you homeschool your child only three hours a day for five days a week, that comes out to fifteen hours a week. Three hundred hours divided by fifteen hours a week of homeschooling comes out to twenty weeks, or about five months.

Let me emphasize this point—it could take you, or a tutor you hire, as little as five months to teach your child to read, write, and do simple arithmetic. Again, to be even more conservative, most children could learn these skills in one year if you or a tutor concentrated your instruction on these basics. Public schools take eight to twelve years of children's lives, yet they turn out millions of high-school graduates who can barely read or add and who need remedial English classes if they attend college.

David Colfax and his wife Micki are teachers turned ranchers who taught their four sons at home in the 1970s and 1980s, and three of their sons eventually went to Harvard. They co-authored a book titled *Homeschooling For Excellence*, which describes their home-schooling experience. In their book, they compared the time a child wastes in public school to the time average home-schooling parents need to teach their children the basics. Here's what they wrote:

> The numbers are straightforward and irrefutable. The child who attends public school typically spends approximately 1100 hours a year there, but only twenty percent of these—220—are spent, as the educators say, 'on task.' Nearly 900 hours, or eighty percent, are squandered on what are essentially organizational matters.
>
> In contrast, the homeschooled child who spends only two hours per day, seven days a week, year-round, on basics alone, logs over *three times* as many hours 'on task' in a given year than does his public school counterpart. Moreover, unlike the public school child, whose day is largely taken up by non-task activities, the home-schooled child has ample time left each day to take part in other activities—athletics, art, history, etc. . . . [15]

So according to the authors, if home-schooled children study for only two hours a day, year round, they will get three times more educational hours on academic basics like reading, writing, and arithmetic than public-school students get.

Not only does teaching your child the basics at home take far less time than you thought, but teaching these skills is even easier today because parents now have all the education resources available to them that I've already noted. Also, wonderful bookstores like *Barnes & Noble* and *Borders* have whole sections full of books about teaching your child to read, write, and do basic math, as well as books that will interest and challenge young readers.

Once your children learn to read well, the whole world of learning opens to them. They can explore any subject that interests them, and read ever more difficult material by themselves in books or on the computer. For a small subscription fee, your children can study the entire *Encyclopedia Britannica* on the Internet. They can access almost every major library in the world through the Internet, including the Library of Congress. If your kids love to read and learn, bookstores, free public libraries, and the Internet provide unlimited resources.

Once your children read well, you can point them towards your local library or bookstore, supervise their studies, and see where their interests take them. Your job is to introduce your kids to as many different subjects and resources as possible. Have them take art classes at the local YMCA, library, or arts and crafts store. Introduce them to different kinds of music. See if they enjoy a music lesson on the piano, guitar, or drums. Give them classic novels by great authors to read.

When you take your children to your local library, have them check out books on science, history, biographies, or other subjects that might interest them, such as dinosaurs, airplanes, or the American Revolution. Suggest books on different subjects. See which subjects excite them and which books they discard with a yawn. Give them more of what excites them. Watch their passion for learning grow at its own pace with your enthusiastic support. This is true self-education guided by you, the loving parent. As I noted earlier, your children could be ready to attend college by the time they are fourteen years old. In Renaissance Italy in the 1500s, bright fourteen-year-old boys attended the great universities in Padua and Florence.

The key point is that you have many options and a vast amount of education resource material available to help you homeschool your children. When you take advantage of this material, home-schooling can be fairly easy and take less time than you think.

How Do I Homeschool My Children If I Have to Work?

If you're a single parent or a married couple on a tight budget so that both parents have to work, you may worry about finding the time and energy to homeschool your children, but it can be done. It comes down to planning and scheduling your time. Most home-schooling parents teach their children about two to four hours a day and turn out well-educated kids. So the problem is how to squeeze in about ten to twenty hours a week for home-schooling.

Here are some suggestions:

1. Can you work part-time, leaving yourself time for home-schooling?

2. Can you find a job in your local neighborhood so that you don't waste one to three hours commuting every day?

3. Can you work from home? Computers, the Internet, fax machines, and e-mail all make working from home relatively easy today. Thousands of companies now offer this option to their workers. You could offer to work for slightly less money if your boss resists this arrangement.

4. Can you start a home business that would give you more free time?

5. Can you do all your home-schooling on weekends? If you can arrange concentrated six-to-ten-hour sessions on Saturday and Sunday, you'll be free to work at your job during the rest of the week. Or you might try a combination of weekday and weekend home-schooling sessions.

6. Can you change your work schedule so that you work in

the afternoon or at night and teach your children in the morning?

7. If you have no other alternatives, home-schooling could be done in the evening, say from 7 to 10 P.M., or a combination of weekday nights and weekend sessions.

8. If you're married, get your husband or wife to help with the home-schooling. That gives each parent more time flexibility. Both parents should be involved in home-schooling if possible.

9. If you have older children, ask them to help their younger brothers or sisters in their home-schooling studies.

10. If your child is old enough and responsible enough, take him or her to the local library to study for the morning or afternoon. Most local libraries now have rows of computers connected to the Internet and lots of books for your child to read. Let your child explore the subjects that interest him or her. The same applies to local bookstores. Barnes & Noble or Borders bookstores have tons of special reading material for kids and even a cafe where your children can eat breakfast or lunch while they explore all the wonderful books around them. Children usually learn more from their own reading than from dumbed-down public-school textbooks.

11. Take turns with other parents in your neighborhood who homeschool their children. Having each parent take a turn home-schooling the other's children a few days a week, based on availability, gives each parent more work-time flexibility.

12. Tutors can also be shared. Get together with a few neighborhood parents and chip in to pay math or reading tutors to teach three or four kids together at a set time every week. The tutors could use each parent's home in turn as a mini-school. When a group of parents share the costs, tutors become more affordable for everyone.

13. Churches and synagogues have been education centers for American children since colonial days. Have a meeting with some of your neighbors about going to a local church and asking it to start a small school to teach children reading, writing, and arithmetic. Offer donations to the church to cover the

expense of tutors or teachers. Your local pastor, priest, or rabbi might like this idea and start the school to increase attendance by getting more parents interested in his church or synagogue. Also, your church might start a local day care center. If it agrees to this, you could homeschool your child when you get home from work, or with weekend sessions.

14. Here's another suggestion. Local YMCAs can be found in most major cities. These YMCAs (or JCCs if you're Jewish) have wonderful classes for children of all ages. Become a member of your local YMCA or JCC. For a $300 to $500-a-year membership fee, you can get all kinds of help with your children. The Ys and JCCs also have organized sports activities and arts and crafts classes for children. You pay a little extra for these services, but you'll pay far less than for a private day care center. Go to your local YMCA or JCC and inquire about their activities and classes for children. When you come home from work, you can pick up your child, eat supper, relax for an hour, and then begin home-schooling classes.

15. You also might try getting together with a group of neighbors and going to your local YMCA or JCC to talk with the supervisor about starting more formal learn-to-read classes. You can suggest paying a small increase in your membership fees to pay for the tutor the YMCA or JCC would hire. The supervisor might find this idea appealing because it would be good for business. By expanding the classes and services they offer, YMCAs or JCCs can get more parents as members and make more profits.

16. What about grandparents? They love your children, and often they get bored just sitting around being retired. If they live nearby, ask them if they would like to help homeschool their grandchildren while you're at work. They will probably thank you for asking. Having grandparents help with home-schooling can bring the whole family close together again, and helps your children socialize with and appreciate older people. Also, Grandma and Grandpa may enjoy being taught how to use the computer by their grandchildren.

17. Look to your immediate family or circle of close friends

or neighbors for people you could ask or pay to help watch and/ or homeschool your children during the day. If you live near a married sister who stays home with her children, ask her if she would help you homeschool your child. If possible, consider moving near a close relative who would be willing to help. If you have a close friend who stays at home, ask her if you can pay her to take care of and help homeschool your child while you work.

18. Retired senior citizens are another source of potential low-cost tutors in your neighborhood. Contact local senior citizen groups, or put ads in the local paper. In every town and city in America, thousands of retired people already volunteer their time teaching children to read in local YMCAs, churches, and schools. Tap this vast potential of bored retired people who like children and would love to tutor them. Being around children makes most older people feel young again, and many times you do *them* a favor by asking (or paying) them to watch over or teach your children.

19. While or after you homeschool your children, you can give them real-life education and a taste of the work-world through apprenticeships. As noted earlier, many of our Founding Fathers, such as Ben Franklin, George Washington, and John Adams, learned a trade as apprentices. Franklin was apprenticed to a printer, Washington to a surveyor, and Adams to a lawyer. Apprenticeship was the equivalent of today's high school work-study programs.

With your teenager's approval, ask a local accountant, builder, lawyer, architect, engineer, car mechanic, bank manager, or restaurant owner if your older child can work with him or her as an apprentice or intern during the day. Your teenager would receive no pay, but he or she could learn valuable on-the-job skills, including talking to customers, creating bills and invoices, getting along with a boss, and being punctual and responsible at work. Apprenticing is also a way to introduce your children to different careers to see which ones they like or don't like. If children know firsthand from work experience that they don't like or are unsuited to a particular career, they won't waste years studying it in college.

20. You might get together a group of co-workers where you work and approach your boss or supervisor to create a small day-care center in the office, if there is a room that can be put aside for this purpose. You can suggest to your group that each worker-parent accept a small cut in pay to cover the cost of a day-care teacher to watch over and instruct the children. Your boss might like this idea, as it would not take money from the company and would insure loyal, happy workers. Keep thinking of incentives your group can offer your boss that would make it worth his while to consider your idea. Incentives can be a small pay cut or your willingness to work overtime without overtime pay.

21. With email, a fax machine, computer, printer, and a high-speed Internet connection, most clerical work can be done at home today. You can take the work into the office one day a week or even e-mail the work to your office. Business phone calls can even be routed to your home phone. With today's technology, many employers see that it pays to have their employees work from home. If your boss is against this idea, think of ways to make this arrangement worthwhile to him or her. Again, offer to take a small cut in your salary or benefits or rearrange your time schedule if you can do so without inconveniencing your employer. A boss who considers you a reliable and competent employee may agree to a work-at-home arrangement to keep a valued employee happy. If your boss rejects this idea, you might start quietly looking for another job with a company that will give you the flexibility you want and need.

22. Once your children learn to read well and use computer programs and the Internet, your home-schooling options increase dramatically. The learning software or Internet school you select becomes their teacher, giving your children individualized, step-by-step instruction. When your kids are old enough, they can spend all morning or afternoon on the computer, learning to their heart's content while you're at work.

Your job when you come home from work would be to check on their progress, answer their questions, encourage them, and find more advanced books or learning software as their skills improve. Books, education software, and Internet schools can be your children's home-schooling classroom. Once your kids get into learning this way, you will have the time you need to work.

These are some of the ways you can arrange the time to homeschool your children, even if you have to work. Once you make the decision to start home-schooling, you can take advantage of these many options.

Who Will Watch My Children While I'm Working?

If you work, and homeschool your kids at night, on weekends, or part-time during the day, who will watch your children while you work? What if you can't afford high-priced licensed day care? First, re-read all the home-schooling options listed in the previous section. Here you'll find many suggestions about who could watch your children while you work, such as grandparents, older children at home, trusted neighbors, adult relatives who live nearby, local YMCAs or church day-care centers, retired couples in your neighborhood, a small day-care center where you work, and working from home.

Many of these relatives, neighbors, YMCAs, or local churches can serve a dual purpose of both watching your children while you work and teaching your child reading and other skills. Also, most older children can occupy themselves at home on the computer or in a local library while you're at work, without adult supervision.

Another option is to create your own day-care system with neighbors. Before public schools became mandatory, parents built family, church, and community ties with trusted neighbors to arrange convenient childcare among themselves. You can do the same. Organize a group of trusted neighborhood parents and friends, and rotate day care centers in each other's homes. If you get a group of five neighborhood parents, have each parent take turns supervising the children in her home for one day a week or one week at a time. This system can save all parents in the group a huge amount of money for day care.

Also, there are usually some parents in the neighborhood who don't work. Ask them if they would like to earn extra money baby-sitting your children and the children of other working parents in the neighborhood. Many non-working parents, especially in poorer neighborhoods, would be happy to make extra money this way (of course, you would only approach a non-working parent that you know and trust).

If you try these options, you should be able to find no-cost or low-cost day care for your children while you work.

What about Time for Myself?

If you're a single working mother and decide to homeschool your children, make sure you're good to yourself. When you come home from work, let yourself relax and wind down from work before you start the lessons. You will be your children's coach and teacher, so your mind should be clear and alert. After a while you'll get used to your home-schooling schedule, and both you and your children will look forward to it.

Be patient with yourself. If you've never taught reading or math to a child, do some research to find the best books, programs, and computer software available. Engage your children as partners in this learning process. See which programs they enjoy and learn most quickly from. Also, many home-schooling parent organizations have Internet sites filled with information to help you through the process (see the Resources section).

What Will Home-schooling Be Like?

How you homeschool your children is entirely up to you, which is one of home-schooling's greatest benefits. You have complete flexibility and total control over what, when, and how you teach your children. If one book, Internet school, or software program doesn't work out, you can quickly change to another until you find one that works best for you and your kids. You can set up a flexible home-schooling schedule based on whether you work part or full-time, are a single working parent, or a stay-at-home mother. After teaching your children the basics, you can work out a flexible curriculum based on what subjects interest them. The books, Internet schools, and home-schooling Internet sites listed in the Resources section include guidelines for creating your home-schooling program. They also have real-life stories about parents who home-schooled their kids.

If you're new to home-schooling or uncertain of your ability to teach your children, you can start by relying on Internet schools to take much of the burden of home-schooling off your back. As I noted earlier, these schools offer everything from specialized tutoring to accredited, full-curriculum programs. A good Internet school will give your children a thorough, structured curriculum for reading, math, and many other subjects, leading to a high-school diploma. Also, these schools can give your children independent evaluations of their work and progress, so your kids are not totally dependent on you for home-schooling.

If you prefer to give your child a more independent, wider-ranging education, you can do most of the home-schooling yourself without using an Internet school. Instead of following a set curriculum, you and your child can explore a whole world of subjects by using books from your local library and book store, computer learning software, Internet resources, outside tutors, field trips to local museums, education videos, and many other resources. The resources you use will often depend on which ones work best for each child, which subjects your child shows an interest in, and each child's learning style.

The following letter to college admission boards by Caitlin Guthrie Freeman describes her experiences as a home-schooled student. Her letter will give you an idea of what home-schooling can be like for your children. This is just one home-schooling student's experience, but it reveals the typical enthusiasm and passion for learning that home-schooling can release in your child:

I am writing this letter in the hope of answering the two questions that you might have for any homeschooler: why do I homeschool and how do I do it?

After graduating from the Antioch School, a private alternative school connected with Antioch College, I decided to spend my seventh grade year at Ridgewood, a private prep school. This was instead of going on to Yellow Springs Junior High like most of my friends. I chose Ridgewood primarily for one reason: the students. They were happy, lively, accepting, and seemed very interested in their work.

Although I received very good grades, and did very well academically at Ridgewood, I found that my learning was very controlled and prescribed. At the Antioch School I had always been encouraged to take charge of my own learning. But at Ridgewood everyone was expected to move along with everyone else, plodding at a universal pace that was too fast for some and infinitely too slow for others. It was expected that we would accommodate our learning for the good of the class; no one was allowed to move out of the mundane rhythm and learn for themselves. Our minds were not our property, they belonged to a communal brain bank and no one could make a withdrawal without their other classmates taking out the exact same amount. For example, although grammar had always been very easy for me, and though I had always received "A"s, I was still often expected to complete four grammar assignments per night along with everyone else in the class, whether or not I needed them. I often found I did not have the time for my own interests or my own learning.

I left Ridgewood for the last time in June of 1993 with a firm idea in my head: I was not going back the next year; I was going to homeschool. My parents and I had discussed this at length during the second half of my seventh grade year. There was so much I wanted to do, so many things I wanted to accomplish that I knew would not be possible if I remained at Ridgewood. So, that last day, after saying farewell to my friends and telling them I would not be returning the next year, I finally started to live my life.

That first year of homeschool was filled with such an incredible sense of elation. I had the sense of limitless time, and the feeling I could learn everything and accomplish anything. Each day I had hundreds of little grab bags set before me, each filled with something new to experience, new to learn. I was free and encouraged to plunge my eager hands into as many of these grab bags of knowledge as I could. I became enamored of archaeology and paleontology, and poured at length over my many references and fact finders.

I read Isaac Asimov's *The Realm of Algebra* as part of my math course. I discovered a love of Shakespeare and that I had a knack for learning and comprehending his rich language after being cast in *Twelfth Night*. I worked on a public access television show and got to conduct a special television interview with children's author, Virginia Hamilton. I began singing with the Dayton Choral Academy. I also discovered opera that year, and found that I could not get enough of Le Nozze di Figaro, Faust, and Die Zauberflote. I became a member of the Yellow Springs High School Drama Club, and acted in my first pre-professional musical, *Jesus Christ, Superstar*, under the superb direction of Marcia C. Nowik. It was an amazing year, filled with freedom, learning, field trips, theatre performances, and all sorts of other experiences.

Today, as I look back on that first homeschool year, I realize that, although I have matured and changed, my love and drive for acquiring knowledge is still as strong

—I am still as elated by the process of learning as I was in eighth grade. I am still just as busy; my days are still as packed with activity as when I was fourteen.

This I hope, gives a sense of why I home school. Now let me explain how I do it. In between the intense bursts of driven energy that make up all my classes, I relax, or read, or work with my friends. Some are homeschoolers, some are not, some live in Yellow Springs, and some live hundreds or even thousands of miles away and keep in touch with me over the Internet. My life is far from being socially empty as some believe homeschoolers' lives must be. I converse on-line each day with people I met while at Interlochen Arts Camp, and consider them to be some of my best friends. Really good friends are hard to come by, and it really doesn't matter whether they are across the country or right next door.

My homeschooling friends have taught me that there are about as many ways to homeschool as there are homeschoolers. I have one friend whose work is completely unstructured. She learns by employing only hands on techniques (creating a budget or measuring ingredients to bake a cake is her math program; her English and grammar come from reading and writing). There are many homeschoolers who employ this unschooling approach to learning, and for many it is very successful.

I have another friend, however, whose entire life is structure. She works completely out of text books and school curricula, reading only to write book reports, studying and learning only for the next homework assignment. She studied at home with an extremely accelerated curriculum for two years, and then graduated to go to college at the age of fifteen.

Although I chose to homeschool to free my schedule, to open up new possibilities for learning, and to allow myself more time to accomplish my own work, being busy creates its own schedule. I have to have a definite routine to accomplish what I want to. It is a routine I set for myself—or that is often set for me by my many outside classes: French, Italian, voice lessons, Shakespeare, Theatre and Horseback.

If I do have a free space that has not been scheduled with a class or my homework, I always seem to find something to fill it. I keep to a regular practice schedule for voice, and always do math and French each weekday morning. I read, write, do science or history, and often do more French in the afternoon. In addition, I have my lessons.

It is a bit of a paradox. I both have what seems like unlimited time to complete projects, and extreme time constraints brought on by my homework, lessons, and classes. However, I do have a flexibility which allows me to prioritize and alter my schedule when some opportunity comes up. This January, for instance, I may be traveling to New York City to attend the 10th Anniversary performance of *The Phantom of the Opera* by Andrew Lloyd Webber. But there is always daily practice and the responsibilities of classes, homework, rehearsals and performances. I am always busy.

Many of my classes are basically self taught in that I am both the teacher and the student, although they are supported by my parents or by weekly lessons with a teacher or tutor. But I have to find a way to use and build on what we've done together between my lessons.

An example of how I organize my homeschool is the way in which my writing course is done. My parents assign me essay topics or research projects, and help provide some of the information or books I might need to get started. I am currently researching the English translations of *Le Fantome de l'Opera* (The Phantom of the Opera) by Gaston Leroux. Over eighty pages were omitted in the Alexander Teixeiros de Mattos translation, and I am trying to find out why. In addition, in the different translations that I have read, each translator seems to have a different style and a different understanding of the French language which colors the way the story is perceived by the reader.

I am also working on translating part of the original text into English. I would like to be able to find the time to translate the entire book and create my own definitive translation of *Le Fantome*. This is something that I am really looking forward to.

I believe choosing to homeschool has been one of the most positive decisions I have made in my life. It has given me freedom of time and choice, the freedom with which to explore my interests, to follow tangents and delve into a subject. Because of homeschooling I have been able to focus on the theatre and music and language in a way that is denied to most people my age. I have learned early to appreciate the wisdom of Shakespeare, the beauty of opera, and the heart and soul of theatre. I know I would not have been able to do this without the vehicle of homeschool supporting and carrying me along the way."[16]

Caitlin's letter should give you some idea of the options and flexibility you have in designing a home-schooling program, as well as how exiting, rewarding, and effective home-schooling can be for your children. Every child's interests will be different, but that is the beauty of home-schooling. After learning to read and write, each child can study whatever subjects excite them. Learning becomes a joyful and rewarding experience, instead of the mindless drudgery it is in most public schools.

Many of the home-schooling general-information Internet sites and parent-organization web sites in the Resources section can also give you an idea of what home-schooling would be like. They have many true stories by home-schooling parents who describe their home-schooling experiences, and offer home-schooling tips. Also, two wonderful books I can recommend will also give you an idea of what home-schooling can be like. They are: *Homeschooling For Excellence*, by David and

Micki Colfax (Warner Books), and *The Unschooling Handbook*, by Mary Griffith (Prima Publishing).

What About College Admissions?

If you homeschool your children, you can feel assured that many colleges will welcome their applications for admission. Not every college and university accepts home-schooled students, but many do. Home-schooled students have been accepted by over 1000 different colleges and universities across the country, including MIT, Harvard, Princeton, and Stanford University.[17]

Many colleges now routinely accept home-schooled students, and some even actively seek them out. Home-schoolers typically submit a portfolio of their work to the college, instead of the standard transcripts. In a letter describing its policy towards home-schooled students, George A. Shriller, Jr., former director of admissions at Boston University, stated: "Boston University welcomes applications from home-schooled students. We believe students educated at home possess the passion for knowledge, the independence, and the self-reliance that enable them to excel in our intellectually challenging programs of study."[18]

The Right to Homeschool

Parents in all fifty states now have the legal right to homeschool their children. This right is confirmed by the U.S. Constitution and the Supreme Court. Although the Constitution does not specifically mention a parent's right to homeschool his or her children, that right is recognized by the Tenth and Fourteenth Amendments. The Tenth Amendment reads: "The powers not delegated to the United States by the Constitution, nor prohibited by it to the States, are reserved to the States respectively, or to the people." Because the Constitution does not delegate any power to the federal government to regulate education, that power is reserved to the states or the people, meaning the voters, including parents.

The Fourteenth Amendment guarantees that all citizens have the right to liberty, which cannot be taken away without due process. In its 1925 Pierce v. Society of Sisters decision (which still stands), the Supreme Court upheld the right of parents to control their children's education. The decision affirmed the "fundamental right" of parents to "direct the upbringing and education of their children under their control."[19] The Justices declared unanimously that "the child is not the mere creature of the state" and "those who nurture him and direct his destiny have the right, coupled with the high duty, to recognize and prepare him for additional obligations."[20]

Unfortunately for home-schooling parents, this same Supreme Court decision also held that states have an "interest" in education. It held that to protect this alleged interest, states have the power to require children to attend school, and the power to regulate schools to ensure that they were doing a good job. So the Court said states can't have a legal monopoly on education, but can force children to attend school and can regulate these schools. The Pierce decision therefore upheld parents' rights with one hand, and struck them down with the other. This decision opened the Pandora's box that let all fifty state governments regulate home-schooling.[21]

Home-schooling is a great success, and that's why many school authorities are hostile to it. Home-schooling parents are a direct challenge to the public-school monopoly. Many school authorities can't stand the fact that untrained and unlicensed parents give their kids a better education than so-called public-school experts. It's easy to see why home-schoolers' success humiliates the failed public schools by comparison. Home-schooling parents also humiliate public-school officials who claim that only certified or licensed teachers are qualified to teach children. Also, many school officials resent home-schoolers because, as I noted earlier, the typical public school loses about $7300 a year in tax money for each child that leaves the system.

For these reasons, until fairly recently, most state legislatures either outlawed home-schooling or tried to strangle it to death with regulations. In 1980, only Utah, Ohio, and Nevada officially recognized parents' rights to homeschool their children. In most other states, legislators continually harassed or prosecuted home-schoolers under criminal truancy laws and educational neglect charges.[22] By 2004, however, pressure from parents, Christian home-schooling organizations, and recent court rulings pushed all fifty states to enact statutes that allow home-schooling, as long as certain requirements are met. These requirements vary for each state.[23]

In spite of these statutes, many states and school authorities still harass home-schooling parents. Here's a typical example:

A Virginia couple was arrested for legally home-schooling their child. Gerald and Angela B. [last name omitted for privacy] were arrested on March 17, 2000, after truancy charges were filed against them by a local public school administrator. The B. [family], however, point out that they followed proper procedures to have their son, Brett, legally schooled at home, and therefore were not in violation of truancy laws. Virginia law requires home schoolers to notify the local public school superintendent of intent to home school. The B. [family] had submitted the proper notice on February 25, 2000. Bryan A. [last name omitted for privacy], assistant principal at [the] . . . Elementary School, filed the charges against the B. [family].

Virginia law, however, stipulates that only school superintendents, not other school administrators, can file truancy charges. In this situation, A. [assistant principal] went around the superintendent and straight to the courts. The Home School Legal Defense Association maintains that, if A. [assistant principal] had followed the law, the B. [family] could have avoided the humiliation of public arrests. Two days after the arrests the charges were dropped.[24]

Because the Supreme Court gave local governments the right to regulate home-schooling, parents can still be harassed by local school officials. To protect your legal rights, you should seriously consider joining the Home School Legal Defense Association (HSLDA). You can join at their web site, http://www. hslda.org. Founded in 1983, HSDLA provides its members with legal representation against local school officials who may demand to supervise parents' home-schooling or periodically test their home-schooled children. The Rutherford Institute is another well-known organization dedicated to protecting parents' rights and providing legal help to home-schooling parents. Their website is http://www.rutherford.org.

One way to avoid state regulations is to use an Internet-based independent-study school. As noted previously, these Internet schools provide a full curriculum of subjects leading to a high school diploma. Because many of these schools are accredited with their respective states as private schools, state school authorities usually won't bother parents whose children are enrolled in one of these schools. If you don't want to restrict your child's home-schooling to the set curriculum of accredited Internet schools, you can pursue parent-directed home-schooling. You then have to be aware of and conform to your state's home-schooling regulations. You can find these regulations on the HSDLA web site.

Home-schooling Can Also Benefit Parents

Home-schooling not only benefits kids, it can also give new skills to parents, and even make them better parents. In learning to homeschool their children, many parents learn skills that personally benefit them also. For example, if you're planning to homeschool your child, you should know or learn how to type, use a computer, and access the Internet. These skills will open a vast world of education and other valuable resources both for you and your child.

Learning to type, if you don't already know how, will make your work at the computer faster and easier. You can teach yourself using an instruction book or take an adult education course at your local college or business school. There are also many excellent, easy-to-use software programs that can teach you to type step by step as you sit at your computer. One such program is *Mavis Beacon's Typing for Kids*, part of a software series that include more advanced typing programs you can use once you've mastered the basics.

You could learn to type together with your child, as a fun project. Have a friendly competition to see who learns to type faster. Typing is more than just a useful skill that will help both you and your child work much faster on the computer keyboard. It is also a marketable skill that, along with a computer and a high-speed Internet connection, can help you earn extra income by working from home.

If you don't feel confident that you can learn the computer and Internet yourself, don't worry. You can learn by taking courses at your local library or community college. There are even easy-to-use computer software programs for beginners that teach you how to use the computer, word-processing programs, and the Internet. Many people are afraid of technological gadgets, but once your computer is set up and you learn the basics, you'll find that the computer is fun and easy to use. Like your kids, you may even become a computer junkie. If you learned how to cook, drive a car, or balance your checkbook, you can easily learn to use a computer and the Internet.

Learning to use a computer also opens up a vast reservoir of information that can help you in many other areas of your life, and give you more financial resources to homeschool your children. On the Internet, you can find life insurance quotes, mortgage refinancing quotes to get the lowest interest rates, vital health information, employment opportunities, and much more. This vast resource of information could help you save money, earn more money, or help you find a better or higher-paying job. These personal benefits from the Internet could eventually make it easier and more affordable for you to home-school your kids.

To advance your own education, you can take distance-learning courses from accredited high schools and colleges. Distance learning lets you earn a college degree from home through the Internet while home-schooling your children.

Don't let the wonder and power of the computer and Internet pass you by. Learning to use a computer and the Internet can change your life and your children's lives. We should all humbly thank and appreciate those geniuses who invented and developed computers, software, and the Internet.

In the next chapter, I will go into even greater detail about ways to homeschool your children.

9

Home-schooling:
The Whole World Can Be
Your Child's Classroom

If you to decide to personally homeschool your children rather than use an Internet school, your next question will probably be, "Now what?" If you have no formal teaching experience, how do you go about home-schooling your children? Where do you start? Taking full responsibility for your children's education may seem scary, but there are many resources available to help you give your child a great education at home, with or without Internet schools or tutors. This chapter will explore many of these resources, and give you the tools to find others.

Knowing that you have many resources available can help you feel more secure in your ability to homeschool your child. Believe that you are just as bright and capable as other home-schooling parents and that you can give your child a wonderful, enriching education at home. You can also increase your confidence by practicing home-schooling techniques *before* you take your child out of public school.

Home-schooling is the least expensive and most natural

way to educate your child. Below you will find many ideas on ways to teach your children reading, math, and other subjects. These ideas are simply a starting point for you. Read some of the many excellent books on home-schooling I list in the Resources section. These books are written by authors who are experts in, and very knowledgeable about home-schooling, and will give you lots of great ideas and resources for home-schooling your children.

Reading

One of the first skills you should teach your children is reading. Once your children learn to read, the whole world opens to them. Many parents think that teaching their child to read is a difficult and mysterious task. It isn't. As I noted earlier, most children can learn to read fairly quickly. It only requires that you use the right methods, such as phonics and reading constantly to your children, and avoid the wrong methods such as whole-language instruction. Just as colonial parents taught their children to read by pointing out letters, letter sounds, words, spelling, and grammar, and reading out loud to their children, you can do the same with your children.

Each child is unique and will learn with a different style and at a different pace. According to Mary Griffith, author of *The Unschooling Handbook*:

How much assistance each child wants or needs varies enormously. What seems to be important is for parents to provide plenty of support: answering all those questions about letters and sounds, playing word games, offering comparisons between new words and ones they already know. For most unschooling families [unschooling is a less structured form of homeschooling], this sort of wordplay is not a conscious exercise they deliberately work into a certain number of hours every day; it's a natural effect of sharing their pleasure in using and enjoying language.[1]

Each child learns to read at a different age and speed. Some children love books from the first time you read to them at age one or two. Others don't gravitate to reading until age six or seven because they prefer art or other activities. Watch your children's reactions as you try different reading approaches. Use what works and excites them and discard what bores them. Because each child learns at his own pace, don't be alarmed if your children aren't reading at the age you think they should. Albert Einstein didn't talk until he was three years old and didn't read until he was eleven.[2]

Read to your child constantly. Kids love to hear stories, so reading becomes associated with fun and with your love and attention. Stories bring children adventure and fascinating facts and ideas about the world. Many stories can also teach kids moral values, such as Aesop's Fables, Grimm's fairy tales, and the stories of Hans Christian Anderson. When you read to your children, you immerse them in words and the sounds of words. They can also learn grammar by seeing and hearing how words are strung together.

While you read to them, they will ask many questions about the words and story, which will lead to further questions, more words, and trips to the dictionary or encyclopedia. You can also ask your children questions as you read to them. Ask them to point out letters, make letter sounds, and try to put the letter sounds together into words. This back-and-forth interaction also gives you clues to each child's learning style.

Make a game out of learning the alphabet and letter sounds. Use alphabet songs and letter blocks, and programs like Alpha-Phonics or Turbo Phonics. Ask your kids to name letters and read words wherever you go, inside or outside the home. Point out road and store signs, read recipes with them, show them food labels in the supermarket, read the instructions on their favorite toys. Surround your children with words.

Children often want to read material related to activities that fascinate them. If your children enjoy cooking, airplane models, or science projects, they'll want to read recipes, instructions for putting the plane together, or the ingredients to mix in their chemistry experiment. The more activities your children enjoy, the more they will want to read.

As you teach your children to read, engage all their senses. Many studies show that the more senses we use in learning facts and skills, the more we retain what we learn. Use teaching materials that engage a child's sense of touch, taste, smell, and sound, as well as sight. Alphabet songs link sound and rhyme to letters and words. You could buy an inexpensive calligraphy pen set, so your child can make artistic letters in different colored inks. Cut letters out of different materials, so your child associates touch with these letters. Bake letter cookies, so your child associates taste and smell with letters and words. The more senses you engage, the fuller your children's experiences and the faster they learn.

All of us, including children, have a dominant sense that we use to learn. Many people are visual learners who have to see or read new material to absorb it. Visual learners don't absorb spoken instructions well or they forget spoken material quickly. They need to see facts or ideas written on paper to study and absorb them. In contrast, people whose dominant sense is hearing often learn better by listening than by reading. They have trouble paying attention to written material. Kinesthetic people, who often become artists, engineers, architects, or surgeons, learn best through physical manipulation of objects. These people have to get their hands busy to fully absorb new material.

Give your children different kinds of teaching materials for the same skill or subject and see which materials your child gravitates to and learns best from. Then use learning materials and methods that take advantage of your child's strongest learning sense or senses.

For example, if your child is a visual learner, use visual teaching aids such as big letters with different colors, children's stories with illustrations, or computer software that lets the child see big letters on the computer screen as he or she types. An auditory learner, in contrast, might learn fastest by hearing you read, using alphabet or word rhymes, repeating letter sounds out loud, or associating funny sounds with letters or words (like growling for a "g"). Have a touch-oriented child use alphabet blocks and magnetic letters to "build" words or string them together, or fingerpaint letters and words.

Take advantage of your child's primary learning style, but also use teaching materials that engage their other senses to reinforce the lessons. For example, alphabet blocks and finger-painting use both sight and touch. Alphabet rhymes use sound and sight. Illustrated books that you read to your child use sight and sound. Cooking with your child uses sight, touch, smell, and taste as your child reads the instructions, mixes ingredients, and smells and then tastes the food. When your children use all their senses, especially the dominant one, they have more fun and learn faster than they would just listening to a teacher.

There are dozens of fine learn-to-read books, programs, and computer software to choose from that make learning to read fun and exciting for your kids (see the Resources section). There are also tutors and step-by-step courses on the Internet that teach children to read.

Your local library and bookstore are also great resources. Barnes & Noble, Borders, and other large bookstores have children's reading-instruction books of all kinds and grade levels, and audio books your child can listen to. You and your child can spend all day in these stores and never exhaust the possibilities. If you work and have limited time, many bookstores are open on week-ends and in the evening. You can also order books on the Internet from these bookstores' web sites, and from other Internet sites such as Amazon.com.

My favorite play is *The Miracle Worker* by William Gibson. In one scene, young Helen Keller's mother thanks Annie Sullivan, Helen's stubborn, dedicated teacher, for teaching Helen cleanliness, telling Annie that cleanliness is next to godliness. Annie retorts, "Cleanliness is next to nothing, she [Helen] has to learn that everything has its name! That words can be her *eyes* to everything in the world outside her, and inside too. What is she without words? With them she can think, have ideas, be reached, there's not a thought or fact in the world that can't be hers."[3] The glorious gift of reading can be for your children what it was for Helen Keller. By teaching your children to read, you can give them the world.

Math

Basic math is another important skill that children should learn. It involves not only calculation skills like addition and multiplication, but mathematical ideas like sorting, grouping, fractions, progressions of numbers, spatial relations, and much more. Children have mathematical abilities wired into their brains, much like their innate ability to learn language and reading, but these abilities must be guided and nurtured.

As with reading, each child will have his or her own learning style in learning numbers, computation, and math concepts. As you introduce math materials and ideas, keep a sharp lookout for the learning materials and styles that your child responds to best. As with reading, use study materials that take advantage of your child's dominant learning sense and make learning fun.

Surround your child with numbers and math ideas as much as possible. Building blocks, Lego toys, and log houses all involve counting, sorting, and combining real-world objects based on numbers and math operations. Board games like dice, Yahtzee, Monopoly Junior, Dominoes, Connect Four, and Chutes and Ladders are a fun way to get your child to understand math ideas. For older children, card games like Blackjack, poker, cribbage, or even solitaire teach mathematical concepts like addition, subtraction, sorting, patterns, and probability.

Besides board and card games, there are also many math manipulation toys. Pattern blocks, Geoboards, and Cuisinaire rods can teach children shapes, numbers, fractions, geometry, and the decimal system in an entertaining way. Balances introduce the concept of weight, rulers introduce the idea of distances and units of measure, and graph paper with squares of different sizes can help teach about proportion. Crafts using beads, marbles, paper shapes, or even loose change or Popsicle sticks can all be used for math lessons on counting, sorting, and shapes. Even jelly beans or M&M candies can be used for lessons on numbers, adding, subtracting (by eating the candies), or sorting by groups of colors.

Older children can learn basic or more advanced math skills with such products as *Saxon* or *Miquon* math workbooks, which offer a structured approach that is popular among many home-schooling parents. Both series teach arithmetic and other math-related ideas step-by-step, increasing the complexity with each new workbook. You can combine these formal math-teaching materials with real-life lessons. For example, by cooking with your children, you can introduce fractions and percentages, addition, subtraction, and division as you measure out flour or other ingredients, slice a pie, and so on.

Many other subjects such as geography, science, astronomy, music, even history can be linked to math lessons. Geography requires knowledge of distances and directions, lengths of rivers, or heights of mountains. Science, of course, depends on math and measurement. With chemistry experiment kits, your child can mix and measure materials. With electricity experiment kits, he or she can measure amps and voltage. Astronomy is about distances, shapes of planets and orbits, speed of motion through space, and distances to galaxies far, far away. Music lessons can involve math because music itself is patterns of sound based on mathematical relationships between notes.

Math is all around you in your daily activities, which you can use for math lessons. Giving your children a fixed allowance and letting them buy things with the allowance introduces ideas about both math and money. Children quickly learn the practical value of addition and subtraction if they spend too freely and use up all their allowance for the week.

Taking trips with your children gives you an opportunity to teach them lessons about time and distance, how far the car can go on a full tank of gasoline, and so on. Shopping can teach them about weights, shapes of cans and cereal boxes, and addition and subtraction of money at the checkout counter. Gardening can teach them about times to water flowers, and distances between seeds in a seedbed. Pointing out different trees in the neighborhood can lead to lessons about telling trees apart by their width, height, thickness of their trunks, and shape of their leaves.

As with reading, learn-math books and computer resources for math instruction are readily available. Use an Internet search engine like Google or Yahoo to look for math-teaching books, software, tutors, or Internet schools and you will find hundreds of listings. These resources teach both math ideas and computation skills step-by-step, for children of all ages and skill levels. They make learning math fun, and your children learn at their own pace with you by their side to help and guide them.

Science

Science is much more than the dry facts that public-school children have to memorize and regurgitate on the next test. It's the study of the physical world around us. By observing plants, rocks, bugs, lightning, magnetism, and all the other wondrous objects and forces of Nature, a child can learn how to think like a scientist—to observe, predict, and experiment. Science is one of humankind's greatest achievements. It has given us antibiotics, electricity, airplanes, elevators, automobiles, skyscrapers, and abundant food. Scientists and inventors like Louis Pasteur, Thomas Edison, the Wright brothers, and Bill Gates are real heroes who have raised our standard of living to unheard-of levels, compared with life as it was only a few hundred years ago.

You can teach your children about science in the same way you teach them math—with formal teaching materials and experiments, and by letting them experience science in their daily lives. Immerse your children in chemistry, biology, physics, astronomy, computers, and other sciences to see which subjects excite them the most. Every child is a born scientist. From their earliest days, children eagerly seek to learn everything they can about the world around them. They constantly touch, smell, probe, examine, and experiment with every object within their reach. When learning to walk, children learn about gravity and balance, and test whether they can walk by moving their legs and arms in a certain way. They experiment with new ways to keep their balance, such as holding onto a chair.

As your children get older, you can immerse them in science with relatively inexpensive science toys and kits that let them explore their world. These include a telescope, microscope, magnifying glasses, Lego building blocks, electricity and chemistry kits, planters for flowers and vegetables to learn biology, and model airplane kits to learn about flight. Your local mall usually has a child-learning store with a variety of science kits. You can also search the Internet for children's science toys and kits.

As with math, your kids can learn science from everyday activities you share with them. Cooking is one big chemistry kit. It lets your children experiment with heat, cold, taste, texture, density, fluidity, acidity, measurement, and chemical interactions such as what happens when you mix vinegar with baking soda. Gardening introduces children to biology, plant life, photosynthesis, food and nutrition, plant reproduction, and much more. When your children get a cut or a cold, you can show them illustrated books about germs, the body, medicine, and blood circulation.

Of course, your local bookstore and library have many fascinating and colorfully illustrated science books for children of all ages, as well as biographies of Pasteur, Edison, and other great scientists to inspire them. Older kids who become fascinated by a particular science can read more advanced books on biology, physics, chemistry, astronomy, and electronics.

Your children can spend endless hours on the Internet exploring a vast range of scientific topics from ants to volcanoes.

They can explore these subjects at their leisure, twenty-four-hours a day. The Internet puts the great libraries of the world at their fingertips. As noted earlier, the *Encyclopedia Britannica* now has a computer software edition, so your child can study science articles on every subject under the sun.

Another way to bring science into your children's lives is to take them on field trips. Science and natural history museums will fascinate them and expose them to the history of science. Go to a construction site and talk about foundations, building materials, heating, electrical, and plumbing systems, and what beams and columns do. Terrific television programs like *Nova* and cable networks like the *Science Channel* can also spark your children's passion for science.

Of course, you won't know all the answers to your children's probing questions. But you can use their questions as a springboard to show them how to research a subject in more depth using the library or the Internet, so they have the tools to explore subjects on their own.

Again, as with math and reading, gear your science instruction to each child's age and learning style. Use learning materials that appeal to your children's strongest sense, so they can learn quickly. Make learning fun, and engage their curiosity and endless desire to understand the world around them.

If your children need more advanced instruction as they get older, think about finding a local tutor or mentor. Place ads on college bulletin boards for student-tutors who major in the science that fascinates your child. Also, ask the local public school if your child can use its science facilities for lab experiments. As noted earlier, many states have laws that allow home-schooled children to use public-school science labs.

History

Unfortunately, in most public schools today, history instruction has degenerated into memorizing facts and dates from dumbed-down textbooks, and classes that try to brainwash children with anti-American values. Today's politically-correct history textbooks are often propaganda pieces that promote multiculturalism and oppose such traditional Western values as family, religion, and individual rights.

Author Charles J. Sykes talks about the anti-American bias in today's history textbooks:

At one time, American history textbooks emphasized an almost uncritical triumphalism, in which Americans were presented as innocent, noble champions of all that is good. While that picture needed revision, it has now been virtually turned on its head. Where Americans were once portrayed as champions of human freedom, they are now frequently portrayed as a nation of hypocrites, who routinely fell short of their ideals and mocked their pretensions with their racism, their rape of the land, and their colonialist ambitions. In this new vision, the story of America becomes a story of victims and victimizers, and history is rewritten, in part, to compensate the victims for their oppressors' wrongs and their neglect. An exercise in celebration thus becomes an exercise in self-contempt and skepticism.[4]

Here's what Patrick, a California parent, said about his children's history textbooks: "Texts? I can't think of one that's really worth warm spit. Lots of books about history [in the library], but texts? Awful. Texts are to history what library paste is to a gourmet meal."[5]

Real history is not so much about *what* happened as about *why* it happened. History is the story of the human race—our cultures, economic systems, political beliefs, and government systems. Studying history helps children understand human nature because history *is* human nature acting through human societies over time.

Studying real history can give your children answers to important questions, such as: Why do groups and cultures act as they do? Why do nations make war on one another all the time?

Why do different peoples at different times form primitive societies, city-states, monarchies, or republics? Why do cultures have religious beliefs? How do human nature, geography, and economic and political forces combine to determine whether a society becomes a democracy, monarchy, theocracy, or totalitarian tyranny? How and why do societies grow more complex? What happens when societies become bigger? How do advances in human knowledge such as agriculture and medicine, affect human history? Why did democracies and republics like ancient Greece and Rome eventually turn into dictatorships or tyrannies? What is the purpose of government? Why do we need it? Why was the American Revolution so important in human history? and Why do we need a Bill of Rights? These are some of the questions that students of history ask. You won't find many discussions of such issues in government-funded public-school classrooms.

Your children can learn real history from hundreds of excellent books in bookstores and your local library. Children don't have to learn history in chronological order. Introduce different historical periods to your kids at different times and see what interests them. Do your children like to read about the Stone Age, ancient Egyptian mummies, medieval knights, England fighting the Spanish Armada, the French Revolution, Patrick Henry and the American Revolution, or Laura Ingalls Wilder's *Little House on the Prairie* books about life on the American frontier?

As your children get older, try to relate what is happening today to similar events in past historical periods. Try to link historical events to broad principles of human behavior and economic and political ideas. Talk to them about the "why" of history.

As their reading and comprehension improves, have your children take out books from the library that describe specific historical periods, people, or events in greater depth. Let your kids read exciting adventure novels like *The Three Musketeers*, *Treasure Island*, and *A Tale of Two Cities* to spark their interest in the novel's historical period. Movies like *Ivanhoe, Mutiny on the Bounty,* and *Back to the Future* can also stimulate your child's interest in history. Biographies of famous people, such as Edison, Washington, Napoleon, and Genghis Khan, are a great way to introduce your child to a specific historical era and the forces that shaped it.

Besides books, there are many other history resources you can turn to. Cable television has the History Channel, which has fascinating history documentaries. Look at old maps and atlases with your child and study how geography has affected history. Living-history field trips to places like colonial Williamsburg, Valley Forge, or the battlefield at Gettysburg are fun as well as educational.

Engage your children in current events. Reading newspapers and news magazines like *Time, Newsweek,* and *U.S. News and World Report* with your children can become a daily lesson in history, politics, and economics. Try to gear your history sessions to each child's age, interests, current reading abilities, and learning style.

Understanding history will also be important to your children in later life, when they are grown-up citizens. America's future is in the hands of our children, who will become the next generation's citizens, lawyers, teachers, senators, and business leaders. If no one teaches our children the values of liberty, individual rights, and limited government that America was founded on, then America's future, and our children's freedom, is in great danger.

The Arts

Children love the arts. There are endless possibilities to get your child drawing, making music, or doing crafts. Materials your children can experiment with include crayons, finger paint, collages, clay, Play-Doh, wood, stained glass, and paper, pencils and pens. In addition to drawing and crafts, art-related activities include singing, playing a musical instrument, dancing, playacting, and puppet making.

You can find a vast number of arts and crafts or music books for children of all ages at a good bookstore or your local library. You can also have your child read biographies of great artists, and books that show collections of paintings by different artists. The Internet is a vast source of arts and crafts books and materials you can buy from online book and art stores like Barnes & Noble, Borders, and Amazon.com. There are also many Internet sites where your child can look at paintings, sculptures, or buildings, and read stories about artists.

As with reading, math, and science, you can involve your child in art activities throughout the day. I mentioned using calligraphy to make word art. You and your children can make craft projects throughout the year, such as birthday cards for friends and relatives, Easter eggs, Halloween costumes, Christmas decorations, and much more. Buy an inexpensive digital camera to get your children interested in photography. Take them on field trips to art museums. Go with them to art shows, local plays, or music recitals. The more art activities you introduce to your children, the greater chance they will find something they love to do with art.

Many years ago, when my nephew was only five years old, I gave him a small electronic piano keyboard that cost me twenty dollars. He loved playing this little toy piano so much that his mother decided to give him piano lessons. He went on to study piano professionally and he now teaches piano for a living. You never know what activity will spark a child's passion and lead to a possible career. Your job as a parent is to surround your children with such activities, notice their reactions, and help them go to the next level.

Be careful about pushing your kids too hard into an art activity you want them to do rather than one that sparks their interest. How many thousands of children have been turned off to music by parents who dragged them to piano lessons when they weren't ready or interested? Let your children show you what activities they love, and take it from there.

Using Internet Resources

Here are some tips for finding anything fast on the Internet, including home-schooling Internet sites. When you use a search engine like Google, Yahoo, or Alta Vista, type in the exact words that describe what you are looking for as your search criteria. For example, if you want to find general homeschool sites, type "homeschooling" in the search engine, usually in the blank white strip next to the word "search." If you want to find homeschool parent organizations, type in those exact words. If you want to find magazines about home-schooling, type in "home-schooling magazines." If you want educational materials to teach your child to read, type in something like "homeschool resources," "educational materials," or "learn-to-read computer software."

Using the exact words that describe what you are looking for will give you better search results. If one combination of words doesn't give you the results you want, change the words around or think of other words that better describe what you are looking for. Soon you will become an expert at surfing the Internet, which will save you much time.

If you want to look up a particular education game, software, or company, type in its exact name. For example, if you want companies that sell the educational game Yahtzee or alphabet blocks, type "Yahtzee" or "alphabet blocks" in the search box. Many companies today have their own Internet sites, which you can find by typing the company's name into your search engine. Most of the time you will get dozens of listings related to what you are looking for.

Also, most Internet sites contain links to other web pages with similar material. On a website homepage, search for sub-headings that say "Links" or something similar. Clicking on this Links button will take you to yet another list of useful Internet sites. Keep doing this on every site, and soon you will have hundreds of web sites that give you valuable resources for home-schooling, or whatever else you are searching for.

You can find many general-information Internet sites

on home-schooling by typing "homeschooling" or "online schools" into your search engine. These sites have practical, up-to-date information on Internet schools, state home-schooling laws, parent-support groups, teaching materials and supplies, and much more. Many useful Internet sites appear in the home-schooling Resources section at the end of this book.

Home-schooling Legal Help

If you are going to homeschool your child, it is important that you join the Home School Legal Defense Association (discussed in Chapter 8). Membership presently costs about $100 a year. The HSLDA has a staff of lawyers who are experts in home-schooling laws. You can call them immediately if a school official demands to test your child, inspect your home-schooling records, or otherwise harasses you. Their lawyer will talk directly to the school authorities, and if necessary, represent your case in court. Your $100-a-year membership fee covers most legal services you might get from HSLDA.

HSDLA's web site (http://www.hslda.org) also has articles and resource material on many legal and political issues surrounding home-schooling, as well as comprehensive information on home-schooling regulations for every state (you should study and know your state's regulations). Read their web site at least once a month to keep track of any changes in regulations in your city or state.

Using the resources and suggestions indicated above and in the Resources section that follows will help you homeschool your children. By taking your children out of public school and using these wonderful education alternatives, you can protect your children and give them the future they deserve.

Conclusion

Education should be a joy for children, not a mind-numbing waste of time. As we've seen, public schools can kill that joy, cripple children's ability to read, warp their values, waste twelve years of their lives, and sometimes put kids in grave danger from violence, drug pushers, and taking Ritalin.

For almost eighty years, school authorities have been tying to "reform" the public-school system. From the "progressive" schools in the 1920's to the "whole-language" reading advocates today, public schools have tried one fad after another, only to see each new education gimmick fail. They all failed because the underlying *structure* of the public-school system remained the same—it is a compulsory, government-controlled system that stays in business through force and deception.

Unlike your grocer, department store, or local car mechanic, public schools get their customers and their money by *force*. Also, the public-school near-monopoly essentially kills any real competition. It strangles an education free market that could give parents real school choice and children a joyous, rewarding education.

I have also argued in this book that parents should *not* depend on public-school authorities to fix the system from within. In most cases, school authorities, employees, and teacher unions *like* the system the way it is, precisely because they personally benefit by it.

Tenure gives public-school teachers and principals *almost absolute job security*. Public schools *stay in business no matter how bad they are,* because taxes prop them up. Most public-school employees get higher salaries than average workers in their town or city. Most also get generous benefits and pensions that other workers in the private sector don't enjoy.

With this kind of setup, is it any wonder that public-school employees, their unions, and politicians who get campaign contributions from teacher unions will fight to the death to keep the public schools intact? Is it any wonder that they fight against vouchers, charter schools, home-schooling, or other options parents use to escape the public schools?

Most public-school employees might care about your children, but parents should *not* expect them to go against their own self-interest. Most teachers, principals, and administrators are decent, dedicated people, but public-school employees and their unions will not relinquish their power or cut their own economic throats for your children's sake.

As a result, we cannot fix this system from within, not in a hundred years. The only way to fix the public schools is to *scrap* them.

One goal of my book was to convince parents that the public-school system is beyond repair, and that they should look elsewhere to give their children a decent education. Parents who want to give their children an exciting and rewarding education should consider *taking their children out of public school*.

Parents, you have the power to give your kids a great education that will fill them with a love of learning and unleash their extraordinary potential. But to do this, you have to leave the failed public schools behind and take advantage of the wonderful, low-cost education alternatives I discussed in this book. Your children can have a bright future and rewarding life if you take charge of their education now, before it is too late. Isn't that what you want for your children?

Resources

The following pages list many resources that you can use to homeschool your children. These include books, general-information home-schooling Internet sites, Internet schools, on-line tutoring sites, teaching-materials Internet sites (including computer software), Internet libraries, parent support-group sites, legal help sites, and college testing, preparation, and admissions Internet sites. Use these resources to the fullest so that you feel more confident about home-schooling your children.

Books

The following books can give you a thorough overview of home-schooling, techniques to use, legal issues, teaching methods and materials that have worked for other parents, how to use the computer and Internet for home-schooling, and many other helpful topics. Many home-schooling general information sites (the next section) will also feature books on how to homeschool.

Armstrong, Thomas. *Awakening Your Child's Natural Genius: Enhancing Curiosity, Creativity, and Learning Ability*, (J. P. Tarcher, 1991). A wonderful book on practical activities at home to inspire your children to learn, be creative, and awaken the natural curiosity and genius that all kids have.

Armstrong, Thomas. *In Their Own Way: Discovering and Encouraging Your Child's Personal Learning Style* (J. P. Tarcher, 1987). Offers practical ideas on discovering and working with your children's particular learning styles. Also, Armstrong, Thomas. *Seven Kinds of Smart: Identifying and Developing Your Many Intelligences* (Plume, 1993).

Blumenfeld, Samuel L. *Homeschooling: A Parent's Guide To Teaching Children* (Replica Books, 1999). This excellent book describes what home-schooling is all about, and helps parents decide whether home-schooling fits their family lifestyle. It covers important aspects of home-schooling, such as: why parents choose to homeschool, how to create and implement a personal style of education for your kids, what subjects to teach and how to teach them, how to handle the socialization issue, how to deal with school authorities, and much more. The book also gives full-time working parents useful, practical information on how to home-school their children.

Cohen, Cafi. *And What about College?* (Holt Associates, 1997). This book is a great help for home-schooling parents seeking college admission for their children. It has practical advice and details on how to describe your child's homeschool education through model letters, resumes, and transcripts that colleges will accept for admission. It offers great advice on how to put your children's home-schooling records in the best possible light to greatly increase their chance for admission to college. This is a must book for home-schooling parents and teenagers ready for college.

Deci, Edward L. *Why We Do What We Do: Understanding Self-Motivation* (Penguin, 1996). This book is a fascinating discussion of how our reasons for doing things affect our abilities. This book will help you understand how to motivate your children to learn.

Gold, Laura Maery, and Joan M. Zielinski. *Home-School Your Child for Free: More Than 1,200 Smart, Effective, and Practical Resources for Home Education on the Internet and Beyond* (Prima, 2000). The Internet is an open door to the biggest library the world has ever seen—and it's all at your fingertips, free. This book is a great source of information, adventure, and educational experiences for the entire family. You'll discover online lesson plans arranged by subject, teaching tips, and success stories from other home-schooling parents. The book has complete curriculum plans for a comprehensive education from preschool through high school. It also has legal guidelines and compliance requirements for home educators, and much more. A great resource book.

Griffith, Mary. *The Unschooling Handbook: How to Use the Whole World as Your Child's Classroom* (Prima, 1998). This wonderful book about "unschooling," a less programmed form of home-schooling, really does show parents how to use the whole world as their children's classroom. It has specific sections on teaching your child reading, art, math, science, and history. It has great advice on how to tell whether your child is learning, how to keep records, and ways to get your child into college. A wonderful introduction to home-schooling and unschooling.

Harris, Gregg, and Sono Harris. *The Home School Organizer* (Noble, 1995). This is an important book that shows you how to organize and keep track of all your lessons, curriculum, children's progress, and other home-schooling details. This book is also a must for legal purposes, if or when local school authorities ask for home-schooling progress records.

Holt, John. *How Children Fail* (Dell Books, 1964). This is a brilliant book about how public schools cripple children's creativity, potential, and desire and ability to learn.

Holt, John. *How Children Learn* (Perseus Publishing, Revised Edition, 1999). This book gives a fresh and insightful look at how children learn. Holt shows how learning is a natural process for children, and how parents can best help their children to learn.

Klicka, Christopher J. *The Right Choice: Home Schooling* (Noble, 1995). This terrific book describes not only the great benefits of home-schooling, but the great dangers of keeping your children in public school. It also makes a brilliant legal and constitutional case for home-schooling and against public schools.

Leppert, Mary, and Michael Leppert. *Home-schooling Almanac, 2002—2003: How to Start, What to Do, Where to Go, Who to Call, Web Sites, Products, Catalogs, Teaching Supplies, Support Groups, Conferences, and More!* (Prima, 2001). This comprehensive guide for new home-schooling parents is divided into three main sections: "Nuts and Bolts" helps identify the learning style of your children. It reviews teaching styles, and uses an easy, question-and-answer format that gives information on commonly asked home-schooling topics. The "Products" section sorts educational teaching materials by subject, rather than age or skill level, which makes it easy to find various products. The "Resource Guide" gives contact information for home-schooling conferences and organizations in every state, and homeschool certification requirements for all states.

Llewellyn, Grace. *Freedom Challenge: African-American Homeschoolers* (Lowry House, 1996). This book is a collection of essays by African-American and other minority parents about their experiences in home-schooling and unschooling their children.

Llewellyn, Grace. *The Teenage Liberation Handbook: How to Quit School and Get a Real Life and Education* (Lowry House, 1991). A great book for any parent who wants to get her teenage children excited about life, learning, and home-schooling. It thoroughly covers many ideas about unschooling and home-schooling and has many resources for further study.

Orr, Tamra B. *A Parent's Guide to Home Schooling* (Mars, 2002). Lively and readable, and includes a huge amount of information on home-schooling. Includes essays and practical advice by both experts and home-schooling parents "in the trenches." Orr is also the author of *101 Ways to Make Your Library Home-schooling Friendly,* and *125 Things Homeschoolers Can Do on the Internet.*

Papert, Seymour. *The Connected Family: Bridging the Digital Generation Gap* (Longstreet Press, 1996). The author talks about many ways to use the computer to teach your children different subjects. It's aimed at parents who have no previous computer knowledge.

Perelman, Lewis J. *School's Out: Hyperlearning, the New Technology, and the End of Education* (Avon Books, 1993). This book enthusiastically and thoroughly explains how the computer and Internet can be a great resource for teaching your child at home.

Pride, Mary. *The Big Book of Home Learning: Preschool and Elementary, vol. 2* (Alpha Omega, 1999). This thorough resource book on home-schooling for preschool and elementary grade children covers resource material, lesson plans, and curriculums for reading and other subjects.

Reed, Donn. *The Home School Source Book* (Brook Farm Books, 1991). A great resource book that is part catalog, part essays about teaching your children at home. Contains many teaching resource ideas.

Rupp, Rebecca. *The Complete Home Learning Source Book: The Essential Resource Guide for Homeschoolers, Parents, and Educators Covering Every Subject from Arithmetic to Zoology* (Three Rivers Press, 1998). A comprehensive source book that gives parents and teachers information on all the resources needed to plan a well-balanced curriculum for the home or the classroom, from preschool through high school. It is a thorough reference guide for home-schooling, including teaching materials, curriculum, books, magazines, lesson plans, learning kits, hands-on materials, and much more.

Rupp, Rebecca. *Good Stuff: Learning Tools for All Ages* (Holt Associates, 1997). This book lists a wide variety of nontextbook learning materials for home-schooling, such as games, cards, posters, books, and catalogs, all divided into different subjects.

Rupp, Rebecca. *Home Learning Year by Year: How to Design a Homeschool Curriculum from Preschool through High School* (Three Rivers Press, 2000). This book gives a comprehensive guide to designing a homeschool curriculum, from one of the country's leading home-schooling experts. The book presents a structured plan to ensure that your children learn what they need to know, at the right time, from preschool through high school.

Walberg, Herbert and Bast, Joseph L. *Education and Capitalism: How Overcoming Our Fear of Markets and Economics Can Improve America's Schools* (Hoover Institute Press, 2003). This enlightening book shows how a free-market education system can improve our schools and give children a superior education.

Ward, Ann. *Learning at Home: Preschool and Kindergarten*, (Noble, 1995). This is one of a series of learning-at-home books by Ann Ward, previously an experienced elementary-school teacher before she became a home-schooling mom. She offers her own step-by-step curriculum packed with daily teaching plans for up to ten subjects. Thorough and easy to use, and a great resource for new home-schooling parents.

Wise, Jessie, and Susan Wise Bauer. *The Well-Trained Mind: A Guide to Classical Education at Home* (W. W. Norton, 1999). One of the most thorough books on home-schooling your children. Gives a wealth of information, specific advice, curriculum material, and lesson plans for math, reading, and other subjects, and can be a parent's constant guide for home-schooling children of all ages.

General Information
Home-schooling Internet Sites

These are great sites that give detailed information on many aspects of home-schooling, including Internet schools, tutors, home-schooling education materials, state regulations, and much more. To find additional Internet sites on Google, Yahoo, and other search engines, use search phrases like "homeschooling," "homeschool resources," or "home education."

1. A to Z Home's Cool Homeschooling: http://www.gomilpitas.com/home-schooling
2. EducationRevolution: http://www.educationrevolution.org

3. Homeschool World: http://www.home-school.com

4. Homeschool Central: http://www.homeschoolcentral.com

5. Home School Corner: http://www.e-tutor.com/homeschool/index.htm

6. Jon's Homeschool Resource page: http://www.midnightbeach.com/hs

7. Family Education Network: http://familyeducation.com

8. E-tutor, at homeschool corner.com: http://www.e-tutor.com/homeschool/index.htm

9. Home School Zone: http://www.homeschoolzone.com

10. Ask Eric (Educator's Reference Desk): http://www.eduref.org

11. Teach at Home: http://www.teach-at-home.com

12 EduPuppy: http://www.edupuppy.com

13. EdHelper.com: http://www.edhelper.com

14. American Homeschool Association: http://www.americanhomeschoolassociation.org

15. Home School Internet Resource Center: http://rsts.net/home/index.htm

16. Education World: http://www.educationworld.com

17. Net HomeSchool: http://www.nethomeschool.com

18. NHERI (National Home Education Research Institute): http://www.nheri.org.

19. NHEN (National Home Education Network): http://www.nhen.org.

20. Homeschool of Fish, Homeschool Cheap on the Cheap: http://www.homeschooloffish.com/homeschoolcheap.htm

21. HomeSchool.com: http://www.homeschool.com

22. Educating.net: http://www.educating.net

23. John Holt website, *Growing Without School*: http://www.holtgws.com.

24. Home Ed Magazine: http://www.home-ed-magazine.com.

25. FamilyEducation.com: http://familyeducation.com/

home.

Internet Schools

Here you will find many kinds of Internet schools. Some are full virtual schools. Others are Internet divisions of brick-and-mortar private schools. Some offer only accredited high-school programs, others have middle-school and high-school programs, and some offer a full 1st -12th grade education. Many are state-accredited schools that offer fully structured academic programs leading to a high school diploma. Others have a less structured curriculum or offer courses or tutoring on various subjects. You will also find university-affiliated 1st-12th grade and high-school programs, and Christian-based 1st-12th grade schools.

Also, many of these schools will test your children's current academic skill levels in reading and math. Research these sites to find Internet schools that best suit your children's age, abilities, and interests, and the tuition costs you can comfortably afford. To find additional Internet school sites, use search phrases like "online high-school," "online K-12 school," "internet schools," "virtual schools," and "university high-school programs."

High-School programs
1. Compuhigh: http://www.compuhigh.com.
2. Dennison Online Internet School: http://www.dennisononline.com.
3. Keystone National High School: http://www.keystonehighschool.com.
4. Citizen's High School: http://www.citizenschool.com
5. James Madison Online High School: http://www.pcdihomestudy.com/jm/index.shtml.
6. Thompson Education Direct: http://www.educationdirect.com/index.html.
7. Alger Learning Center: http://www.independent-learning.com.

8. The American School: http://www.americanschoolof-corr.com.

9. Intelligent Education, Inc.: http://www.intelligented.com.

10. EdAnywhere (also has a homeschool program): http://www.edanywhere.com.

11. North Atlantic Regional Schools: http://www.narson-line.com.

12. Phoenix Academy: http://www.phoenixacademies.org.

13. Thompson Education Direct: http://www.educationdi-rect.com.

14. Indiana University High School program: http://scs.indiana.edu.

15. University of Nebraska-Lincoln High School program: http://class.unl.edu.

16. University of Texas at Austin High School program: http://www.utexas.edu/cee/dec/uths/index.shtml.

17. The University of Oklahoma Independent Learning High School: http://isd.ou.edu/accreditation.htm.

Grades K-12

18. North Texas Academy (grades 4 –12): http://www.northtexasacademy.com.

19. The Learning Odyssey (grades K – 6):

20. Willoway 3D Learn (grades 5 - 12): http://www.willoway.com.

21. Advanced Academics (grades 7 -12, works with your local public-school district who may pay for tuition at Advanced Academics): http://www.advancedacademics.com.

22. North Dakota University Division of Independent Study (grades 1 -12): http://www.dis.dpi.state.nd.us.

23. Texas Tech University Extended Studies (grades K – 12): http://www.dce.ttu.edu.

24. University of Missouri-Columbia Independent Study Program (grades 1- 12): http://indepstudy.ext.missouri.edu.

25. Stanford University Education Program For Gifted Youth (grades 1- 12): http://www-epgy.stanford.edu.

26. University of Arizona Academic Outreach (grades 1 -12): http://www.eu.arizona.edu/corresp.

27. Allendale Academy (grades K-12): http://www.members.tripod.com/euty.

28. Clonlara School (grades K -12): http://www.clonlara.org.

29. K12 (grades K-12, nationwide Internet *charter* schools and homeschool program): http://www.k12.com.

30. The Trent Schools (grades 1-12): http://www.the-schools.com.

31. Oak Meadow (grades K–12, plus curriculum material for homeschooling parents): http://www.oakmeadow.com.

32. Bradford Grove school (grades 1-12): http://www.branfordgrove.com/home.html.

33. Active Learning Academy (grades 1-12): http://www.my-ala.com.

34. The Sycamore Tree (grades K-12 homeschool program): http://www.sycamoretree.com.

35. Homeschool.com (grades 1-8): http://www.homeschool.com.

36. Home Study International (grades K-12): http://www.hsi.edu

37. Alpha Omega Academy (grades 3-12): http://www.aop.com.

38. Laurel Springs School (grades 1-12): http://www.laurelsprings.com.

39. Eldorado Academy (grades K-12): http://www.eldoradoacademy.org.

40. Sycamore Academy (grades 3-12): http://www.sycamoretree.com/school.htm.

41. Christa McAuliffe Academy (grades K-12): http://www.cmacademy.org.

42. Bridgeway Homeschool Academy (grades K-12): http://www.homeschoolacademy.com.

43. USA International Online School (grades K-12): http://www.usainternationalonlineschool.com.

44. Internet Home School (grades 1-12): http://www.in-

ternethomeschool.com/#IHS.

45. Internet Academy (grades K-12): http://www.iacademy.org.

46. Waterford Academy (grades K-12 homeschool program): http://www.childu.com.

47. Royal Academy (grades K-12): http://www.homeeducator.com/HEFS/royalacademy.htm.

Christian-affiliated schools (grades K-12)

48. Country Christian School (grades 1–12): http://www.countrychristianschool.net.

49. Aaron Academy (grades 1–12): http://www.aaronacademy.com.

50. Agape Christian Academy (grades 1- 12): http://www.agapechristianacademy.org.

51. Alpha-Omega Academy (grades K –12): http://new.aop.com.

52. Ariel Christian Academy (grades 3 –12): http://www.arielchristianacademy.com.

53. Crossroads Christian Schools (grades K-12): http://www.crossroadschristianschool.com.

54. Deseret Academy (grades K-12): http://www.deseretacademy.org.

54. Eagle Christian School (grades 7 -12): http://www.eaglechristian.org.

56. Home Study International (grades K-12): http://www.hsi.edu.

57. Lincoln Christian Academy (grades 1-12): http://www.cwd.com/lca.

58. Northstar Academy (grades 7-12): http://www.northstar-academy.org.

Online Tutoring

These are Internet sites that offer tutoring in math, reading, science, and other subjects, or help you locate a tutor. Some of these sites also offer online testing of your children's current academic skill levels in reading and math. Also look on the general information sites for tutor services. To find additional sites, use Internet search phrases like "online tutors," "K-12 tutors," or "math or reading tutors."

1. Score Education Centers (grades K-10, tutoring centers) : http://www.escore.com.
2. eSylvan.com (grades 3-9, specializing in reading and math instruction): http://www.esylvan.com.
3. E-Tutor.com: http://www.e-tutor.com.
4. Bridgeway Cyber Academy: http://www.bridgewaycyberacademy.com.
5. LessonTutor.com: http://www.lessontutor.com.
6. Click A Tutor: http://www.clickatutor.us.
7. Huntington Learning Center (local brick-and-mortar tutoring centers): http://www.huntingtonlearning.com.
8. Tutor2000.com (nationwide tutor referral service): http://www.tutor2000.com.
9. Education For Kids.com: http://www.education-for-kids.com.
10. Tutor Find: http://www.tutorfind.com.
11. Tutor At Work.com: http://www.tutoratwork.com.
12. E-Homework Help: http://www.ehomeworkhelp.com.
13. CompassLearning Odyssey: http://www.childu.com.

Home-schooling Teaching Materials

Parents who want more direct control over their children's home-schooling curriculum can buy books, games, course curriculum material, computer software, and other teaching materials for math, reading, science, history, and many other subjects. The following Internet sites sell a wide range of home-school teaching materials. To find additional Internet sites, use search phrases like "learn to read," "learn math," "children's learning materials," and "homeschool teaching materials."

1. Turbo Reader: http:// www.turboreader.com
2. Alpha-Phonics: http://www.howtotutor.com.
3. Go Phonics Reading Program: http://www.gophonics. com.
4. Core Curriculum of America (grades K-12): http:// core-curriculum.com.
5. Homeschool SuperCenter: http://homeschoolsuper-center.com.
6. Pearson at School: http://www.pearsonatschool.com.
7. Headsprout (teaches reading fundamentals, ages four to seven): http://www.headsprout.com.
8. Hooked on Phonics/Hooked on Math (reading and math): http://www.hop.com
9. A+ Math (fun math instruction): http://www.aplus-math.com.
10. eSylvan Learning Center (reading, math): http:// www.educate.com.
11. Frontline Phonics (guarantees results): http://www. frontlinephonics.com.
12. Funnix Reading Tutor: http://www.funnix.com.
13. The Rayment Reading Method (free): http://www. indepthinfo.com/read/method.shtml.
14. Starfall (learn to read): http://www.starfall.com.
15. The Brain Store (learn math K-12 grades): http:// www.toonuniversity.com.
16. Math.com (math resources): http://www.math.com
17. 1 on 1 School Supplies (reading, math, software, re-sources): http://www.1on1schoolsupplies.com.
18. Amazing Toy Store (Leap Frog math, reading, much more): http://www.amazingtoystore.com/leapfrog.html.
19. 3Moms (homeschool curriculum material): http:// www.3moms.com.
20. ABC Home-School Supplies: http://www.home-schoolinghelp.com.
21. Brain Pop (reading, math lessons): http://www.brain-pop.com.
22. Enchanted Learning (reading, math material): http://

www.enchantedlearning.com.

23. ACE-Educational.com (home-schooling resources): http://www.for-home-schooling.com.

24. Fun Brain (math, reading materials, lessons): http://www.funbrain.com.

25. Geographia (learning geography): http://www.geographia.com.

26. Home Schooling (books, software, other): http://www.startup-page.com.

27. Robinson Curriculum (homeschool curriculum materials): http://www.robinsoncurriculum.com.

28. Homeschool Book Depot (low-cost books on all subjects) http://www.homeschoolbookdepot.homestead.com.

29. KiddSmart.com (books, lessons, etc., for ages one to six): http://www.kiddsmart.com.

30. Learning Streams (books, software, lessons): http://www.learningstreams.com.

31. Mental Edge (tests to discover child's current reading and math levels): http://www.learningshortcuts.com.

32. Time2Read (reading program): http://www.time2read.com.

33. The Resourceful Homeschooler (books, software, other teaching materials): http://www.resourcefulhomeschooler.com.

34. School.net (teaching resources, all subjects): http://www.school.net.

35. Family Learning Organization (testing and assessment of your child's skills): http://www.familylearning.org/testing.html.

36. SheHomeSchools (books, other resources): http://www.shehomeschools.com.

37. History Place (history articles): http://www.historyplace.com.

38. The Home School Source (books, other materials, lending library): http://www.thehomeschoolsource.com.

39. The Homeschool Highway to Learning (books, lessons, other resources): http://members.aol.com/homehwy/

home.html.

40. Homeschooler's Curriculum Swap (swap books, software, other materials with other parents): http://www. theswap.com.

41. Educating.net (extensive learning materials, all grades): http://www.educating.net/grade.asp.

42. Homeschool Books: http://homeschool.itgo.com/ parenthelpsandresources.html.

43. L.A.M.B. Company curriculum: http://www.lambco. com/home.htm.

44. ShillerMath: http://www.shillermath.com.

Internet Libraries

The following sites are Internet libraries and research sites for children of all ages, covering a wide range of subjects. To find additional sites, try using search terms like "Internet library," "Internet research,' "research," or "encyclopedia."

1. Awesome Library: http://www.awesomelibrary.org.
2. eLibrary: http://www.ask.elibrary.com.
4. World Wide School library: http://www.worldwide-school.org/about.html.
5. How Stuff Works: http://www.howstuffworks.com.
6. Internet Public Library Kidspace: http://www.ipl.org, or http://www.ipl.org/div/kidspace.
7. Internet Mathematics Library: http://mathforum.org/ library.
8. InetLibrary: http://www.inetlibrary.com.
9. World eBook Library: http://www.netlibrary.net.
10. Library of Congress: http://www.loc.gov.

Home-schooling Parent Associations

The following Internet sites are especially useful for parents who want to talk to and connect with other home-schooling parents and groups. Parents can use these sites to learn the experiences, problems, and knowledge gained by other home-schooling parents. To find additional sites, try using search terms like "homeschool association," "homeschool parent organization," "homeschooling parents," or "homeschooling families." Also, most of the general-information homeschool sites listed earlier have links to homeschool associations.

1. American Homeschool Association: http://www.americanhomeschoolassociation.org.

2. National Home Education Network: http://www.nhen.org.

3. Finding Homeschool Support on the Internet: http://www.geocities.com/Athens/8259.

4. Homehearts: http://www.homehearts.com.

5. Homeschool Help for Parents: http://www.homeschoolhelpforparents.com.

6. Homeschool Social Register: http://www.homeschoolmedia.net.

7. Home-schooling Friends: http://www.home-schooling-friends.org.

8. Kaleidoscapes: http://www.kaleidoscapes.com.

9. Home School and Private School Organizations: http://www.learning4liferesources.com.

10. Teach at Home Organization List: http://www.teach-at-home.com.

11. HomeschoolAssociations: http://www.creativeartsinaction.com/homeschool_associations.htm.

12. Homeschool World/groups: http://www.home-school.com

13. National Association of At-Home Mothers: http://www.athomemothers.com.

14. Family Unschoolers Network: http://www.unschooling.org.

15. The Homeschool Review: http://www.thehomeschoolreview.com.

16. Education World: http://db.education-world.com.
17. Busy Parents Online: http://www.busyparentsonline.com.
18. Unschooling.com: http://www.unschooling.com.

Legal Help For Home-schooling Parents

The following organizations offer legal help to parents to deal with school authorities and know their state's homeschooling regulations. To find additional Internet sites, search with phrases like "legal help for homeschooling parents," or homeschool legal organizations."

1. Home School Legal Defense Association (HSLDA): http://www.hslda.org.
2. The Rutherford Institute: http://www.rutherford.org.

College Testing, Preparation, and Admission Requirements

When your teenage children are ready to apply to college, the following Internet sites give you practical and detailed information on the college admissions process for home-schoolers. To find additional sites, search with phrases like, "homeschool college admissions," "college test preparation," and "college admissions." Most of the general-information homeschool sites listed earlier also have college admissions information.

1. Kaplan Test Prep and Admissions: http://www.kaptest.com.
2. Colleges That Admit Homeschoolers: http://learninfreedom.org/colleges_4_hmsc.html.
3. Homeschool Teens and College: http://www.homeschoolteenscollege.net.
4. Homeschool Central: http://homeschoolcentral.com/

high.htm.

5. Peterson's College (extensive information): http://www.petersons.com.

6. Scholar Stuff: http://www.scholarstuff.com.

7. National Association for College Admissions Counseling: http://www.nacac.com.

8. College Confidential: http://www.collegeconfidential.com.

9. Super College: http://www.supercollege.com.

10. XAP College Counseling: http://www.xap.com.

11. Test Prep: http://www.testprep.com.

12. The Admissions Office: http://www.theadmissionsoffice.com.

13. Apply4Admissions: http://www.apply4admissions.com.

14. Homeschoolers College Admissions Handbook (book): http://www.homeschoolzone.com/hsz/cohen6.htm.

15. College Admissions for Homeschoolers: http://www.love2learn.net/hsinfo/admision.htm.

16. Colleges That Admit Homeschoolers: http://learninfreedom.org/colleges_4_hmsc.html.

17. Homeschool Magazine: http://www.homeschoolmag.com.

18. College Planning: http://www.openhere.com/edu/higher-education/college-entrance.

Notes

Preface

1. Joe Williams and Alison Gendar, "State Test Scores Show Racial Divide," *New York Daily News*, March 28, 2002.

Chapter 1

1. L. H. Butterfield, ed., *Diary and Autobiography of John Adams* (Cambridge: Harvard University Press, 1961), quoted in Klicka, The Right Choice, p. 119.

2. Carl Bridenbaugh and Jessica Bridenbaugh, *Rebels and Gentlemen* (Oxford, UK: Oxford University Press, 1982), p. 99, quoted in Klicka, *The Right Choice*, p. 119.

3. Daniel Webster, "Discourse on Education," (1851), quoted in Klicka, *The Right Choice*, pp. 119–20.

4. Sheldon Richman, *Separating School and State: How to Liberate America's Families* (Fairfax, VA: Future of Freedom Foundation, 1994), p. 38.

5. Pierre Dupont, *National Education in the United States of America*, (University of Delaware Press, 1923), pp. 3–5, cited in Christopher J. Klicka, *The Right Choice: Homeschooling* (Gresham, OR: Noble Publishing, 1995), p. 119.

6. Sheldon Richman, *Separating School and State: How to Lib-*

erate America's Families (Fairfax, VA: Future of Freedom Foundation, 1994), p. 38., and Barbara Miller Solomon, "The Reader's Companion to American History, Education: IV. Women's Education," accessed from website www.college.hmco.com/history/readerscomp/rcah.

7. Ibid., pp. 38-39

8. John Gatto, *The Underground History of American Education* (New York: Oxford Village Press, 2001), p. 52.

9. Ibid., p. 53.

10. Ibid., pp. 61–62.

11. Ibid., p. 53.

12. Ibid., p. 53.

13. Ibid., p. 54.

14. Ibid, p. 54 .

15. Joe Williams and Alison Gendar, "State Test Scores Show Racial Divide," *New York Daily News* March 28, 2002.

16. David Boulton, "Children of the Code," A Social-Education Project and PBS Television Documentary Series," accessed from http://www.childrenofthecode.org, January 29, 2004.

17. G. Reid Lyon, quoted in David Boulton, interview, "Children of the Code," September 11, 2003, accessed from http://www. childrenofthecode.org/interviews/lyon.htm, January 29, 2004.

18. G. Reid Lyon, interview, "Children of the Code," September 11, 2003, accessed from http://www.childrenofthecode.org-/interviews/lyon.htm, January 29, 2004.

19. Donald L. Nathanson, quoted in David Boulton, interview, "Children of the Code," September 8, 2003, accessed from http://www.childrenofthecode.org/interviews/nathanson.htm   , January 29, 2004.

20. National Institute for Literacy, "National Adult Literacy Survey," 1992, accessed from http://nces.ed.gov/naal/design-/about92.asp, April 12, 2004.

21. Grover Whitehurst, quoted in David Boulton, interview, "Children of the Code," September 10, 2003, accessed from http:// www.childrenofthecode.org/interviews/whitehurst.htm, Jan. 29, 2004.

22. David Boulton, "Children of the Code," September 10, 2003, accessed from http://www.childrenofthecode.org-/cotcintro.htm, Jan. 20, 2004.

23. Andrew J Coulson, *Market Education: The Unknown History*, (Transaction Publishers: Somerset, NJ, USA, 1999), pp. 40-44, and Ellie Crystal, "Ancient Greek Education," website accessed from http://www.crystalinks.com/greekeducation.html, Feb 10, 2004.

24. Andrew J. Coulson, *Market Education: The Unknown History*, (Somerset, NJ: Transaction Publishers, 1999), pp. 40-44.

25. Ibid, pp. 54-57.

26. Ibid., pp. 61-64

27. Ibid., p. 85

28. Gatto, *The Underground History of American Education*, pp. 26-27.

29. Ibid, p. 28.

30. Ibid., p. 32.

31. Klicka, *The Right Choice*, pp. 155–63.

32. Franz de Hovre, "German and English Education: a Comparative Study," quoted in Murray N. Rothbard, *Education, Free and Compulsory: The Individual's Education* (Auburn, AL: Ludwig von Mises Institute, 1999), p. 27.

33. John Gatto, "Our Prussian School System," p. 10, quoted in Richman, p. 41.

34. John Taylor Gatto, *Dumbing Us Down: The Hidden Curriculum of Compulsory Schooling* (Philadelphia: New Society Publishers, 1992), p. 25.

35. Gatto, "Our Prussian School System," quoted in Richman, p. 42.

36. Ibid.

37. Andrew J. Coulson, *Market Education: The Unknown History*, (Somerset, N.J. (USA): Transaction Publishers, 1999), p. 150

38. National Center for Education Statistics, "Report for Year 2000 on Crime in Public Schools," Washington, D.C., 2000, accessed from www.nces.ed.gov, Sept. 30, 2003.

39. PRIDE Surveys, Inc, "PRIDE National Survey," year 2000–2001, accessed from www.pridesurveys.com, Aug. 20, 2003.

Chapter 2

1. Christopher J. Klicka, answer to author inquiry, Home

School Legal Defense Association, November 2003.

2. Pacific Justice Institute, press release, "Homeschoolers Threatened by Pending Bill," April 16, 2003, quoted in *HEM News and Commentary*, accessed from http://www.home-ed-magazine.com/nc/303/42103.html, June 25, 2003.

3. Christopher J. Klicka, *The Right Choice: Home Schooling* (Gresham, Oregon: Noble Publishing, 1995), p. 57.

4. "FRC Equips Moms and Dads with School Survival Guide, A Tool for Keeping Parents Aware and Involved," *PR Newswire*, September 24, 1996, accessed from http://www.aegis.com/news/pr/1996 /pr960926.html, Jan. 4, 2004.

5. Ibid.

6. Pacific Justice Institute, press release, "Elementary Schools Sued for Unlawful Pro-Homosexual Presentations," January 31, 2002, accessed from http://www.restoringamerica.org/archive/education/sued_for_prohomopresentation.html, Jan. 10, 2004.

7. James L. Fletcher Jr., "Sex Education and the Biblical Christian," Journal of Bible Ethics in Medicine website, accessed from http://www.bmei.org/jbem/volume4/num2/fletcher_sex_education_and_the_biblical_christian.pdf, February 11, 2003.

8. Jeff Rense, "Provable Accusations against American Public Schools," *Sightings*, October 14, 1999, accessed from http://www.rense.com/politics5/pbsc.htm, Oct 13, 2003.

9. Brian Kamenker and Scott Whiteman, "Kids Get Graphic Instruction in Homosexual Sex," *Massachusetts News*, May 2000, accessed from http://www.massnews.com/past_issues-/2000/5_May/maygsa.htm, Oct. 20, 2003.

10. Ibid.

11. Parents' Rights Coalition, "In Newton, MA., Gay Teenage Sex Book Assigned to English Class," article not dated, accessed from http://www.parentsrightscoalition.org/book.htm, January 10, 2003.

12. Parents' Rights Coalition, "Trampling on Parents' Rights, A Few of the Stories," article not dated, accessed from arentsrightscoalition.org/Horror_Stories.htm, January10, 2003.

13. Charles J. Sykes, *Dumbing Down Our Kids: Why America's Children Feel Good about Themselves but Can't Read, Write, or Add* (New York: St. Martin's Griffin, 1995), p.171; and Senator Gilbert J. DiNello, Chairman, "Final Report: The Senate Select Com-

mittee to Study the Michigan Model for Comprehensive School Health Education," December 1992, pp. 6, 23, accessed from http://www.equip.org/free/DN118.htm, June 23, 2003.

14. Denise McArthur, "Don't Teach; Just Join Kids as Co-learners," *Stars and Stripes*, July 31, 1997.

15. Jerry Moore, "Lack of Community Involvement," comment posted April 9, 2000, *Jerry Moore's School Talk*, accessed from http://www.myshortpencil.com/schooltalk/messages/2/68.html, Feb 12, 2003.

16. "Parents Rights Bill," *Parents' Rights Coalition*, accessed from http://www.parentsrightscoalition.org/prbill_text.htm, Feb. 3, 2004).

17. Sykes, *Dumbing Down Our Kids*, p.175.

18. Ibid.

19. Ibid., p.178.

20. Paul Craig Roberts, "The U.S. Child and Family Services Gestapo Targets Parents," *Capitalism*, December 16, 2000.

21. Ibid.

22. John C. Greene, "Columbine, Moodus, and Public Education," *Ship of State*, May 14, 2000, accessed from http://www. shipofstate.com/archiv, May 30, 2003.

23. Debra J. Saunders, "Did Your Mom Eat Your Homework? Schools Shift the Blame for Academic Failure to Parents," *Policy Review*, Spring 1995.

24. Klicka, *The Right Choice*, pp. 48–49.

25. William Kirk Kilpatrick, *Why Johnny Can't Tell Right from Wrong* (New York: Simon and Schuster, 1992), p. 16, quoted in Sykes, *Dumbing Down Our Kids*, pp. 160–61.

26. Sykes, *Dumbing Down Our Kids*, pp. 157–58, from Garry Abrams, "Youth Gets Bad Marks in Morality," *Los Angeles Times*, Nov. 12, 1992.

27. Sykes, *Dumbing Down Our Kids*, pp. 157–58.

28. Ibid., p. 158.

29. Berit Kjos, *Brave New Schools* (Eugene, OR: Harvest House, 1995), p. 15.

30. Ibid., p. 22.

31. Pacific Justice Institute, "Letter to Subscribers," March 7, 2003, accessed from www.pacificjustice.org, Aug. 20, 2003.

32. "A Journey Beneath Your Feet," in *READ*, *Weekly Reader*

Corporation, cited in Kjos, p. 87.

33. Dan Dekock, *Honor:A Simulation of Coming of Age*, (Carlsbad, CA: Interaction Publishers, 1988), p. 46, cited in Kjos, p. 89.

34. "Fun with Chinese Horoscopes, Teacher Created Materials, Inc.," 1992, and Vincent Rogers, "Education, Teaching Social Studies: Portraits from the Classroom," *National Council for the Social Studies Bulletin, no. 82*, p. 20, cited in Kjos, p. 89.

35. Kjos, p. 90. These occult practices were taught to seniors in preparation for a Mountain View High School graduation celebration. For several years afterwards, according to Kjos, more occult practices were added.

36. Reported by a teacher in a public elementary school in San Jose, California, cited in Kjos, p.90.

37. Starhawk, *The Spiral Dance: A Rebirth of the Ancient Religion of the Great Goddess* (San Francisco: HarperSanFrancisco, 1979), pp. 62, 123–24, cited in Kjos, p. 90.

38. Kjos, p. 91

39. Louise Derman-Sparks and the ABC Task Force, *Anti-Bias Curriculum: Tools for Empowering Young Children* (Washington, DC: National Association for the Education of Young Children, 1989), and a copy of the original program, cited in Kjos, p. 91.

40. Kjos, p. 91.

41. Lester Kirkendall and other SIECUS board members, "Sexuality and Man," a collection of articles (New York: Scribner, 1970), cited in Kjos, p. 92.

42. Kjos, p.92.

43. Aldous Huxley, *Brave New World* (New York: HarperCollins, 1932), p. 28.

44. Thomas Sowell, "Indoctrinating the Children," *Forbes*, February 1, 1993, p. 65.

45. Recalled by Ashley, one of the tenth-grade students asked to do this assignment, Kjos, p. 55.

46. Ibid.

47. Ibid., p. 28.

48. Deborah Sharp, "A Culture Clash Divides Florida," *USA Today*, May 18, 1994, quoted in Kjos, , p. 33.

49. "The Columbus Controversy: Challenging How History Is Written," (Macmillan-McGraw Hill School Publishing, 1991),

videotape, cited in Kjos, p. 35.

50. National Center for History in the Schools, "United States History Standards for Grades 5–12, Era 2, Colonization and Settlement," *National Standards For History, Basic Edition*, 1996,accessed from http://www.sscnet.ucla.edu/nchs/standards, Sept. 20, 2003.

51. Thomas Sowell, "Twisted History," *Townhall.com*, December 17, 2003, accessed from http://www.townhall.com/columnists/-thomassowell/ts20031217.shtml, Sept. 3, 2003.

Chapter 3

1. John Gatto, *Dumbing Us Down* (Philadelphia: New Society Publishers, 1992), p. 13.

2. Beverly Jankowski and Joan Wittig, "Because We Care about Children," quoted in Charles J. Sykes, *Dumbing Down Our Kids* (New York: St. Martin's Griffin, 1995), pp. 105–06.

3. Jayna Davis, "What Did You Learn in School Today?" KFOR-TV, Oklahoma City, May 27,1993, and June 6, 1993, cited in Sykes, *Dumbing Down Our Kids*, pp. 105–06.

4. Sykes, *Dumbing Down Our Kids*, p. 102.

5. George A. Clowes, "Reading Is Anything but Natural," interview with G. Reid Lyon, *School Reform News*, July 1999, accessed from http://www.heartland.org/archives/education/jul99/lyon.htm, February 27, 2004.

6. Sykes, p. 102.

7. Ibid., pp.101–02.

8. Ibid., p.102.

9. "California Rediscovers Phonics," *NCPA Daily Policy Digest*, February 12, 2002.

10. Sykes, *Dumbing Down Our Kids*, p.101.

11. Quoted in Howard Witt, "New Age Teaching Spells Trouble in California," *Chicago Tribune*, May 14, 1995, and Berit Kjos, *Brave New Schools* (Eugene, OR: Harvest House, 1995), p. 61.

12. Sykes, *Dumbing Down Our Kids*, pp. 106–07.

13. Ibid., p. 92.

14. Ibid., p. 115.

15. Bas Braams, "Chancellor Klein's Math Problems," *New*

York Sun, February, 6, 2003.

16. Sykes, *Dumbing Down Our Kids,* p. 115, and Jean Merl, "Say Goodbye to Chalkboard Math Drills," *Los Angeles Times,* April 30, 1994.

17. Sykes, *Dumbing Down Our Kids,* p. 116.

18. National Center for Education Statistics, "State Results for the NAEP 2003 Mathematics Assessment," cited in Sykes, *Dumbing Down Our Kids,* p. 116.

19. Sykes, *Dumbing Down Our Kids,* p. 123.

20. Gary Hull, *Caution: Textbooks Are Hazardous to Your Child's Mind in Math, History, and Literature; Today's Textbooks Actively Undermine a Child's Capacity to Think, Rational Education,* accessed from http://education.aynrand.org/textbook.html, Sept. 6, 2004.

21. Jill Tomlinson, Hilda, *The Hen Who Wouldn't Give Up* (New York: Harcourt, Brace, Jovanovich, 1980), cited in Hull, *Caution: Textbooks Are Hazardous to Your Child's Mind.*

22. Hull, *Caution: Textbooks Are Hazardous to Your Child's Mind,* accessed from http://education.aynrand.org/textbook.html, Sept. 6, 2004.

23. Nancy Montgomery, "Textbooks Too Easy, Too Dull, Experts Say," *Seattle Times,* March 3, 1996, cited in Hull, *Caution: Textbooks Are Hazardous to Your Child's Mind.*

24. Andrew J. Coulson, *Market Education: The Unknown History,* (Somerset, (USA):Transaction Publishers, 1999), p. 170.

25. Sykes, *Dumbing Down Our Kids,* pp. 30–31.

26. John Jacob Cannell, "How Public Educators Cheat on Standardized Achievement Tests: The Lake Wobegon Report," from Albuquerque: *Friends for Education,* 1989, cited in Sykes, *Dumbing Down Our Kids,* pp. 143–45.

27. Ibid.

28. Ibid.

29. Ibid.

30. Gary W. Phillips and Chester E. Finn Jr., "The Lake Wobegon Effect: A Skeleton in the Testing Closet?" *Educational Measurement: Issues and Practice 7, no. 2* (Summer 1988), cited in Sykes, *Dumbing Down Our Kids,* p. 145.

31. Myron Lieberman, *Public Education: An Autopsy* (Cambridge: Harvard University Press, 1993), pp. 82–83.

32. Sykes, *Dumbing Down Our Kids,* pp. 146–47.

33. Ibid, p.147.

34. Jonathan Kozol, *Savage Inequalitites: Children in America's Schools* (New York: HarperPerennial, 1992), p.46, cited in Andrew J. Coulson, *Market Education:The Unknown History*, (Somerset, (USA): Transaction Publishers, 1999), p. 22.

35. Andrew J. Coulson, , *Market Education: The Unknown History*, (Somerset, (USA): Transaction Publishers, 1999), p. 22.

36. Charles J. Sykes, "Soccer Moms vs. Standardized Tests," *Center for Education Reform*, December 6, 1999, accessed from http://www.edreform.com/index.cfm?fuseAction=document&do cumentID=460&sectionID=70&NEWSYEAR=1999, Nov. 20, 2003.

37. Ibid.

38. Gail Russell Chaddock, "Adverse Impact?" *Christian Science Monitor*, November 30, 1999, accessed from http://csmonitor. com/cgi-bin/durableRedirect.pl?/durable-/1999/11/30/p14s1.htm, December10, 2002.

39. Jay Greene, Senior Fellow at the Manhattan Institute for Policy Research, "New York Dropouts Uncounted," *New York Daily Sun*, Sept. 17, 2003.

40. Alan Bonsteel, "Public Schools Hiding Actual Dropout Counts," *Los Angeles Daily News*, "Their Opinion," April, 22, 2004.

41. Jay Greene, Senior Fellow at the Manhattan Institute for Policy Research, "New York Dropouts Uncounted," *New York Daily Sun*, Sept. 17, 2003.

42. Jonathan Kozol, *Savage Inequalities: Children In America's Schools*, (New York: HarperPerennial, 1991), p. 113.

43. Carl Sommer, *Schools in Crisis: Training for Success or Failure?* (Houston, TX: Cahill Publishing, 1984), p.11.

44. Susan Schwartz, "Promote or Retain? Questions about Tougher School Standards," October 1, 1999; updated December 5, 2000, accessed from http://www.aboutourkids.org-/aboutour/ articles/-promoteorretain.html, June 3, 2003.

45. Ibid.

46. Andrew J. Coulson, *Market Education: The Unknown History*, (Somerset, N.J.: Transaction Publishers, 1999), pp 194.

47. Jim Lehrer, "Cheating Teachers," *Online NewsHour*, April 26, 2000, accessed from http://www.pbs.org-/newshour/bb/educa-

tion/jan-june00/teachers_4-26.html, Sept. 10, 2003); and American School Board, "Investigation Reveals Cheating on High-Stakes Testing," February 2000, accessed from http://www.asbj.com, Sept. 10, 2003.

48. Diane Spoehr, conversation, in Sykes, *Dumbing Down Our Kids*, pp. 241–42.

49. PA Parents Commission, "To Tell the Truth: Will the Real OBE Please Stand Up?" April 1993, cited in Sykes, *Dumbing Down Our Kids*, p. 242.

50. State of Kentucky, "Proposed Education Goals," cited in Sykes, *Dumbing Down Our Kids*, p. 247.

51. State of Pennsylvania, Proposed Education Goals, cited in Sykes, *Dumbing Down Our Kids*, p. 248.

52. Sykes, *Dumbing Down Our Kids*, p. 248.

Chapter 4

1. Adam Myerson, "Culture Is Not An 'Excuse': High Achievers Show How It's Done," *Philanthropy*, March 2002, accessed from http://www.philanthropyroundtable.org/magazines/2000-09/meyerson.html, June 14, 2003.

2. Jay P. Greene and Greg Forster, "Public High School Graduation and College Readiness Rates in the United States," *New York: Manhattan Institute for Policy Research*, September 2003.

3. Charles J. Sykes, *Dumbing Down Our Kids* (New York: St. Martin's Griffin, 1995), p.32.

4. Jaime Escalante, quoted in Chester E. Finn Jr., *We Must Take Charge: Our Schools and Our Future* (New York: Free Press, 1991), p. 108, and Sykes, *Dumbing Down Our Kids*, pp. 57–58.

5. Sykes, *Dumbing Down Our Kids*, pp.286–87.

6. Professor William Fischel, "How Judges Are making Public Schools Worse," *City Journal*, Summer, 1998, pp.30-42, accessed from http://www.act60org.fischel2.htm, Aug.20, 2003.

7. Carl Sommer, *Schools in Crisis: Training for Success or Failure?* (Houston, TX: Cahill Publishing, 1984), p. 5.

8. Ibid.

9. Ibid.

10. Ibid., p. 6.

11. Dave Evans, "Mayor Names City's 12 Most Dangerous Schools," *ABC News*, January 5, 2004, accessed from http://abclocal.go.com/wabc/news/ourschools/wabc_ourschools_ 010504danger.html, Sept. 15, 2003.

12. United Federation of Teachers, "School Based Option: Staffing and Transfer Plan," UFT, accessed from http://www.uft.org/?fid=154&tf=674; and UFT, "Seniority Transfers," accessed from http://www.uft.org/?fid=154&tf=676, April 1, 2003.

13. Joe Calderone and Russ Buettner, "Failing Schools: Uncertified Teachers Flood Poor Nabe," *New York Daily News*, November 8, 1999.

14. Connie Mabin, "School Voucher Programs Growing Slowly," *Daily News (Cleveland)*, June 29, 2003, accessed from http://www.childrenfirstamerica.org/-DailyNews/03Jun/0629031.htm, March 10, 2004.

15. Ibid.

16. Kathleen Lucadamo, "Lawsuits a Possibility for Choice Struggle," *New York Sun*, December 3, 2002.

17. Sue Kirchhoff, "Federal Deficit Hits Record $374.2 Billion," *USA Today*, Oct., 20, 2003.

18. Dale McDonald, "Annual Report on Catholic Elementary and Secondary Schools: United States Catholic Elementary and Secondary School Statistics, 2003–2004," *National Catholic Education Association*, accessed from http://www.ncea.org/newinfo/catholicschooldata-/annualreport.asp, March 5, 2004; and Jeanne Sahadi, "Can You Really Afford Private School?," *CNN/Money*, February 9, 2004, accessed from http://money.cnn.com/2004/02/06/pf/-private_school/index.htm, Feb. 23, 2004.

19. Center for Education Reform press release, "Number of Operating Charter Schools Up Ten Percent," February 11, 2004, accessed from http://www.edreform.com/index.cfm?fuseActio n=document&documentID=1704, Jan. 23, 2004; and "Strong Charter School Laws Boost Achievement," *Center For Education Reform*, February 11, 2004, accessed from http://www.edreform.com/index.cfm?fuseAction=document&documentID=1703, Jan. 23, 2004.

20. Bruno V. Manno, "Yellow Flag," *Education Next*, accessed from http://www.educationnext.org/20031/16.html, July 20, 2003.

21. Ibid.

22. Ibid.

23. Ibid.

24. Ibid.

25. Center for Education Reform, "Charter Schools 2002: Results from CER's Annual Survey of America's Charter School," accessed from http://edreform.com/_upload/-survey2002.pdf, Dec. 10, 2003.

26. Chester E. Finn, Jr., "The War on Charter Schools," *National Charter School Clearinghouse Conference*, Sept. 14, 2002, accessed from http//www.nationalcharter-schoolclearinghouse.net/newsletter/conference/keynote.htm, June 15, 2004.

27. Patrik Jonsson, "White Teachers Flee Black Schools," Special to the *Christian Science Monitor*, January 21, 2003.

28. Gary Orfield, Mark D. Bachmeier, David R. James, and Tamela Eide, Harvard Project on School Desegregation, "Deepening Segregation in American Public Schools," *BAMN: Coalition to Defend Affirmative Action and Integration;* and "Fight for Equality by Any Means Necessary," (*BAMN*), December 10, 2002, accessed from http://www.bamn.com/resources/97-deepingseg.htm, Feb. 23, 2004.

29. Brian Carovillano, "U.S. Schools Resegregating, Study Says, Children Come First," January 21, 2003, accessed from http://www.childrencomefirst.com/schoolsresegregating.shtml, Mar. 20, 2004.

30. Lucadamo, "Lawsuits a Possibility for Choice Struggle," *The New York Sun*, Dec. 3, 2002.

31. Elissa Gootman, "City Will Limit Chance To Leave Failing Schools," *The New York Times*, July 17, 2004.

32. Joe Williams, "Clueless That Kids' Schools Are Failing," *New York Daily News*, December 20, 2002.

33. Sam Dillon, "Private Teachers Are Struggling In Public Schools," April 16, 2004, accessed from *International Herald Tribune Online* website, www.iht.com/articles/515461.html, June 16, 2004.

34. Krista Kafer, "Implementation Watch: Students' Rights Under the No Child Left Behind Act," WebMemo #113, June 19, 2002, accessed from the *Heritage Foundation* website, www.heritage.org/Research/Eduction/WM113.cfm, June 20, 2004.

35. Sam Dillon, "Private Teachers Are Struggling In Public

Schools," April 16, 2004, accessed from *International Herald Tribune Online* website, www.iht.com/articles/515461.html, June 16, 2004.

36. Ibid.

37. Ibid.

38. C. Harlow, "Education and Correctional Populations," Washington, DC: *Bureau of Justice Statistics Special Report*, April, 2003 and 2001.

39. Marnie S. Shaul, U.S. Government Accounting Office, February, 2002, accessed from *Alliance For Excellent Education* website, www.all4ed.org/whats_at_stake/-index.html, June 23, 2004.

40. Jackie Cissell, "Slap in the Face of the Reverend Floyd Flake," *National Center for Public Policy Research*, March 1998, accessed from http://www.nationalcenter.org/-/NVFlakeCissell398. html, Dec. 18, 2003.

Chapter 5

1. Lawrence H. Diller, "Extreme Ritalin," *Salon.com*, March 31, 2000, accessed from http://dir.salon.com/health/feature/-2000/03/31/ritalin/index.html, June. 15, 2003.

2. Leonard Sax, "Ritalin: Better Living through Chemistry?" *World and I*, accessed from http://www.worldandi.com/public/-2000/november/sax.html, December 8, 2000.

3. Terrance Woodworth, "DEA Congressional Testimony," May 16, 2000, accessed from http://www.usdoj.gov/dea/pubs/cngrtest/ct990311.htm, Dec. 5, 2003.

4. Peter R. Breggin, *Talking Back to Ritalin: What Doctors Aren't Telling You about Stimulants and ADHD*, rev. ed. (Cambridge: Perseus Publishing, 2001), p. 128.

5. Bruce Wiseman, "Testimony presented to the Pennsylvania House Democratic Policy Committee," Philadelphia, September 26, 2002.

6. Breggin, *Talking Back to Ritalin*, pp. 296–304.

7. ADHD Parents Support Project, "50 Conditions Mimicking ADHD," 2000, accessed from http://adhdparentssupportgroup.homestead.com/50conditionsmimicingADHD.html, Sept.

3, 2003.

8. Breggin, *Talking Back to Ritalin*, pp.331–32.

9. Ibid., pp. 13–14.

10. Peter R. Breggin, "Vital Information about Ritalin, Attention Deficit-Hyperactivity Disorder, and the Politics Behind the ADHD/Ritalin Movement," accessed from http://www.breggin.com/ritalinbkexcerpt.html, January 16, 2003.

11. William Carey, "Paper presented at Consensus Conference," University of Pennsylvania, 1998, p. 35, cited in Breggin, *Talking Back to Ritalin*, pp. 13–14, .

12. Breggin, *Talking Back to Ritalin*, pp. 13–14.

13. Ibid., p. 15.

14. Ibid., p. 24

15. Woodworth.

16. U.S. Drug Enforcement Administration, "1995 Report on Methylphenidate (Ritalin)," accessed from http://www.methylphenidate.net/, cited in Breggin, *Talking Back to Ritalin*, p. 102.

17. U.S. Drug Enforcement Administration.

18. Ibid.

19. Sax.

20. Breggin, *Talking Back to Ritalin*, p. 12.

21. Ibid, p. 335.

22. Ibid., p. 36.

23. Ibid., p. 109.

24. Ibid., pp. 335–336.

25. "Ritalin," *Physician's Desk Reference Medical Dictionary* (Montvale, NJ: Medical Economics, 1996), p.848.

26. Ibid., p. 848.

27. Breggin, *Talking Back to Ritalin*, p. 7.

28. Lawrence D. Smith, "Death from Ritalin: The Truth behind ADHD," accessed from http://www.ritalindeath.com, January 16, 2003.

29. Ibid.

30. William Norman Grigg, "Drugging Our Kids," accessed from http://www.thenewamerican.com/tna/-2003/08-25-2003/vol9no17_drugging_print.htm, March 24, 2003.

31. Wiseman, testimony.

32. Mary Eberstadt, "Why Ritalin Rules," *Heritage Founda-*

tion Policy Review, April & May 1999, No. 94, accessed from Heritage Foundation website, www.policyreview.rog/apr99/eberstadt. html, April 20, 2003.

33. Teacher comment, "Free-thinking and Linking by Joanne Jacobs," January 11, 2004, accessed from http://www.joannejacobs.com, January 11, 2004.

34. Megan Rosenfeld, "On Ritalin, in Need of a Third Opinion," *Washington Post*, April 8, 2001, accessed from http://www.cannabisnews.com/new/thread 9310.shtml, April, 4, 1003.

35. Karen S. (parent), comment, January 11, 2004, *ParentCenter*, accessed from http://www.parentcenter.com/bbs, January 11, 2004.

36. Bobby Brown, "Our Story," accessed from http://www.bsuccessful.com/ourstory.htm, January 16, 2003.

37. Rick Karlin, "Ritalin Use Splits Parents, School," *Times Union* (Albany, NY), May 7, 2000.

38. Parents' comments, *New York Post*, August 10–12, 2002, accessed from http://www.nypost.com/commentary, Oct. 23, 2003.

39. "Parents Speak Out against Schools Coercing Them to Place Children on Psychiatric Drugs," *Ablechild.org*, 2001, accessed from http://www.ablechild.org/voices.htm, January 8, 2004.

40. Associated Press, "Mom Says School Made Her Give Ritalin to Son," *Ablechild.org*, August 9, 2002, accessed from http://www.ablechild.org/newsarchive/mom_says_school_made_her_8-9-02.htm, April 18, 2003.

41. Mary Eberstadt, "Why Ritalin Rules," Heritage Foundation, *Policy Review*, April and May 1999, accessed from www.policyreview.org/apr99/eberstadt.html.org/apr99/-eberstadt.html, June 19, 2004.

42. Andrew J. Coulson, *Market Education: The Unknown History* (Somerset, N.J.: Transaction Publishers, 1999), p. 204.

43. Ibid

44. Neil Bush, "My Son Was a Victim of School Rx: Ritalin," *New York Post*, August 14, 2002, Alliance for Human Re-search Protection, accessed from http://www.ahrp.org/-infomail/0802/14. htm., Oct. 15, 2003.

45. Breggin, *Talking Back to Ritalin*, pp. 217–18.

46. Ibid., p. 249.

47. Diagnostic and Statistical Manual of Mental Disorders,

4th ed. (DSM-IV), cited in *Misunderstood Minds*, 2000, accessed from http://www.pbs.org/wgbh/misunderstoodminds, January 14, 2004.

48. Omnisaurus, "Child Medication Safety Act of 2003—Finally!!," *Livejournal.com*, April 5, 2003, accessed from http://www.livejournal.com, May 23, 2003.

49. "Child Medication Safety Act of 2003 (Introduced in Senate)," Ablechild.org, May 2003, accessed from http://ablechild.org/flegislation.htm, May 23, 2003.

50. Samuel L. Blumenfeld, "Child Medication Safety Act of 2003: Blocked by Liberal Senators," *NewsWithViews.com*, November 25, 2003, accessed from http://www.newswithviews.com/Blumenfeld/Samuel14.htm, June 4, 2003.

51. U.S. Sentencing Commission, "Special Report to the Congress: Cocaine and Federal Sentencing Policy," February 1995, pp. iii and 150, accessed from http://www.ussc.gov-/crack/exec.htm, Jan. 4, 2004.

Chapter 6

1. Albert Shanker, quoted in David Boaz, "The Public School Monopoly," Vital Speeches of the Day, June 1, 1992, p. 507, and G. Gregory Moo, *Power Grab: How the National Educa-tion Association Is Betraying Our Children* (Washington, DC: Regnery, 1999), p. 222.

2. "Living in Japan: Education," japan-guide.com, June 9, 2002, accessed from http://www.japan-guide.com/e/e2150.html May 21, 2003.

3. Mike Lynch, "Free To Choose: The U.S. Supreme Court's Decision Is a Victory for Children," reasononline.com website, June 27, 2002, accessed from http://www.reason.com/ml/ml062702a.shtml, Nov. 15, 2003.

4. "Comparison of 2002 School Taxes on an $800,000 Home." Wealthy taxpayers pay even more: $7,290 for an $800,000 home, according to the Westchester County [New York] Tax Commission, NYS Offices of Real Property Services,

5. Rod Paige, U.S. Secretary of Education, Forward to "Research, School Choice 2003: Overview," Heritage Foundation,

not dated, accessed from www.heritage.org/-Research/Education/ Schools/-schoolchoice_overview.cfm, April 26, 2004.

6. D. T. Armentano, "Monopoly," Future of Freedom Foundation, May 1992, accessed from http://www.fff.org/-freedom/0592c. asp, Jan. 9, 2004.

7. Ray Lehmann, "Going Postal: Messing with the U.S. Mail," *Libertarian Republicans Speak Out*, accessed from http:// www.afn.org/~afn04641/lehmann1.html, June 20, 2003.

8. National Center for Education Statistics, "Digest of Education Statistics 2002," accessed from http://www.capenet.org/facts. html, Feb. 20, 2004.

9. U.S. Census Bureau, "Economics Statistics Briefing Room," November, 24, 2003, accessed from http://www.whitehouse.gov/ fsbr/ income.html, March 9, 2004.

10. Dick Armey, "Tax Freedom Day: A Day to Celebrate?," accessed from http://flattax.house.gov/armey, May 2, 1996.

11. U.S. Census Bureau, "New Residential Sales," accessed from http://www.census.gov/const/price_indexes.pdf, Sept. 3, 2003.

12. George C. Eads, "Health Insurance: Is Your Family Protected?" *National Academies Op-Ed Service Archive*, January 24, 2003, accessed from http://www4.nas.edu/onpi/-oped. nsf/onpi/oped.nsf/(Op-EdByDocID)/-C1D540DED8363CE1-85256CB8007AE90B?-OpenDocument, Feb. 23, 2004; and Economic and Social Research Council, "Statistics Report," August 1, 2001.

13. Nancy Coleman, "Working Mothers Face Double Bind over Time and Wages," *Economic Policy Institute Press*, May 8, 2002, accessed from http://www.epinet.org/-ctent.cfm/press_re-leases_mothers050802.html, June 23, 003.

14. Isabel Paterson, *The God of the Machine*, (1943 reprint, Caldwell, ID: Caxton Printers, 1964), p. 274.

15. Andrea Holland LaRue, "Summary of State Teacher Tenure Laws," from 'The Changing Face of Teacher Tenure,'" Report presented to the faculty of the Graduate School of the University of Texas at Austin, August 1996, American Federation of Teachers (AFT) Department of Research, accessed from http://www.aft. org/research/reports/tenure/laruetab.htm, Sept. 4, 2003.

16. Charles J. Sykes, *Dumbing Down Our Kids* (New York: St.

Martin's Griffin, 1995), pp. 234-35.

17. Walter Olson, "Time to Get Off the Tenure Track," *New York Times*, July 8, 1997, accessed from http://www.walterolson. com/articles//teactenr.html, July 10, 2003.

18. Gerald A. Pound, "Tenure Law Is Impediment to School Reform," Michigan Education Report, May 12, 2000, accessed from http://www.mackinac.org/pubs/mer/article.asp?ID=2874, Sept. 29, 2003.

19. Press release, Pacific Research Institute, January 1, 2001, "America's Debate," posted November 17, 2003, accessed from http://www.americasdebate.com/forums/index. php?showtopic=372, Oct. 23, 2003.

20. National Education Association, *NEA 2000-2001 Handbook 2001* (Washington, DC: NEA, 2000), p. 324.

21. "2003–2004 NC Public School Salary Schedules," *North Carolina Public Schools*, January 26, 2004, accessed from http:// www.ncpublicschools.org/salary_admin/salinfo.htm, Nov. 20, 2003.

22. C. S. Lewis, *God in the Dock: Essays on Theology and Ethics* (reprint, Grand Rapids, MI: William B. Eerdman, 1994).

23. Sheldon Richman, *Separating School and State* (Fairfax, VA: Future of Freedom Foundation, 1994), p. 48.

24. John Dewey, *My Pedagogic Creed*, accessed from http:// www.infed.org/archives/e-texts/e-dew-pc.htm, June 23, 2003.

25. Joel H. Spring, *The American School, 1642—1985: Varieties of Historical Interpretation of the Foundations and Development of American Education* (New York: Longman, 1986), pp. 168–69.

26. National Education Association, *NEA 2000-2001 Handbook*, p. 10.

27. Fred Bayles, "In Mass., Those Who Can't Spell or Write, Teach," *USA Today*, June 24, 1998.

28. Thomas Sowell, *Inside American Education: The Decline, the Deception, the Dogmas* (New York: Free Press, 1993), pp. 24–25.

29. Ibid., p. 25.

30. Ibid, p. 25.

31. Sykes, *Dumbing Down Our Kids*, pp. 85–87.

32. Paul Craig Roberts, "Education's Nemesis," *Washington Times*, February 18, 2003, accessed from http://www.washtimes. com/commentary, June 23, 2003.

33. Sykes, *Dumbing Down Our Kids*, pp. 90–91.
34. Peter R. Breggin, *Talking Back to Ritalin* (Cambridge: Perseus Publishing, 2001), p. 257.
35. Sowell, p. 27.
36. Sykes, *Dumbing Down Our Kids*, pp.28.

Chapter 7

1. Paul Craig Roberts, "Judicial Blackboard Jungle," *Washington Times*, December 9, 1999.
2. David Ayers, "Public Education Is Doomed," part 1, *Homeschool World*, 1994, accessed from http://www.home-school.com/Articles/PubEdDoomed1.html, Oct. 12, 2002.
3. George Will, "Causes of Education Failures Can Be Found 'Elsewhere,'" *Staten Island Advance*, January 8, 2002.
4. Nina H. Shokraii, "Why Catholic Schools Spell Success For America's Inner-City Children," Heritage Foundation, June 30, 1997, accessed from http://www.heritage.org/Research/UrbanIssues/BG1128.cfm, Jan. 23, 2004.
5. Dale McDonald, "Annual Report on Catholic Elementary and Secondary Schools: United States Catholic Elementary and Secondary School Statistics 2002–2003," National Catholic Education Association (NCEA), accessed from http://www.ncea.org/newinfo/catholicschooldata/annualreport.asp, Feb. 2, 2004.
6. Lawrence M. Rudner, "Education Policy Analysis Archives, The Scholastic Achievement and Demographic Characteristics of Home School Students in 1998," ERIC Clearinghouse on Assessment and Evaluation, 1999, accessed from http://epaa.asu.edu/epaa/v7n8, May 29, 2003.
7. Peter Brimelow, "Income Gap," *Forbes*, July 27, 1998.
8. James Bovard, "Teachers Unions: Are the Schools Run for Them?" *Freeman Magazine*, July 1996, p. 497, accessed from http://www.theadvocates.org/freeman/9607bova.html, Nov. 3, 2003.
9. AFT press release, "Beginning Teacher Salaries Improve as Shortage Abates," July 11, 2003, accessed from http://www.aft.org/press/2003/071103.html, Sept. 28, 2003; and U.S. Bureau of Labor Statistics, "National Compensation Survey: Occupational Wages in the United States, July, 2002," June 2003, accessed from

http://www.bls.gov/ncs/ocs/sp/ncbl0539.pdf, Nov. 15, 2003; and Martin L. Gross, *The Conspiracy of Ignorance: The Failure of American Public Schools*, (New York: HarperCollins Publishers, 1999), p.9; and U.S. Bureau of Labor Statistics, "National Compensation Survey: Employee Benefits in Private Industry in the United States, March 2003," April 2004.

10. National Association of Catholic School Teachers (NAC-ST), "2001–2002 NACST Lay Teacher Salary Survey," accessed from http://www.nacst.com/salsurvey/-20012002survey/home. htm, March 11, 2004.

11. U.S. Department of Labor, "2002 National Occupational Employment and Wage Estimates," Bureau of Labor Statistics, November 26, 2003, accessed from http://www.bls.gov/oes/2002/ nat.htm, March 11, 2004.

12. Bruce Bartlett, "Reducing Class Size Doesn't Improve Outcome," National Center for Policy Analysis, November 2, 1998, accessed from http://www.ncpa.org/oped/bartlett/-nov298. html, Sept. 5, 2003.

13. Ibid.

14. "Better Teachers versus Smaller Classes," National Center for Policy Analysis, originally published as "Teacher Quality Trumps Quantity When It Comes to Helping Kids," *USA Today*, January 29, 1999, accessed from http://www.ncpa.org/pi/edu// pd012999c.html, March 17, 2004.

15. "The Class-Size Reduction Program: A First-Year Report," Washington, DC: U.S. Dep't. of Education, 2000.

16. Casey J. Lartigue Jr., "Politicizing Class Size," Cato Institute, *Education Week*, September 29, 1999, accessed from http:// www.cato.org/research/education/articles/classsize.html, Sept. 4, 2003.

17. Susan Hewitt, "Smaller Classes a Waste," *West Australian*, February 19, 2002.

18. Charles J. Sykes, *Dumbing Down Our Kids* (New York: St. Martin's Griffin, 1995), p. 19.

19. Shokraii, "Why Catholic Schools Spell Success for America's Inner-City Children," Heritage Foundation, accessed from http://www.heritage.org/Research/UrbanIssues/-BG1128.cfm, July 12, 2003.

20. Samuel Casey Carter, *No Excuses: Lessons from 21 High Per-*

forming, High-Poverty Schools (Washington, DC: Heritage Foundation, 2001), accessed from http://www.noexcuses.org/pdf/noexcuseslessons.pdf, pp. 43, 74, 93, July 20, 2003.

21. Samuel Casey Carter, quoted in "Researcher Finds 7 Traits Common to Successful, High-Poverty Schools," *School Reform*, October 16, 2002, accessed from http://www.schoolreform.smartlibrary.org/NewInterface/segment.cfm?segment=2234, Dec. 22, 2002.

22. Gail Russell Chaddock, "In Voucher Report Card, Black Pupils Gain," *Christian Science Monitor*, August 30, 2000.

23. Bob Chase, speech before the National Press Club, November 16, 2001.

24. Daniel Wolff, a parent activist in Nyack, New York, quoted in *Education Week*, May 1, 2002.

25. Marquette University professor Howard L. Fuller, who organized the March 3–5, 2000 conference on Expanding and Enhancing Educational Options for African-Americans, quoted in George A. Clowes, "Black Leaders on a Mission for Parent Power," *School Reform News*, May 2000.

26. Michael Scherer, "Theodore J. Forstmann," *Mother Jones.com*, March 5, 2001, accessed from http://www.motherjones.com/-news/special_reports/-mojo_400/210_forstmann.html, Sept. 4, 2003.

27. Theodore J. Forstmann, testimony before the House Committee on the Budget, U.S. House of Representatives, Washington, DC, September 23, 1999.

28. Chase, speech.

29. Will, "Causes of Education Failures Can Be Found 'Elsewhere.'"

30. Ibid.

31. AFT press release, "Coalition Files Suit Challenging Ohio's Charter School Program," May 14, 2001, accessed from http://www.aft.org/press/2001/051401.html, Feb. 5, 2004.

32. Ann Mabbott, "Our Responsibility to Educate Immigrant Children," faculty opinion column, *Hamline Magazine*, fall 2002, accessed from http://www.hamline.edu/gse/sltl_html/Mabbott2.htm, July 9, 2003.

33. Drew Lindsay, "PepsiCo Backs Off Voucher Plan in Jersey City," *Education Week*, November 15, 1995, p. 3., cited in Andrew

J. Coulson, *Market Education: The Unknown History* (Somerset, N.J.: Transaction Publishers, 1999), p. 259.

34. Andrew J. Coulson, *Market Education: The Unknown History* (Somerset, N.J.: Transaction Publishers, 1999), p. 226.

35. Ibid., pp. 226-228

36. AFT Center on Accountability and Privatization, "Tools to Fight Privatization," accessed from AFT website www.aft.org, April 22, 2003.

37. McDonald, "Annual Report on Catholic Elementary and Secondary Schools, 2002–2003," accessessed from http://www.ncea.org/newinfo/nceacommunications/cswhighs.asp, Oct. 20, 2003.

38. Casey Lartigue, "Fly-by-Night Public Schools," Cato Institute, May 24, 2002, accessed from http://www.Cato.org/dailys/05-24-02.html, Nov. 10, 2002.

39. National Alliance to End Homelessness, "1.7 Million More Americans Fell below Poverty Line," *Alliance Online News*, September 26, 2003, accessed from http://www.endhomelessness.org/pub/onlinenews/news09-26-03.pdf, Jan 7, 2004.

40. U.S. Census Bureau, "Current Population Survey, Poverty in the United States," table: "Age and Sex of All People, Family Members and Unrelated Individuals Iterated by Income-to-Poverty Ratio and Race: 2002 Below 100% of Poverty—All Races," CPS 2003 Annual Social and Economic Supplement, September 26, 2003, accessed from http://ferret.bls.census.gov/macro/032003/pov/new01_100_01.htm, February 8, 2004.

41. LotteryInsider.com, "Lotteries Are Still The Most Popular Form of Gambling in US," accessed from http://www.lottery-insider.com/stats/uslot.htm, March 4, 2004; and Sharon Sharp, "Lottery Beneficiaries," Public Gaming Research Institute (PGRI), August 20, 1999, accessed from http://www.publicgaming.org/lotben.html, Feb. 6, 2004.

42. Cato Institute, *Policy Analysis*, December 6, 2000, accessed from http://www.Cato.org, Nov. 10, 2002.

43. New York State Department of Law, Charities Bureau, "Pennies for Charity 2002: Where Your Money Goes," New York: Office of NY State Attorney General, 2002.

44. Jay Mathews, "Alternative Schools: Daring to Be Different," *Newsweek*, June 2, 2003.

45. John Taylor Gatto, *Dumbing Us Down* (Philadelphia: New Society Publishers, 1992), p.13.

Chapter 8

1. Jerry Mintz, "Ten Signs That You Need to Find a Different Kind of Education for Your Child," Education Revolution, Alternative Education Resource Organization (AERO), accessed from http://www.educationrevolution.org/tensigthatyo. html, January 1, 2003.

2. Clonlara CompuHigh, accessed from http://www.compuhigh.com, February 20, 2004; and Jeanne Sahadi, "Can You Really Afford Private School?" *CNN/Money*, February 9, 2004, accessed from http://money.cnn.com/2004/02/06/pf/private_school, Nov. 3, 2003.

3. Bob Suter, "Cyberschool Fills a Niche," *Newsday*, March 26, 2002, accessed from http://www.babbagenetschool.com/FAQ's/Newsday_com%20Cyberschool%20Fills%20a%20Niche. htm, Nov. 5, 2003.

4. Shira J. Boss, "Virtual Charters: Public Schooling, at Home," *Christian Science Monitor*, January 8, 2002, accessed from http://www.csmonitor.com/2002/0108/p14s1-1epr.html, March 15, 2004.

5. Christopher J. Klicka, *The Right Choice: Home Schooling* (Gresham, OR: Noble Publishing, 1995), p. 132.

6. Ibid., p. 137.

7. Elaine McCrate, "Working Mothers in a Double Bind," Economic Policy Institute, May 2002, accessed from http://www.epinet.org/content.cfm/briefingpapers_bp124, Feb.8, 2003.

8. John Taylor Gatto, *The Underground History of American Education* (City: Oxford Village Press, 2000/2001), p.52, and from the U.S. Census of 1840.

9. Barry Dean Simpson, "'Free'" Education and Literacy," Ludwig Von Mises Institute, January 28, 2004, accessed from http://www.mises.org/fullstory.asp?control=1425, Oct.14, 2003.

10. Lauri Scogin, "The Home School Court Report," *Home Schoolers Excel 3, no. 1* (January–February 1987), cited in Klicka, *The Right Choice*, p. 126.

11. Isabel Shaw, "Making The Transition from Parent to Homeschool," Family Education.com, March 20, 2004, accessed from http://www.familyeducation.com/article/0,1120,58-28446-0-1,00.html, Nov. 4, 2003.

12. Isabel Lyman, "The Why of Homeschool," Ludwig Von Mises Institute, posted February 25, 2003, accessed from http://www.mises.org/fullstory.asp?control=1167, Jan. 12, 2004.

13. Laura, a parent, comment, November 27, 2000, accessed from http://www.homesteadingtoday.com, June 23, 2003.

14. Gatto, p. 13.

15. David Colfax and Micki Colfax, *Homeschooling for Excellence*, reissued (New York: Warner Books, 1988), pp. 46-47.

16. Caitlin Guthrie Freeman, "Why I Homeschool: Letter to Admissions Officers at Sarah Lawrence, Yale, and Oberlin," July 15, 1997, accessed from http://www.homeschoolteenscollege.com/college%20essays/essay11.htm, Jan. 23, 2004.

17. Patricia M. Lines, "Homeschooling: ERIC Digest," ERIC Clearinghouse on Educational Management, September 2001, accessed from http://www.ericdigests.org/2002-2/homeschooling.htm, Feb. 20, 2004; and Karl M. Bunday, "Colleges That Admit Homeschoolers," 2002, accessed from http://www.learninfreedom.org/colleges_4_hmsc.html, Feb. 10, 2004.

18. Klicka, *The Right Choice*, p. 139.

19. Ibid., p. 340; see also Pierce v. Society of Sisters, 268 U.S. 510, 534-35 (1925) and Wisconsin v. Yoder, 406 U.S. 205, 232 (1972).

20. Klicka, *The Right Choice*, p. 380.

21. "Decision: Pierce v. Society of Sisters (1925), Children, Education, and Privacy," *Agnosticism/Atheism* website, accessed from http://www.atheism.about.com/library/decisions/privacy/bldec_PeirceSociety.htm, February 21, 2004.

22. Klicka, *The Right Choice*, p. 380.

23. Ibid., p. 381.

24. National Center for Public Policy Research, "Parents Arrested for Legally Having Son Home-Schooled," *CNSNews.com*, March 19, 2003, accessed from http://www.conservative-news.net/ViewNation.asp?Page=\Nation\archive\200303\NAT20030319a.html, Jan 23, 2004.

Chapter 9

1. Mary Griffith, *The Unschooling Handbook: How to Use the Whole World as Your Child's Classroom* (Rocklin, CA: Prima Publishing, 1998), pp. 95–106.

2. The Life and Times of Albert Einstein, accessed from http://trillian.com/bio/Einstien.htm, Feb. 3, 2004.

3. William Gibson, *The Miracle Worker* (New York: Bantam Books, 1962), p. 101.

4. Charles J. Sykes, *Dumbing Down Our Kids* (New York: St. Martin's Griffin, 1995), pp. 134–35.

5. Patrick, a parent in California, quoted in Griffith, *The Unschooling Handbook*, p. 127.

Selected Bibliography

- Adams, Charles, *For Good and Evil: The Impact of Taxes On the Course of Civilisation*, Madison Books, 1993.
- Armstrong, Thomas, *The Myth of the A.D.D. Child*, Plume Books, 1997.
- Blumenfeld, Samuel L., *How To Tutor*, The Paridigm Co., 1973.
- Blumenfeld, Samuel L., *Homeschooling: A Parents Guide To Teaching Children*, Carol Publishing Group, 1997.
- Breggin, Peter R., M.D., *Talking Back To Ritalin*, Perseus Publishing, 2001.
- Colfax, David and Micki, *Homeschooling For Excellence*, Warner Books, 1988.
- Coulson, Andrew J., *Market Education: The Unknown History*, Transaction Publishers, 1999.
- Diller, Lawrence H., M.D., *Running On Ritalin*, Bantam Books, 1998.
- Fortkamp, Frank E., Ph.D., *The Case Against Government Schools*, American Media, 1979.
- Gatto, John Taylor, *Dumbing Us Down*, New Society Publishers, 1992.
- Gatto, John Taylor, *The Underground History of American Education*, The Oxford Village Press, 2000.
- Goldberg, Bruce, *Why Schools Fail*, Cato Institute, 1996.
- Gorn, Elliot J., editor, *The McGuffey Readers, Selections from*

the 1879 Edition, Bedford/St. Martin's Press, 1998
• Griffith, Mary, *The Unschooling Handbook: How To Use the Whole World As Your Child's Classroom*, Prima Publishing, 1998.
• Gross, Martin L., *The Conspiracy of Ignorance*, HarperCollins, 1999.
• Holt, John, *How Children Fail*, Pitman Publishing, 1964.
• Holt, John, *How Children Learn*, Penguin Books, 1967.
• Holt, John, *The Underachieving School*, Delta Books, 1969.
• Kilpatrick, William, *Why Johnny Can't Tell Right From Wrong*, Touchstone Books, 1992.
• Kjos, Berit, *Brave New Schools*, Harvest House Publishers, 1995
• Klicka, Christopher J., *The Right Choice: Home Schooling*, Noble Publishing Associates, 1995.
• Kozol, Jonathan, *Savage Inequalities: Children In America's Schools*, HarperPerennial, 1992.
• Kramer, Rita, *Ed School Follies: The Miseducation of America's Teachers*, Backinprint.com Book, 1991.
• Lieberman, Myron, *Public Education: An Autopsy*, Harvard University Press, 1993.
• Lieberman, Myron, *The Teacher Unions*, The Free Press, 1997.
• Moo, G. Gregory, *Power Grab:How the National Education Association is Betraying Our Children*, Regnery Publishing, 1999.
• National Education Association, *2000-2001 Handbook*, National Education Association, 2000.
• Richman, Sheldon, *Separating School and State*, Future of Freedom Foundation, 1994.
• Rickenbacker, William F., editor, *The Twelve-Year Sentence: Radical Views On Compulsory Schooling*, Fox & Wilkes Publishers, 1974.
• Rothbard, Murray N., *Education: Free & Compulsory*, Ludwig Von Mises Institute, 1971.
• Ruwart, Dr. Mary J., *Healing Our World*, SunStar Press, 1992.
• Schlafly, Phyllis, *Chld Abuse In The Classroom*, Pere Marquette Press, 1984.
• Sommer, Carl, *Schools In Crisis: Training For Success or Failure?*, Cahill Publishing Co., 1984.

• Sowell, Thomas, *Inside American Education: The Decline, The Deception, The Dogmas*, The Free Press, 1993.

• Sowell, Thomas, *Education: Assumptions Versus History*, Hoover Institution Press, 1986.

• Stormer, John A., *None Dare Call It Education*, Liberty Bell Press, 1999.

• Sykes, Charles J., *Dumbing Down Our Kids*, St. Martins Press, 1995.

• Walberg, Herbert J., and Bast, Joseph L., *Education and Capitalism*, Hoover Institution Press, 2003.

About the Author

Joel Turtel specializes in writing about political and education issues. He has been an avid reader and researcher in political philosophy for over 40 years. He owned a consulting company for fifteen years in which he had to interact with government agencies, and deal with their regulations on a daily basis. As a result, he gained first-hand knowledge of the deep-rooted problems that government regulations cause businesses of all kinds. After selling his consulting company in 1991, he became a full-time writer. His first book, published in 1996, was "The Welfare State: No Mercy For the Middle Class." His current book was the result of over three years of research and writing.

Index